ECONOMICS OF CRIME
THEORY AND PRACTICE

Daryl A. Hellman • Neil O. Alper

Professors of Economics
Northeastern University

PEARSON

Custom
Publishing

Printed in the United States of America

10 9 8 7 6 5

ISBN 0-536-10661-4

2005160147

MT

Please visit our web site at *www.pearsoncustom.com*

PEARSON CUSTOM PUBLISHING
75 Arlington Street, Suite 300, Boston, MA 02116
A Pearson Education Company

Contents

Preface

The purpose of the book is to provide an introduction to the economics of crime. As such, it can be used in a variety of ways: as a supplement to an introductory course in microeconomics, as a basic framework on which to build an advanced course in the economics of crime and some other "issues" course, or as the primary textbook in an economics of crime course directed to an audience with a limited background in economics. Our primary intention for the book was to fulfill the latter purpose.

For many years we have been teaching an undergraduate course in the economics of crime in which a large percentage of the students are not economics majors. Although most of these students have had a course in the principles of economics, some have not had both micro- and macroeconomics, some had difficulty with introductory economics, and some have limited recall of, or interest in, the material encountered in their previous economics courses. For this reason we have written the book for an audience which has had only limited exposure to economics. We therefore include brief definitions of many concepts and terms (e.g., price elasticity of demand) the first time they are used in the book. The level of analysis is intended to be such that a student with no previous training in economics can comprehend the material with the help of an instructor. More sophisticated analyses or advanced issues are occasionally suggested, or contained or referenced in footnotes. Thus the material in the book can be made to challenge the more advanced student as well.

Throughout the book the emphasis is on presenting a consistent framework in which to analyze and develop public policy for dealing with crime. Public policy and social issues are emphasized, sometimes at the expense of detailed institutional or descriptive material or more advanced theoretical constructs. The development of an economic framework for analysis and the presentation of empirical studies to support it are aimed toward policy. What are the implications of the analysis for public policy? What policy options are available? How effective would those alternatives be? What information do we need to make intelligent decisions? Our intention is to develop a few recurring themes and a way of analyzing crime in society. Our hope is that the student will come away from the course with a new perspective on crime and with a general approach to the analysis of crime and of possible ways of dealing with it which can be applied to new situations or data.

The first half of the book is devoted to developing a theoretical framework. Chapter 1 provides a brief introduction to the subject matter. Although in teaching the course we begin by devoting a substantial amount of time to a discussion of the dimensions of the crime problem, data sources, and so forth, we have abbreviated this discussion in the introductory chapter. The instructor can, of course, supplement Chapter 1 with additional current statistics and issues. Development of the theoretical framework begins in Chapter 2 with a discussion of the economic impact of criminal activity. Chapter 3 describes an economic theory of criminal behavior. Using these two chapters as a foundation, Chapter 4 discusses various aspects of the optimum allocation of resources to the criminal justice system. This is the most difficult chapter in the book for students without a background in economics. However, once Chapter 4 has been mastered, the battle has been won, and the rest of the material in the book should readily fall into place.

Chapters 5 through 9 apply the theoretical material to an analysis of various categories of crime: crimes against property, crimes against persons, crimes without victims, the markets for illegal drugs and organized crime. The final chapter highlights some of the major themes and issues in the economics of crime.

Preparation of this edition and earlier editions of this book would have been impossible without the support and assistance of many individuals. Mariko Geronimo deserves special thanks for her assistance in preparing the most recent edition. We would like to thank several anonymous reviewers for their thoughtful and constructive comments. We would also like to remember those who assisted in the past, including Nasreen Akanda, Gustavo Aristabal Maria DaCosta, and David Walsh for their careful bibliographic work and David Agdern, Jennifer Dawson, Cheryl (Noakes) Fonville, Sylvia

Goldberg, Sheila Palma, Pauline Sayers, and Ellen Shoner for their expeditious handling of the typing chores. Additionally we would like to thank Linda Woods and Steven Morrison for identifying some very important material for us.

Daryl A. Hellman
Neil O. Alper

1

Introduction to the
Economics of Crime

Crime is a major social concern which has received increasing attention in recent years. In this book we are going to try to analyze the reasons for the crime problem and evaluate various public policies for dealing with it. While an adequate understanding of criminal behavior, as well as policy design, may require a multidisciplinary perspective, the focus of this book will be on an economic approach to understanding criminal behavior and designing effective policies for dealing with the problem of criminal activity.

To the **economist,** crime is rational behavior—a choice that is made by a person or persons in deciding how best to spend their time. In making the choice, individuals consider what they stand to gain and what they stand to lose; that is, they consider the benefits and costs of using their time in different ways—working legally, working illegally, or not working at all. One implication of this approach is that individuals have some knowledge, not necessarily perfect, of the benefits and costs associated with different actions.

Because of the assumption of rationality, economists would hypothesize that punishment deters crime. This does not mean that in every instance in which punishment increases we can expect to see crime decrease. The reason for this, as we will see in Chapter 3, is that there are other factors which also affect crime rates—other benefits and costs to the individual which must be considered. In addition, as we will also see, the concept and measurement of punishment costs is somewhat complicated. But economists would argue that, other things being equal, an increase in expected punishment costs should decrease crime.[1] Finally, of course, there may be instances in which the assumption of rationality is not appropriate, for example, in "murders of passion." The extent to which an economic approach is useful in analyzing such crimes is discussed in Chapter 6.

The economic model can be compared with those of other social sciences. To the sociologist, crime is deviant behavior. The deterrent effect of punishment concerns the role of sanctions in generating conformity. Much of the earlier empirical research on the question of the ability of punishment to deter crime has been done by sociologists and social psychologists, albeit with a different perspective and perhaps sometimes with different expectations regarding its effectiveness.[2] Sociologists or psychologists may also focus on other aspects of the role of punishment, such as the importance of the type of norm being sanctioned, the motivation behind the deviant behavior, the importance of perception of sanctions, or the impact of class, race, age, or sex on deviant behavior.[3]

Some of the concerns of sociologists, psychologists, political scientists, and other social scientists who study criminal behavior can be incorporated within the economic model. This is because economists argue that the gains and costs of criminal behavior include psychic elements. These psychic costs and benefits become a catchall for all kinds of psychological, sociological, and political phenomena. For example, one possible gain to a juvenile from the crime of vandalism is peer approval. The gain to a radical political activist from a bank robbery may be a chance to make claims against the political system which must regulate conflict. To the economist, these are examples of psychic gains from crime. These are not emphasized in the economic model, nor are they examined, and appropriately so; they are topics for investigation by other disciplines. But their inclusion in the economic model and their recognition in empirical work permits the establishment of links between the research of economists and that of criminologists and other social scientists interested in studying criminal behavior.[4]

Our economic analysis begins in Chapter 2 with one economic aspect of criminal activity—the economic impact of crime. This is an important part of our analysis because it will suggest what we stand to gain by reducing crime, and therefore, the amount it is worth spending on law enforcement and criminal justice. In this chapter the tools of supply and demand are introduced.

In Chapter 3 an equally important economic aspect of the analysis of crime is addressed—development of an economic explanation of criminal behavior. This is essential for the design of public policy to reduce crime, for the first step in such design must be an understanding of why crimes are committed.

The following chapters defines the problems of economic choice which are faced in the production of law enforcement and criminal justice, and describes tools for implementing those choices. The remaining chapters apply the theoretical framework developed in the earlier chapters to an analysis of various types of criminal activity.

While the theoretical framework to be developed here is intended to be applicable to a wide variety of criminal activities, the specific analyses or examples are limited to certain categories of crime. There are a large number of activities, or behaviors, which are classified as criminal. The Heritage Foundation estimates that there are well over 3,300 separate federal crimes[5] and there are a much larger number of state and local ones.[6] Some crimes involve bodily harm; others involve stealing, public morals, or government revenues; still others involve regulation of the economy or creation of hazardous conditions. Some of the newest crimes are those associated with the Internet and the World Wide Web and are known as **cybercrimes**.

The focus of this book will be on a limited number of criminal activities, although these activities represent those for which the most data are available and in which the public seems to be most interested. Specifically, the crimes analyzed are the FBI index crimes, **white collar crime, "victimless" crimes, and organized crime.**

FBI INDEX CRIMES

Let us begin with **FBI index crimes.** This term refers to eight specific offenses, and attempted offenses, which are counted by the FBI in compiling an index of serious crimes. These figures are published regularly in *Uniform Crime Reports.* Later we will evaluate the crime index as an indicator of the seriousness of the crime problem. For now, let us simply find out what the index crimes are.

The eight index crimes can be divided into two parts: violent crimes (sometimes referred to as crimes against persons) and property crimes. Four violent crimes are included in the index: murder and non-negligent manslaughter, forcible rape, robbery, and aggravated assault. We will briefly define each of these here. Detailed definitions are contained in the appendix to this chapter.

Murder and non-negligent manslaughter are both forms of willful homicide—the killing of one human being through the willful act of another. Criminal homicide also includes negligent manslaughter—the killing of one human being through the gross negligence of another. Negligent manslaughter, however, is not included among the index crimes. For brevity, this category of crime is sometimes called willful homicide or, more simply, homicide or murder.

Forcible rape refers to the carnal knowledge of a female, forcibly and against her will. Incidents in which physical force is not involved or the victim is under the legal age of consent are not counted in the index. While some state statutes have degenderized this crime, in the FBI counts, the victim is defined as female.

Robbery is the taking or attempting to take anything of value from the care, custody, or control of a person or persons by force or threat of force or violence and/or by putting the victim in fear. Robbery therefore involves a property crime, or theft, aggravated by the use or threat of force against a person(s). Thus, it combines elements of crimes against persons and crimes against property.

Aggravated assault is an unlawful attack by one person upon another for the purpose of inflicting severe or aggravated bodily injury.

Index crimes also include four crimes against property: arson, burglary, larceny–theft, and motor vehicle theft. Arson is the intentional damaging or destruction by means of fire or explosion of someone's property without consent, or of any property with intent to defraud. In 1978 the U.S. Congress mandated that arson be added to the FBI serious crime index. Previously it was not one of the index crimes. Systematic data on arson is just beginning to be available.

Burglary is the unlawful entry into a structure to commit a felony or theft, whether or not force is used. Attempted forcible entries are also counted as burglaries.

Larceny–theft is the unlawful taking, carrying, leading, or riding away of property (except motor vehicles) from the possession or constructive possession of another. Larceny, unlike burglary, does not involve unlawful entry. Larceny includes crimes such as pickpocketing, purse snatching, and shoplifting.

Motor vehicle theft is the theft or attempted theft of a motor vehicle.

These eight index offenses are also referred to as Part I offenses. In Chapter 5 we analyze index crimes against property, including robbery and white collar crimes. Chapter 6 focuses on violent crimes, or crimes against persons. The remaining chapters analyze a few other crimes which are not part of the FBI index—victimless crimes—with a chapter devoted to the markets for two illegal drugs, heroin and cocaine, and a chapter devoted to organized crime.

The most complete crime data are available for the index offenses. The FBI's uniform crime reporting (UCR) program, approved by Congress in 1930, collects, compiles, and publishes national crime statistics on offenses known to the police. Figures are published annually as part of the *Uniform Crime Reports*. Detailed information on offenses, arrests, and charges for criminal offenses is available for the index crimes. In addition, the FBI collects and publishes figures on persons arrested and charged for a wide variety of other crimes, including "victimless" crimes. These crimes are included in what are called Part II offenses.

The FBI is in the process of introducing a redesigned UCR program, called the **National Incident-Based Reporting System (NIBRS),** which will expand the information collected from local law enforcement agencies.[7] The redesigned program collects information on each incident, victim, offender, arrestee, and any property involved with the crime. The crimes include the eight index crimes and 14 additional crime categories. The FBI started accepting NIBRS data in 1989, but as of 2003 only 25 state data reporting programs have been certified to provide data on their crimes. The pace of implementation is hindered by several factors including the lack of resources.

RECENT TRENDS IN THE AMOUNT OF CRIME

Using data from the *Uniform Crime Reports,* it is interesting to look at what has been happening to the number of index crime offenses over the last several years. Table 1–1 shows the total number of offenses in the United States for each of the index crimes for selected years from 1960 to 2003. It is important to realize that these figures represent only offenses known to the police either from citizen complaints or from independent police discovery. The figures, therefore, do not necessarily reflect the actual number of crimes committed.

Figures are given for seven of the offenses separately, for total property crimes excluding arson (burglary, larceny-theft, and motor vehicle theft), for total violent crimes (murder, forcible rape, robbery, and aggravated assault), and for total index crimes (the sum of the seven crimes).

As the figures clearly indicate, the number of reported offenses for all crimes increased substantially over the period from 1960 to 1980 (while not reported in the table, the trend continued through 1981). The percentage increases in each category are listed at the bottom of the table. The early 1980s was a period of decreases in reported offenses through 1984, with increases in each subsequent year through 1991. Explanations for the decrease in criminal activity include a decrease in the proportion of the population most likely to commit crimes, and changes in the certainty and the severity of punishment for criminal activity. Reasons for the increase to record levels in 1991 are unclear, but are believed to be related to increases in drug and drug-related crimes; changes in the attitudes of young people to the use of violence in dealing with conflicts; the lack of supervision at home associated with the

TABLE 1–1

NUMBER OF OFFENSES KNOWN TO POLICE, UNITED STATES, 1960–2003 (SELECTED YEARS)

Year	Total Crime Index*	Violent Crime	Property Crime	Murder and Non-negligent Manslaughter	Forcible Rape	Robbery	Aggravated Assault	Burglary	Larceny—Theft	Motor Vehicle Theft
1960	3,384,200	288,460	3,095,700	9,110	17,190	107,840	154,320	912,100	1,855,400	328,200
1965	4,739,400	387,390	4,352,000	9,960	23,410	138,690	215,330	1,282,500	2,572,600	496,900
1970	8,098,000	738,820	7,359,200	16,000	37,990	349,860	334,970	2,205,000	4,225,800	928,400
1975	11,256,600	1,026,280	10,230,300	20,510	56,090	464,970	484,710	3,252,100	5,977,700	1,000,500
1980	13,408,300	1,344,520	12,063,700	23,040	82,990	565,840	672,650	3,795,200	7,136,900	1,131,700
1985	12,431,400	1,328,800	11,102,600	18,980	87,670	497,870	723,250	3,073,300	6,926,400	1,102,900
1990	14,475,600	1,820,130	12,655,500	23,440	102,560	639,270	1,054,860	3,073,900	7,945,700	1,635,900
1995	13,867,100	1,798,790	12,068,400	21,600	97,460	580,550	1,099,180	2,595,000	8,000,600	1,472,700
1996	13,493,900	1,688,540	11,805,300	19,650	96,250	535,590	1,037,050	2,506,400	7,904,700	1,394,200
1997	13,194,600	1,636,100	11,558,500	18,210	96,150	498,530	1,023,200	2,460,500	7,743,800	1,354,200
1998	12,475,600	1,531,040	10,944,600	16,910	93,100	446,630	974,400	2,330,000	7,373,900	1,240,800
1999	11,634,380	1,426,040	10,208,330	15,520	89,410	409,370	911,740	2,110,740	6,955,520	1,152,080
2000	11,608,070	1,425,490	10,182,580	15,590	90,180	408,020	911,710	2,050,990	6,971,590	1,160,000
2001	11,876,670	1,439,480	10,437,190	16,040	90,860	423,560	909,020	2,116,530	7,092,270	1,228,390
2002	11,877,220	1,426,330	10,450,890	16,200	95,140	420,640	894,350	2,151,880	7,052,920	1,246,100
2003	11,816,782	1,381,259	10,435,523	16,503	93,433	413,402	857,921	2,153,464	7,021,588	1,260,471
Percent Change										
1960–1981	+296.7	+372.1	+289.6	+147.2	+379.9	+449.8	+330.2	+314.4	+287.8	+231.4
1981–1984	–11.5	–6.5	–12.0	–17.0	+2.1	–18.2	+3.2	–21.0	–8.4	–5.1
1984–1991	+25.2	+50.1	+22.2	+32.2	+26.5	+41.8	+59.4	+5.8	+23.5	+61.0
1991–2000	–22.0	–25.4	–21.4	–36.9	–15.4	–40.7	–16.6	–35.0	–14.4	–30.2
2000–2002	+2.3	+0.1	+2.6	+3.9	+5.5	+3.1	–1.9	+4.9	+1.2	+7.4
2002–2003	–0.5	–3.0	–0.2	+1.7	–1.9	–1.8	–3.8	+0.1	–0.5	+1.1

Source: U.S. Department of Justice, Federal Bureau of Investigation, *Uniform Crime Reports for the United States, 1975* (Washington, D.C., 1976), Table 2, 49; *Uniform Crime Reports for the United States, 1986* (Washington, D.C., 1987), Table 1, 41; *Uniform Crime Reports for the United States, 1991* (Washington, D.C., 1992), Table 1, 58; *Uniform Crime Reports for the United States, 1995* (Washington, D.C., 1996), Table 1, 58; *Crime in the United States 1998: Uniform Crime Reports* (www.fbi.gov/ucr/98cius.htm, Table 1.64); *Crime in the United States, 2003: Uniform Crime Reports,* (www.fbi.gov/ucr/03cius.htm, Table 1.70).
*Arson is excluded because sufficient data are not available to estimate totals.

growth of two-earner families and households headed by working women; lack of government supported social programs; and the worsening economy of the early 1990s.[8] From 1991 to 2000, the number of index crimes reported to the police continually decreased, followed by an increase from 2000 to 2002, then a decrease from 2002 to 2003. The decline from 1991 to 2000, which had been across all the index crimes, is associated with a period of increased criminal justice expenditures and harsher, mandatory sentences.

An economist studying the decrease in crime during the 1990s found six factors that many believed played a role in explaining the decline but did not and four factors that he believes do explain the decline. The ones that do not explain the decline are: the strong economy of the 1990s, though he suggests that this may have indirectly impacted criminal activity by increasing government expenditures on the criminal justice system (more on this later in the book); the country's changing demographics, including the aging of the baby boom generation; changes in the strategies used by police to fight crime; changes in gun control laws; new laws allowing people to carry concealed weapons; and the increase in the use of capital punishment. The factors that he found explained the decline are: an increase in the number of police; the dramatic increase in the rate of incarceration in the U.S.; a significant decline in the crack cocaine market; and the Supreme Court's legalization of abortion in 1973.[9] The last is the most controversial and hinges on the idea that children who are not wanted are more likely to commit crime and with legalized abortion there are fewer unwanted children.

The figures in Table 1–1 are somewhat misleading as indicators of changes in the seriousness of the crime problem over that period. For one thing, the population of the country increased over that time (see Table 1–2), so that even if the public were neither more nor less "criminal," we would expect the number of crimes to increase simply because the number of potential criminals—and victims—has gone up.

To correct for this, criminal offense statistics are often reported as a crime rate (i.e., the number of reported offenses divided by the size of the population):

$$\text{Crime rate} = \frac{\text{number of crimes}}{\text{population}}. \qquad (1\text{--}1)$$

The resulting number gives the number of crimes per person, or per capita. When we are looking at national figures, because the denominator is the entire population of the country, which is a very large number, the rate is often expressed as the number of crimes per 100,000 people.

Table 1–2 contains population figures for the United States for selected years from 1960–2003 and crime rates for each of the same categories contained in Table 1–1. The figures were obtained by simply dividing the number of crimes for a particular category and a particular year (from Table 1–1) by the population for that year.

The figures in Table 1–2 present a somewhat different picture. While from Table 1–1 we see that the number of index crimes increased by 249.2 percent from 1960 to 2003, the index crime rate increased by only 115.3 percent over that period. The rate of violent crimes increased faster than the rate of crimes against property—by 195.2 percent compared to 107.9 percent. The crime rate with the largest growth is aggravated assault, with an increase of 242.6 percent. With few exceptions, the rate of crime for each category increased every year during the 1960 to 1981 period and decreased during the 1982 to 1984 period. With the exception of burglary, all the crime rates increased over the seven years starting with 1985, with all but two (murder and burglary) reaching record levels. Since 1991, the overall crime rate has decreased, as have the rates for each of the index crimes listed in Table 1–2. All crime rates in 2000 were at their lowest levels in decades, with the murder, robbery and burglary rates not being this low since the late 1960s. In 2001 most crime rates increased slightly, with the exception of total violent crimes, forcible rape and aggravated assault. Then, in 2002, the downward trend of previous years returned as most crime rates decreased, including both total violent crime and property crime rates. In 2003, almost all crime rates declined. However, while violent crime rates decreased by almost 4% from 2002, the murder rate increased by almost 1.8%. Some experts have attributed this to a surge in street violence due to youth and gang killings.[10]

PROBLEMS IN THE INTERPRETATION OF DATA

Before concluding that the crime problem had increased through 1991 as much as Tables 1–1 and 1–2 suggest, it is important to realize that another thing was increasing very substantially over that period: the number of agencies reporting crimes to the FBI. The national figures on crimes known to the police are obtained from figures voluntarily provided to the FBI by law enforcement agencies, either through a state reporting program or directly by local agencies. In 1960, the number of reporting agencies was roughly 2,500. By 2003, the number of participating agencies had increased to 17,381, covering the entire U.S. population. Thus, there was a substantial increase in the reporting base and, predictably, a substantial increase in reported crimes.

TABLE 1-2
RATE OF OFFENSES KNOWN TO POLICE, UNITED STATES, 1960–2003 (SELECTED YEARS)
(RATE PER 100,000 INHABITANTS)

Year	Population	Total Crime Index[a]	Violent Crime	Property Crime	Murder and Non-negligent Manslaughter	Forcible Rape	Robbery	Aggravated Assault	Burglary	Larceny-Theft	Motor Vehicle Theft
1960	179,323,175	1,887.2	160.9	1,726.3	5.1	9.6	60.1	86.1	508.6	1,034.7	183.0
1965	193,526,000	2,449.0	200.2	2,248.8	5.1	12.1	71.7	111.3	662.7	1,329.2	256.8
1970	203,235,398	3,984.5	363.5	3,621.0	7.9	18.7	172.1	164.8	1,084.9	2,079.3	456.8
1975	213,124,000	5,281.7	481.5	4,800.2	9.6	26.3	218.2	227.4	1,525.9	2,804.8	469.4
1980	225,349,264	5,950.0	596.6	5,353.3	10.2	36.8	251.1	298.5	1,684.1	3,167.0	502.2
1985	237,923,795	5,207.1	556.6	4,650.5	7.9	37.1	208.5	302.9	1,287.3	2,901.2	462.0
1990	249,464,396	5,820.3	731.8	5,088.5	9.4	41.2	257.0	424.1	1,235.9	3,194.8	657.8
1995	262,803,276	5,277.6	684.6	4,593.0	8.2	37.1	220.9	418.3	987.6	3,044.9	560.5
1996	265,228,572	5,086.6	636.5	4,450.1	7.4	36.3	201.9	390.9	944.8	2,979.7	525.6
1997	267,783,607	4,930.0	611.3	4,318.7	6.8	35.9	186.3	382.3	919.4	2,893.4	505.0
1998	270,248,003	4,615.5	566.4	4,049.1	6.3	34.4	165.2	360.5	862.0	2,728.1	459.0
1999	272,690,813	4,266.5	523.0	3,743.6	5.7	32.8	150.1	334.3	770.4	2,550.7	422.5
2000	281,421,906	4,124.8	506.5	3,618.3	5.5	32.0	145.0	324.0	728.8	2,477.3	412.2
2001	285,317,559	4,162.6	504.5	3,658.1	5.6	31.8	148.5	318.6	741.8	2,485.7	430.5
2002	287,973,924	4,118.8	494.6	3,624.1	5.6	33.0	145.9	310.1	746.2	2,445.8	432.1
2003	290,809,777	4,063.4[b]	475.0	3,588.4	5.7	32.1	142.2	295.0	740.5	2,414.5	433.4
Percent Change											
1960–1981	+27.8	+210.4	+269.4	+204.9	+92.2	+275.0	+330.4	+236.5	+224.3	+203.4	+159.4
1981–1984	+3.1	–14.1	–9.3	–14.7	–19.4	–0.8	–20.6	+0.2	–23.4	–11.1	–7.9
1984–1991	+6.8	+17.2	+40.6	+14.4	+24.1	+18.5	+32.8	+49.3	–0.9	+15.7	+50.8
1991–2000	+11.6	–30.1	–33.2	–29.6	–43.9	–24.3	–46.8	–25.2	–41.8	–23.3	–37.5
2001–2003	+1.9	–2.4	–5.8	–1.9	+1.8	+0.9	–4.2	–7.4	–0.2	–2.9	+0.7

Source: U.S. Department of Justice, Federal Bureau of Investigation. *Uniform Crime Reports for the United States, 1975* (Washington, D.C., 1976), Table 2, 49; *Uniform Crime Reports for the United States, 1986* (Washington, D.C. 1987). Table 1, 41; *Uniform Crime Reports for the United States, 1991* (Washington, D.C., 1992), Table 1, 58; *Uniform Crime Reports for the United States, 1995* (Washington, D.C., 1996), Table 1, 58; *Crime in the United States 1998: Uniform Crime Reports* (www.fbi.gov/ucr/98cius.htm. Table 1.64); *Crime in the United States, 2003: Uniform Crime Reports,* (www.fbi.gov/ucr/03cius.htm. Table 1, 70).

[a] Arson is excluded because sufficient data are not available to estimate totals.

9

There are other reasons why comparisons of crime rates from year to year, or even from place to place, can be misleading.[11] Since the offense figures are those known to the police, and since not all crimes are reported to the police, differences in crime rates may reflect differences in the willingness of citizens to report crimes. In 1965 the Crime Commission, concerned about the amount of crime that goes unreported, instituted a national survey to determine how many people had actually been victims of various crimes.[12] By surveying individuals the Commission was able to include in its tally crimes which had occurred but had not come to the attention of the police. By then comparing the national crime rate based on the survey data with the crime rate based on reported crimes, an idea of the percentages of various crimes which are unreported could be obtained. They found that many crimes are underreported; their results suggested that only about half of all index crime offenses are reported.

As a result of the Commission's recommendations, the Department of Justice initiated a national household survey in 1973 to estimate more directly the amount of criminal activity that is not reported to the police. Based on this survey, in 2003 it was estimated that 52 percent of crimes against persons (rape, robbery, and aggravated and simple assault) and 62 percent of crimes against households (burglary, larceny and motor vehicle theft) are not reported to the police.

In Table 1–3 are the detailed estimates from the 2003 survey. Underreporting is not the same for each crime. Motor vehicle theft was the least likely not to be reported; only 23 percent were not reported. Theft was the most likely not to be reported; 68 percent were not reported to the police. We can conclude on the basis of this evidence that approximately 40 percent of all crimes are reported. Another way of saying this is that actual crime rates are almost three times the reported rates. This ratio does vary from year to year and from place to place.

The willingness to report crimes to the police also varies by the gender of the victim. Women are more likely than men to report crimes of violence and just as likely to report property crimes to the police. In 2003, women reported 50 percent of their violent crime victimizations to the police while the men reported only 46 percent of them to the police. For property crime victimizations women and men reported 38 percent.[13]

Racial and ethnic differences exist in willingness to report crimes to the police as well.[14] With respect to crimes of violence, in 2002 whites were less likely to report these crimes to the police than blacks; 47 percent of white victimizations were reported compared to 55 percent of black victimizations.

TABLE 1–3

ESTIMATE OF CRIMINAL ACTIVITY NOT REPORTED TO POLICE FOR THE UNITED STATES, 2003

Crime	Percent Not Reported
Personal crime:	52%
Rape	61
Robbery	39
Assault	40
Property crime:	63%
Household burglary	46
Theft	68
Motor vehicle theft	23

Source: Adapted from U.S. Department of Justice, Bureau of Justice Statistics, *Bulletin: Criminal Victimization, 2003* (Washington, D.C., September 2004), p. 10.

Hispanics were somewhat more likely to report their violent victimizations as non-Hispanics (50 percent of victimizations were reported by Hispanics and 48 percent for non-Hispanics). With respect to property crimes it was the Hispanic population who were slightly less likely to report its property crime victimizations; alomst 39 percent were reported. The non-Hispanic population reported almost 41 percent of its property crime victimizations. Again, the white population was less likely to report its property crime victimizations than the black population; 39 percent of white victimizations were reported compared to 46 percent of black victimizations.

Individuals are not the only ones unwilling to report crimes to the police; it is true of businesses as well. They are generally unwilling to report employee crimes such as fraud and theft but are more willing to report crimes committed by outsiders such as arson, robbery, and burglary.[15] Lack of reporting by businesses may reflect a concern for negative publicity and the costs of dealing with the public criminal justice system. In reaction many businesses have created their own "private" criminal justice systems with private security and punishment, which ranges from reprimands to dismissal.[16] A 1999 survey of businesses found that only one-quarter of **computer crimes,** one of the fastest growing areas of criminal activity in the U.S., are reported to the police. Two explanations given for this are the high-tech industry's distrust of law enforcement agencies, and the fear that any investigation and subsequent publicity will scare customers away.[17]

In an attempt to increase the reporting of crimes some local law enforcement agencies have recently started to allow victims to report certain crimes over the Internet. Palo Alto, California, allows the reporting of certain types of theft (petty, bicycle and grand theft), vandalism and car burglary. The police department in Woodland, California, allows the reporting of vandalism and stolen property, among others.

Another reason why comparison of crime rates can be misleading is that differences in the rates for different years or different cities may reflect changes or differences in recording procedures and standards. Crimes reported to the police must be accurately and consistently recorded in order for reliable comparisons to be made.

There are also some statistical insufficiencies in the FBI data. First, in multiple criminal events only the most serious crime is recorded. Thus, if a woman is robbed and raped, only the rape is recorded as a crime. If a building is destroyed by arson and a person is killed as a result, the crime is counted as a murder. Therefore, a certain number of crimes go unrecorded every year. In addition, in the crime figures no distinction is made between "attempted" and "completed" acts, except for homicide, in which case an unsuccessful attempt is counted as an aggravated assault. The distinction between attempts and completions may or may not be important, depending on how the statistics are used. If the figures are being used as an indicator of the seriousness of the crime problem, in the sense of how often criminal acts are initiated, then perhaps it does not matter whether or not the crime was successfully carried out. If, however, the figures are being used to suggest the harm done to society by criminal acts, or if one is interested in the measurement and evaluation of crime control strategies, the distinction is important. A crime which is not completed is generally less harmful than one which is; and if a crime is not successful, perhaps it reflects public efforts to control crime.

Another issue in measuring the crime problem by calculating crime rates involves the choice of the denominator in equation 1–1. The numerator is the number of crimes, on which we have focused so far. But the denominator, population size, also deserves some attention. Should the entire population of the relevant area (the entire country, a state, or a city) be included or only those age groups which contain potential criminals or victims? If the crime rate is used as an indicator of the seriousness of the crime problem in the sense of frequency of crimes relative to number of potential criminals, then perhaps some age groups should be eliminated from the population figure. One tentative suggestion is to include in the population only persons between the ages of 12 and 20, since arrest data suggest that a disproportionate number of index crimes, particularly robbery, burglary, larceny, and motor vehicle theft, are committed by people in this age group.[18] Such adjustments can make important differences when one is making comparisons over time (if the age structure of the population changes significantly) or making comparisons between states or cities with markedly different age distributions (e.g., Utah, where the median age in 2003 was 27.7 years, versus Maine, where the median age was 40.2 years).[19]

If the crime rate is being used as an indicator of the seriousness of the crime problem in the sense of frequency of crimes relative to number of potential targets, then still another denominator may be appropriate. For forcible rape, perhaps only the number of females in certain age groups should be included. For motor vehicle theft, the number of motor vehicles would seem to be a sensible denominator. The appropriate denominator, then, depends on the crime being considered and the purpose of the study.

A final comment concerns the usefulness of offense statistics as measures of what it is worth to attempt to reduce crime, that is, as a guide in public policy development. The offense statistics simply indicate, at best, how many crimes occurred. The figures do not indicate the harm done to society by the crimes—the extent and cost of bodily injury inflicted or the value of property destroyed or stolen. In Chapter 2 we discuss and compare the economic impact of the various index crimes as well as a limited number of other crimes. Measurement of the harm done to society from various criminal acts gives us an idea of what we can gain by reducing crime and, therefore, the amount it is worth spending on law enforcement and criminal justice. Comparisons of the harm done by various crimes is also useful for policy design, as we will see in Chapter 4 when we discuss the optimum "mix" of crime for any society.

In addition, the FBI index crime statistics are, of course, limited to eight crimes, and while the index is referred to as the "Index of Serious Crimes," other crimes (e.g., child molestation or fraud) may be more serious in terms of harm done than some of those included in the index. Even among crimes against property, fraud and embezzlement have been found to be more serious measured in dollar volume, than the index crimes against property. Thus, the FBI index crime figures have somewhat limited usefulness as indicators of the seriousness of crime in our society. Nevertheless, they continue to be widely publicized and have served as a basis for a great deal of empirical research work. Until 1973 these figures were the only major national source of data on crime.

VICTIMIZATION SURVEYS

In 1967 the President's Crime Commission recommended that a survey technique be used to collect victimization rates and profiles, much as it had done in its experimental survey in 1965. The **National Crime Panel Surveys** were initiated in 1973 under the auspices of the then Law Enforcement Assistance Administration (LEAA), which was established in 1968 as a branch of the U.S. Department of Justice. Now called the National Crime Victimization Survey (NCVS), it is actually conducted by the U.S. Census Bureau, under the auspices of the Bureau of Justice Statistics, using sophisticated sampling techniques. Households have been surveyed annually since 1973 while businesses were surveyed only through 1976.

On the basis of interviewing approximately 56,000 housing units each year encompassing responses from approximately 120,000 persons twelve years old or older, information is collected on the amount of criminal activity affecting households across the United States.[20] The NCVS data provide details on the socioeconomic characteristics of the households victimized by crime and on the reporting of crime to police not available from the FBI's UCR data. In addition to finding out whether or not crimes were reported, the survey also asks for reasons why. Characteristics of the crime can also be determined (e.g., time, place, use of weapon) and in some instances, characteristics of the offender. Finally, because the survey is regularly administered, it provides a vehicle for obtaining other kinds of information about crime and the criminal justice system. Additional questions can periodically be added to the survey to serve particular needs, as was done in 1989 with the School Crime Supplement.[21]

Of course, it is important to keep in mind that the survey results are only as good as the sample design. Because of this, reliable figures are only available for the nation as a whole and for broad geographic categories such as "urban" and "suburban." When the survey was initiated, a group of 39 cities were to be sampled once every three years. Thus, each year the nation as a whole and 13 cities would have been sampled. The city program was dropped after a few years because of the high cost of sampling a sufficient number of households to represent not only the country, but specific cities as well.

The National Crime Victimization Survey provides estimates of the number of crimes committed and the likelihood of individuals or households becoming victimized by crime. The latter is accomplished through the calculation of victimization rates. The victimization rate is essentially the same as the crime rate in the earlier discussion of the UCR data. The differences are that the numerator is the number of crimes reported in the survey by individuals (households), not the number reported to the police, and the denominator is the total population (households) in the U.S. or in the cohort of interest (in thousands), e.g., males.

While the survey was initiated in 1973 it went through a significant revision in 1993 to improve the accuracy of the information collected. One goal of the revision was to develop better screening questions to better stimulate recall of victimization incidents. The result was apparently quite successful, but it made comparisons of information collected prior to 1993 with that from 1993 to the present very difficult. For example, in 1992 when both surveys were used the "old" method led to an estimate of 91.2 personal crime victimizations (rape/sexual assault, robbery, assault and personal theft) per thousand people 12 or older, while the "new" method estimated a rate of 127.5 victimizations per thousand. It is quite apparent that the new method uncovered a considerably larger number of victimizations than the original method.

The number of criminal victimizations and the rate of victimization, like the number of crimes reported to the police and the crime rate, vary from year to year. In 1973 the National Crime Survey, the NCVS prior to 1993, estimated that there were 35.7 million people victimized by crime. Over the next 17 years the number of estimated victimizations rose to 41.5 million in 1981 and then declined to 34.4 million in 1990. In 2003 the estimate from the revised NCVS was that there were 24.2 million victimizations. In comparison, the 2003 UCR indicates that only 11.8 million Index Crimes were reported to the police.

Victimization rates followed a very similar pattern over the period, as illustrated in Table 1–4, though not for every crime in the survey nor at the same rate. The violent crime victimization rate increased from the early 1970s through the early 1980s.[22] It then declined through the early 1990s, when it turned up. It again reached a peak in 1995 and, like the crime rate, has shown a significant decrease through 2003. In fact, it is estimated that the 2003 violent crime victimization rate is at its lowest level since the survey was implemented in 1973. The information in Table 1–4 indicates that criminal victimizations for all the NCVS crimes have declined significantly since 1993, with all categories showing declines of almost 50 percent or more over this period.

As indicated above, the NCVS is capable of providing considerable detail on the characteristics of individuals who are victimized by crime. Table 1–5 reports on victimization rates for 2003. The information in the table shows that there is a great deal of variability in who is victimized by crime. In 2003 male victimization rates for violent crimes were 38 percent higher than

TABLE 1-4
VICTIMIZATION RATES FOR INDIVIDUALS
1973–2003 (SELECTED YEARS)[1]

	Personal Crimes[2]	Crimes of Violence[3]	Rape/Sexual Assault	Robbery	Assault	Personal Theft	Property Crimes[4]	Household Burglary	Motor Vehicle Theft	Theft
1973		32.6	0.9	6.7	24.9	91.1		91.7	19.1	107.0
1975		32.8	0.9	6.8	25.2	96.0		91.7	19.5	125.4
1980		33.3	0.9	6.6	25.8	83.0		84.3	16.7	126.5
1985		30.0	0.7	5.1	24.2	69.4		62.7	14.2	97.5
1990		31.7	0.6	5.7	24.9	68.3		53.8	20.5	86.7
1993	52.2	49.9	2.5	6.0	41.4	2.3	318.9	58.2	19.0	241.7
1994	54.1	51.8	2.1	6.3	43.3	2.4	310.2	56.3	18.8	235.1
1995	48.5	46.6	1.7	5.4	39.5	1.9	290.5	49.3	16.9	224.3
1996	43.5	42.0	1.4	5.2	35.4	1.5	266.3	47.2	13.5	205.7
1997	40.8	39.2	1.4	4.3	33.5	1.6	248.3	44.6	13.8	189.9
1998	37.9	36.6	1.5	4.0	31.1	1.3	217.4	38.5	10.8	168.1
1999	33.7	32.8	1.7	3.6	27.4	0.9	198.0	34.1	10.0	153.1
2000	29.1	27.9	1.2	3.2	23.5	1.2	178.1	31.8	8.6	137.7
2001	25.9	25.1	1.1	2.8	21.2	0.8	166.9	28.7	9.2	129.0
2002	23.7	23.1	1.1	2.2	19.8	0.7	159.0	27.7	9.0	122.3
2003	23.3	22.6	0.8	2.5	19.3	0.8	163.2	29.8	9.0	124.4
Percent Change 1993–2003										
	−55.4	−54.7	−68.8	−58.3	−53.4	−65.2	−48.8	−48.8	−52.6	−48.5

1. The NCVS was redesigned in 1993 making direct comparisons between victimization rates from 1973 to 1992 and 1993 to 2003 difficult. Details on the redesign and comparisons can be found in C. Perkins, et. al., *Criminal Victimization in the United States, 1993* (Washington, D.C.: U.S. Department of Justice, Office of Justice Programs, Bureau of Justice Statistics), May1996.

2. Personal crimes include: rape/sexual assault, robbery, assault and personal theft.

3. Crimes of violence include: rape/sexual assault, robbery, and assault.

4. Property crimes include: household burglary, motor vehicle theft and theft.

Sources: U.S. Department of Justice, Office of Justice Programs, Bureau of Justice Statistics, *Criminal Victimization in the United States: 1973–1990 Trends* (Washington, D.C.); U.S. Department of Justice, Office of Justice Programs, Bureau of Justice Statistics, 1973–1990 Trends (Washington, D.C.), December 1992, various tables; C.M. Rennison, *Criminal Victimization in 1998* (Washington, D.C.: U.S. Department of Justice, Office of Justice Programs, Bureau of Justice Statistics), July 1999, Table 7, 9; and Shannan M. Catalano, *Criminal Victimization 2003*, Washington, D.C., U.S. Department of Justice, Office of Justice Programs, Bureau of Justice Statistics, September 2004.

TABLE 1–5

VICTIMIZATION RATES FOR INDIVIDUALS—2003
(RATES PER 1000 PERSONS 12 OR OLDER)

	Violent*	Rape	Robbery	Assault	Theft
Gender					
Male	26.3	0.2	3.2	23.0	0.4
Female	19.0	1.5	1.9	15.7	1.1
Race					
White	21.5	0.8	1.9	18.8	0.6
Black	29.1	0.8	5.9	22.3	1.7
Other	16.0	0.2	3.4	12.4	0.9
Ethnicity					
Hispanic	24.2	0.4	3.1	20.8	1.1
Non-Hispanic	22.3	0.9	2.4	19.0	0.7
Residence					
Urban	28.2	0.8	3.7	23.8	1.3
Suburban	21.3	1.0	2.3	18.1	0.7
Rural	18.6	0.6	1.6	16.4	0.3

Source: Shannan M. Catalano, *Criminal Victimization 2003*, Washington, D.C., U.S. Department of Justice, Office of Justice Programs, Bureau of Justice Statistics, September 2004.
*Violent crimes include robbery, assault and rape.

female rates. African-Americans were more likely to be victims of violent crimes than whites, and non-Hispanics less than Hispanics. Residents of urban areas had the highest victimization rates for violent crimes followed by suburban residents, with rural residents having been victimized at a rate of 66 percent of the urban residents. While not reported in the table, it is the case that victimization rates generally decrease with age beyond the age of 19. Overall, for the violent crimes listed in Table 1–5 the victimization rate for individuals in the 16–19 age cohort was 53.0, while individuals in the 65 or older cohort had a victimization rate of 2.6. Criminal victimization also decreases with household income for all the violent crimes in the table, from a rate of almost 50 for all violent crime when household income is less than $7,500, to a rate of alomst 18 when household income is $75,000 or more.[23]

Similar patterns exist relative to household characteristics when dealing with crimes that affect household units (i.e., burglary, theft, and motor vehicle theft) rather than individuals. African-American households have victimization rates that are higher than white households for property crimes (17 percent higher), with a motor vehicle theft victimization rate more than double that of white households being the largest difference. The property crime victimization rate for Hispanic households is 26 percent higher than for non-Hispanic households. Urban households have a victimization rate that is almost 60 percent higher than rural households, and household victimization tends to be the highest in the western region of the country and the lowest in the Northeast. Property crimes show the highest rates for households with annual incomes less than $7,500, but do fluctuate considerably as household income increases.[24]

International Crime

Crime is certainly not a problem that is unique to the United States. It has been with all societies from the beginning of time. Table 1–6 provides a limited view of the extent of criminal activity throughout the world. The information is presented as crime rates, thus taking into account the considerable differences that exist in the populations of these countries, while allowing for comparisons to the U.S. crime experience.

In comparing criminal activity in the U.S. to crime throughout the world, it is clear that there are some major differences as well as some close similarities. Violent crime is the area in which crime in the U.S appears to differ most dramatically from crime in other parts of the world. The U.S. homicide rate in 2001 was one of the highest for the countries listed in the table. The U.S. homicide rate in 2001 was 37 percent higher than Canada's.

It is not only homicide where the high level of violence in the U.S. was apparent. In 2001 the U.S. rape rate was the second highest of the countries listed, 10 percent higher than its closest rival, the U.K. The assault rate in 2001 was second highest in the U.S. in comparison to other countries listed.

The evidence also suggests that the property crime rates in the U.S. are not that different from the rest of the world. The information in the table suggests that for theft, excluding automobiles; and for automobile theft there were some countries with higher rates and some with lower ones. What does seem interesting is that the more developed countries, those with higher per capita incomes, apparently had higher rates of property crime than the poorer countries.

Cross-national comparisons of criminal activity are fraught with difficulties.[25] Many of the same problems discussed above relative to the UCR are relevant and perhaps compounded when dealing with a variety of nations. For example **INTERPOL (International Criminal Police Organization),** which

TABLE 1-6
RATE OF OFFENSES KNOWN TO POLICE, SELECTED COUNTRIES
(RATE PER 100,000 INHABITANTS)

Country	Year	Total Crime	Homicide	Rape	Assault	Theft	Auto Theft
Angola	1999	143.5	8.7	—	15.3	38.9	3.7
Argentina	2001	1016.6	8.2	8.9	316.2	602.2	188.0
Australia	2000	—	1.7	197.0	190.0	228.0	730.0
Canada	2001	8572.5	4.1	—	148.5	2758.3	547.6
France	2001	6941.0	3.9	16.4	199.2	4310.3	537.7
Ireland	2001	2389.2	1.6	11.1	85.9	1958.3	4.9
Israel	2001	5888.4	3.4	10.1	42.2	3221.0	472.9
Japan	2001	2209.6	1.1	1.8	26.7	1843.7	49.7
Korea (Rep. Of)	2001	1664.1	2.2	4.3	64.5	386.3	—
The Netherlands	1999	—	1.0	22.0	268.0	593.0	109.4
Russian Federation	2001	2049.6	23.2	5.7	38.5	1190.6	26.5
Scotland	1999	—	2.3	27.7	1192.0	1051.0	582.0
Sweden	2001	13350.3	1.9	23.4	667.4	581.5	674.0
Switzerland	2001	4373.7	2.4	6.3	79.5	3346.5	885.1
UK *	1999	—	1.4	28.9	414.6	858.0	723.9
United States	2001	4160.5	5.6	31.8	318.6	3804.6	430.6

Sources: Interpol (www.interpol.int); and for Australia, The Netherlands, Scotland and the UK, *Cross-National Studies in Crime and Justice*, Bureau of Justice Statistics, U.S. Department of Justice, September, 2004.

*UK is England and Wales.

collects the data reported in Table 1–6, requests information on "serious" assaults. The U.S. interprets this to mean aggravated assaults, but how the other countries around the world interpret it is a function of a number of factors including the laws in that country and who provides the information to INTERPOL. According to Archer and Gartner ". . . the problems of underreporting and different indicators have caused the greatest methodological concern."[26] For example, by comparing survey data with reported crimes, it is estimated that burglary has a 91 percent chance of being reported in The Netherlands, while it has a 49 percent chance of being reported in the U.S.[27] Therefore, any cross-national comparison should be made carefully and with a firm understanding of the differences between the countries being compared.

There are also considerable differences in incarceration rates throughout the world. At mid-2004 the U.S. had the highest incarceration rate in the world with approximately 726 incarcerated inmates per 100,000 people. Comparisons using the most current data available as of 2004 found that Russia had the second highest rate at 587 inmates per 100,000 people. The incarceration rate in England and Wales is less than one-fifth the U.S. rate (143 incarcerated inmates per 100,000 people).[28] The U.S. incarceration rate has been increasing steadily since the 1970s.

With this brief introduction to crime and its dimensions, trends, and data sources behind us, let us turn to a discussion of the economic aspects of crime. We begin in the next chapter with an analysis of the economic impact of criminal activity.

REVIEW TERMS AND CONCEPTS

Crime rate	Organized crime
Crimes against persons	Property crime
Criminal behavior	Psychic benefits
Cybercrime	Psychic costs
Demand	Public policy
Deterrent effect	Punishment costs
Economic benefits	Rational behavior
FBI	Supply
Households-touched-by-crime indicator	UCR
Index crimes	Victimization rate
INTERPOL	Victimless crime
National Crime Victimization Survey	Violent crime
NCVS	White collar crime
NIBRS	

END OF CHAPTER QUESTIONS

1. Compare and contrast the strengths and weaknesses of the two primary sources of information on the amount of crime in the U.S., the FBI's UCR data and the Department of Justice's NCVS.

2. Crime in the U.S. is constantly changing. Describe how it has changed since 1960.

3. Why is it better to report crime *rates* and victimization *rates* when describing criminal activity than the number of crimes and victimizations?

4. In what significant manner does crime in the U.S. differ from crime in much of the rest of the world?

NOTES

1. For a review of studies by economists, as well as other social scientists, of the deterrent effect of punishment on crime, see Charles Tittle, "Punishment and Deterrence of Deviance," in Simon Rottenberg, ed., *The Economics of Crime and Punishment* (Washington, D.C.: American Enterprise Institute for Public Policy Research, 1973), and Gordon Tullock, "Does Punishment Deter Crime?" *The Public Interest,* no. 36 (Summer 1974), 103–111, reprinted in Neil O. Alper and Daryl A. Hellman, *Economics of Crime: A Reader* (Needham, Ma.: Simon & Schuster, 1997). For a very comprehensive work see Alfred Blumstein, Jacqueline Cohen, and Daniel Nagin, eds., *Deterrence and Incapacitation: Estimating the Effects of Criminal Sanctions on Crime Rates* (Washington, D.C.: National Academy of Sciences, 1978).

2. *Ibid.*

3. Paul B. Horton, "Problems in Understanding Criminal Motives," in Simon Rottenberg, ed., *op. cit.*

4. For a discussion of the criminologist's approach to the study of crime and the distinction between causal analysis and policy analysis, see James Q. Wilson, "Criminologists," in *Thinking About Crime* (New York: Basic Books, 1975).

5. "The Federalization of Criminal Law," Taskforce on the Federalization of Criminal Law, American Bar Association, Criminal Justice Section (Washington, D.C., 1998), 94.

6. President's Commission on Law Enforcement and the Administration of Justice, *The Challenge of Crime in a Free Society* (Washington, D.C., 1967). This commission is sometimes referred to as the Katzenbach Commission.

7. Detailed information on the redesigned UCR program comes from "Structure and Implementation Plan for the Enhanced UCR Program," U.S. Department of Justice, FBI, nd, and *Uniform Crime Reports for the United States, 1998* (Washington, D.C.: U.S. Department of Justice, FBI, 1999).

8. James A. Fox, "Murder Most Common," *The Sunday Boston Globe,* January 31, 1993, 65 and 68.

9. Steven Levitt, "Understanding Why Crime Fell in the 1990s: Four Factors that Explain the Decline and Six that Do Not," *Journal of Economic Perspectives,* Vol. 18, no. 1, Winter 2004.

10. From a quote by James Allan Fox, in "Violent Crime Dipped in '03; Murder Rose," by Eric Lichtblau, *The New York Times,* October 26, 2004.

11. For a discussion of some of the problems with the FBI's UCR data, see Marvin E. Wolfgang, "Urban Crime" in James Q. Wilson, ed., *The Metropolitan Enigma* (Cambridge, Ma.: Harvard University Press, 1968).

12. Victimization surveys are now done annually and provide a useful addition to the UCR data. Victimization data are discussed later.

13. Shannon M. Catalano, "Criminal Victimization 2003" (Washington, D.C.: Bureau of Justice Statistics, September 2004), 10.

14. The information in this paragraph is from Cathy Matson and Patsy Klaus, "Criminal Victimization in the United States, 2002, Statistical Tables," (Washington, D.C., Bureau of Justice Statistics, December 2003), various tables.

15. "Private Security: Patterns and Trends," by William C. Cunningham, John J. Strauchs, and Clifford W. Van Meter, U.S. Department of Justice, National Institute of Justice, *Research in Brief,* August 1991, 4.

16. William C. Cunningham, et al., *op.cit.,* 4.

17. Charles Piller, "Cyber-Crime Loss at Firms Doubles to $10 Billion," *The Los Angeles Times,* March 22, 2000, Part C, 1.

18. Roland J. Chilton and Adele Spielberger, "Increases in Crime: The Utility of Alternative Measures," *Journal of Criminal Law, Criminology, and Police Science,* 43, no. 1 (March 1972), 68–74.

19. "Median Age of the Total Population: 2003," (Washington, D.C.: U.S. Census Bureau, www.factfindercensus.gov/).

20. For an overview of the NCVS data and methodology used to collect it, see U.S. Department of Justice, Bureau of Justice Statistics, *Criminal Victimization in the United States,* 1990 (Washington, D.C., 1992).

21. Lisa D. Bastian and Bruce M. Taylor, *School Crime: A National Crime Victimization Survey Report* (Washington, D.C.: U.S. Department of Justice, Office of Justice Programs, Bureau of Justice Statistics, September 1991).

22. Callie Marie Rennison, *Criminal Victimization 1998* (Washington, D.C.: Bureau of Justice Statistics, July 1999), 10.

23. Shannon Catalano, *Criminal Victimization 2003; op.cit.,* Table 6, 7.

24. *Ibid.,* Table 7.8 and Table 8, 9.

25. For an excellent discussion of the problems associated with cross-national comparisons of criminal activity, see Dane Archer and Rosemary Gartner, *Violence and Crime in Cross-National Perspective* (New Haven: Yale University Press, 1984). The book also includes crime rate data for 110 countries and 44 cities around the world starting in 1900 and ending approximately 1970. The length of the series varies by country.

26. *Ibid.,* p. 29. By indicators, the authors mean the unit of measurement such as the number of offenses known, the number of arrests, the number of court cases, or the number of convictions.

27. David Farrington, Patrick Langan, and Michael Tonry, editors, "Cross-National Studies in Crime and Justice" (U.S. Department of Justice, Bureau of Justice Statistics, Washington, D.C., September 2004).

28. Paige Harrison and Allen Beck, "Prison and Jail Inmates at Midyear 2004" (U.S. Department of Justice, Bureau of Justice Statistics, Washington, D.C., April 2005), Table 1, 2; and International Centre for Prison Studies, "Entire World—Prison Population Rates" (www.prisonstudies.org).

APPENDIX TO CHAPTER 1

DEFINITIONS OF TERMS

The following information is taken, with slight revision, from *Sourcebook of Criminal Justice Statistics—1984,* which is published by the U.S. Department of Justice, Bureau of Justice Statistics (Washington, D.C., February 1985), pp. 721–722.

A.   The Crime Index

The following offenses and attempts to commit these offenses are used in compiling the crime index: (1) murder and non-negligent manslaughter, (2) forcible rape, (3) robbery, (4) aggravated assault, (5) burglary, (6) larceny-theft, (7) motor vehicle theft, and (8) arson. (Note: manslaughter by negligence and minor assaults are not included in the crime index.)

B.   Part I Offenses

1. Criminal homicide
   a. Murder and non-negligent manslaughter
   b. Manslaughter by negligence

2. Forcible rape
   a. Rape by force
   b. Attempts to commit forcible rape

3. Robbery
   a. Firearm
   b. Knife or cutting instrument
   c. Other dangerous weapon
   d. Strong-arm, hands, fists, feet, etc.

4. Aggravated assault
   a. Firearm
   b. Knife or cutting instrument
   c. Other dangerous weapon
   d. Hands, fists, feet, etc.—aggravated injury

5. Burglary
   a. Forcible entry
   b. Unlawful entry—no force
   c. Attempted forcible entry

6. Larceny–theft (except motor vehicle theft)
7. Motor vehicle theft
   a. Autos
   b. Trucks and buses
   c. Other vehicles
8. Arson

C. Definitions of Part I Offense Classes

1. **Criminal homicide.** This is the killing of one human being by another. This class consists of two parts: (a) killings due to willful acts (non-negligent) and (b) deaths due to negligent acts. The two subdivisions of the criminal homicide class result from a careful study of the variations found in state statutes.

   a. **Murder and non-negligent manslaughter.** One offense is counted for each person willfully killed by another. As a rule, any death due to a fight, argument, quarrel, assault, or commission of a crime is counted. Suicides, accidental deaths, assaults to murder, and attempted murders are not counted as murder and non-negligent manslaughter. Assaults to murder and attempted murders are counted as aggravated assaults. Certain willful killings are classified as justifiable or excusable under this program. Justifiable homicides are limited to (1) killing of a felon by a police-officer in the line of duty and (2) killing of a felon by a private citizen. A killing is not justifiable or excusable on the basis of self-defense or the action of a coroner, prosecutor, grand jury, or court. These data are police statistics based on a police investigation.

   b. **Manslaughter by negligence.** An offense is counted for each person killed by the gross negligence of another. Traffic fatalities are included. It is not included in the Crime Index.

2. **Forcible rape.** This offense is the carnal knowledge or attempted carnal knowledge of a female, forcibly and against her will. One offense is counted for each person raped or on whom an assault or an attempt to rape has been made. Statutory offenses (no force and victim under the legal age of consent) are not counted. Any rape or attempt accomplished by force is classified as forcible rape regardless of the age of the victim.

3. **Robbery.** Robbery is taking or attempting to take anything of value from the care, custody, or control of a person or persons by force or threat of force or violence and/or by putting the victim in fear. Robbery involves a theft or larceny aggravated by the element of force or threat of force. If no force or threat of force is used, such as in pocketpicking or purse-snatching, the offense will be reported as larceny rather than robbery. Robbery is divided into the following types: (a) firearm; (b) knife or cutting instrument; (c) other dangerous weapon; and (d) strong-arm (hands, fists, feet, etc.).

   a. **Robbery–firearm.** In this category of robbery each "distinct operation" is reported in which any firearm is used as a weapon or employed as a means of force to threaten the victim or put him or her in fear.

   b. **Robbery–knife or cutting instrument.** This category includes each "distinct operation" in which a knife, broken bottle, razor, or other cutting instrument is employed as a weapon or as a means of force to threaten the victim or put him or her in fear.

   c. **Robbery–other dangerous weapon.** A robbery involving a club, acid, explosive, brass knuckles, or other dangerous weapon would be included in this category.

   d. **Robbery–strong-arm (hands, fists, feet, etc.).** This category includes muggings, yokings, and similar offenses in which no weapon is used but strong-arm tactics are employed to deprive the victim of property. This is limited to personal weapons such as hands, arms, feet, fist, teeth, etc.

      In cases involving pretend weapons or in which the weapon is not seen by the victim but the robber claims to have it in his or her possession, the armed robbery is placed in the appropriate category. If an immediate "on view" arrest proves that there is no weapon, the robbery will be labeled "strong-arm robbery."

      In all categories of robbery, attempts are counted in the same way as completed offenses.

4. **Aggravated assault.** Aggravated assault is an unlawful attack by one person on another for the purpose of inflicting severe or aggravated bodily injury. This type of assault is usually accompanied by the use of a weapon or by means likely to produce death or great bodily harm. This category includes the offenses commonly termed assault with intent to kill or to murder; poisoning; assault with a

dangerous weapon; maiming, mayhem, and assault with intent to maim or commit mayhem; assault with explosives; and all attempts to commit the foregoing offenses. Attempt to murder or assault to murder are reported as aggravated assault. All aggravated assaults coming to the attention of police are classified according to whether they involve (a) firearm; (b) knife or cutting instrument; (c) other dangerous weapon; or (d) hands, fists, feet, etc.—aggravated injury.

   a. **Assault–firearm.** Included in this category are all assaults in which a firearm such as a revolver, automatic pistol, shotgun, zipgun, rifle, etc. is used or its use is threatened.

   b. **Assault–knife or cutting instrument.** When a knife, razor, hatchet, axe, cleaver, scissors, glass, broken bottle, ice pick, etc. is used, the assault will be classified in this category.

   c. **Assault–other dangerous weapon.** This category includes assaults resulting from the use of any object or thing as a weapon which does or could do serious injury to a victim.

   d. **Assault–hands, fists, feet, etc. (aggravated injury).** This classification is used to record only those offenses which result in serious or aggravated injury. The assault will be aggravated if the personal injury is serious (e.g., broken bones, internal injuries, or cuts requiring stitches). A severe beating, kicking, etc. of a woman or child by an adult will usually be counted as aggravated assault.

5. **Burglary–breaking or entering.** Burglary is defined as the unlawful entry of a structure to commit a felony or theft. Offenses locally known as burglary include unlawful entry with intent to commit a larceny or felony, breaking and entering with intent to commit a larceny, housebreaking, and safecracking. All attempts at these offenses are also counted as burglary.

   For the purposes of the *Uniform Crime Reports,* structures are considered to include, but are not limited to, the following: dwelling houses, appurtenances to dwellings, garages, churches, schoolhouses, tenements, housetrailers or houseboats which are used as permanent dwellings, mills, barns, vessels, cabins, public buildings, shops, offices, factories, storehouses, apartments, rooms, warehouses, stables, other buildings, ships, and railroad cars. There are three subcategories of burglary: (a) forcible entry; (b) unlawful entry—no force; and (c) attempted forcible entry.

a. **Burglary–forcible entry.** Counted in this category are all offenses in which force of any kind is used to enter a structure unlawfully for the purpose of committing a theft or any felony. Burglary by concealment inside a building followed by an exit from the structure is included in this category.

b. **Burglary–unlawful entry, no force.** The entry in these situations involves no force and is achieved by use of an unlocked door or window. The element of trespass is essential in this subcategory. If the area were one of open access, thefts from the area would not involve an unlawful trespass and would be scored as larceny.

c. **Burglary–attempted forcible entry.** Situations in which a forcible entry burglary is attempted are placed in this category.

6. **Larceny–theft.** Larceny–theft is the unlawful taking, carrying, leading, or riding away of property from the possession or constructive possession of another. All thefts which are not part of a robbery, burglary, or motor vehicle theft should be classified in this category regardless of the value of the article stolen. All thefts and attempted thefts are counted. Larceny–thefts are broken down into pick–pocketing, purse-snatching, shoplifting, thefts from motor vehicles, thefts of motor vehicle parts and accessories, thefts of bicycles, thefts from buildings (where the offender has legal access), thefts from coin-operated devices or machines, and all other larceny not specifically classified.

7. **Motor vehicle theft**. Motor vehicle theft is defined as theft or attempted theft of a motor vehicle. A motor vehicle is defined for this program as a self-propelled vehicle that runs on the surface and not on rails. Taking for temporary use when prior authority has been granted or can be assumed, such as by family members, and unauthorized use by chauffeurs and others having lawful access are not counted as motor vehicle thefts. All cases in which automobiles are taken by persons not having lawful access thereto and are later abandoned are motor vehicle thefts. For the purpose of obtaining a more specific definition of the type of motor vehicle stolen, three subcategories have been established: (a) autos; (b) trucks and buses; and (c) other vehicles.

a. **Autos.** All automobiles which serve the purpose of transporting people from one place to another are included here.

   b. **Trucks and buses.** This breakdown includes vehicles specifically designed to transport people on a commercial basis or to transport cargo.
   c. **Other vehicles.** Examples of this type of vehicle are snowmobiles, motorcycles, motor scooters, trailbikes, etc. Thefts of farm equipment, bulldozers, airplanes, and construction equipment are scored as larceny–thefts.

8. **Arson.** Included in this category are all arrests for violations of state laws and municipal ordinances relating to arson and attempted arson. Any willful or malicious burning or attempts to burn, with or without intent to defraud, a dwelling house, church, college, jail, meeting house, public building or any building, ship or other vessel, motor vehicle or aircraft, as well as contents of buildings, personal property of another, goods or chattels, crops, trees, fences, gates, grain, vegetable products, lumber, woods, cranberry bogs, marshes, meadows, etc., is counted as arson.

   In the event that a death resulted from arson, the incident would be classified as murder; if personal injury resulted, the incident would be classified as aggravated assault.

2

The Economic Impact of Criminal Activity

We begin our discussion of the economic aspects of criminal activity by looking at the **economic impact of crime.** This will be useful because it will give us some idea of what it is worth to prevent crime. Unfortunately, we will find that some aspects of the impact of crime are very difficult, if not impossible, to measure; other aspects, while measurable, are difficult to determine. Regardless of these limitations, assessment of the economic impact of criminal activity is a necessary first step in setting budget priorities and developing effective public policy for the control of crime. At a minimum, our discussion will provide a useful framework for analysis.

MAGNITUDE OF THE IMPACT

Since the late 1960s there have been more than half a dozen studies that have produced estimates of the total annual cost of crime. The estimates range from $19 billion to $2.1 trillion. The differences in the estimates are due to a number of factors including when they were undertaken, the extent of the crimes included and the types of costs examined.[1] They also differ in the way they report the costs.

A recent **National Institute of Justice** study estimated the total cost of crime to be $450 billion, in 1993 dollars ($600 billion in 2005 dollars),[2] based on detailed estimates of the costs of individual criminal victimizations and estimates of the number of victimizations.[3] Before reviewing the estimates from this report found in Table 2–1 it is important to understand the types of costs included in this study. It estimated **"tangible costs"**; these are the costs of the goods and services utilized by the victim and society in reaction to the criminal victimization, and the "quality of life" cost to the victim,

31

including the cost of fear, pain and suffering, or what economists would call **psychic costs,** and the value of the victim's life. Included in the tangible costs are the direct costs of dealing with the crime and its victim(s), such as medical and mental health services, victim services, and police and fire services; and the value of the property damaged or destroyed. Also included among the tangible costs are lost **productivity costs** of people (what economists call **opportunity costs**) including the victims, their families, co-workers and supervisors at the victim's place of work, and bystanders not directly involved in the crime but who are delayed by the crime, such as people stuck in traffic due to an accident caused by a drunk driver.

The cost per criminal victimization (in 2005 dollars) is estimated to be as low as $498 for a larceny and almost $4,000,000 for a fatal crime involving a rape or arson or driving-under-the-influence where the victim dies. In general, the cost per victimization is higher for crimes of violence than for property crimes. For almost all the crimes studied, the quality of life cost is larger than the tangible costs. This is especially true for the victims of violent crimes. Among the tangible costs, the cost of lost productivity is generally the largest cost. In fact, for fatal crimes the productivity cost is 96 percent of total tangible losses.

A more recent and more comprehensive study estimates the annual cost of crime to be $2.1 trillion, in 2005 dollars, or $4,990 for every man, woman and child in the U.S.[4] Some of the additional costs included in this study are the criminals' opportunity costs and the opportunity costs of private crime prevention activities. The time that criminals spend planning and committing the crime represents lost production of goods and services to society, as does the time spent in prison. The time ordinary people spend attempting to prevent crime, such as their participation in a neighborhood watch program or installing locks in their home are also included and are opportunity costs. In fact, the author of this study estimates the annual cost of locking and unlocking doors and looking for the necessary keys is $90 billion ($109 billion in 2005 dollars).[5] The author includes the costs of **private crime deterrence** such as the costs of private guards, alarms, fences, and lighting. The production of all these goods and services utilizes resources and therefore imposes costs on society.

There are two additional types of costs included that make the study more comprehensive. One is what the author calls compliance enforcement. There are many government rules and regulations that are not enforced by the police that are enforced by various inspectors and regulators. For example there are health inspectors who are responsible for enforcing the laws with regard to the cleanliness of public eating establishments like restaurants and college cafeterias.

TABLE 2-1

COST OF CRIME BY TYPE OF CRIME – 2005

	Cost per Victimization			Annual Cost (in millions)		
	Tangible Losses	Quality of Life	Total	Tangible Losses	Quality of Life	Total
Fatal Crime	$1,336,598	$2,634,161	$3,970,759	$44,957	$80,761	$125,718
Child Abuse	10,675	70,492	81,168	9,826	64,609	74,435
Rape	6,865	109,566	116,431	10,095	160,176	170,272
Assault	2,086	10,499	12,585	20,190	103,644	123,834
Robbery	3,096	7,672	10,768	4,173	10,768	14,941
Drunk Driving	8,076	16,018	24,094	18,037	36,343	54,379
Arson	26,247	24,228	50,476	3,580	3,231	6,811
Larceny	498	0	498	12,316	0	12,316
Burglary	1,481	404	1,884	9,463	2,423	11,885
Motor Vehicle Theft	4,711	404	5,115	8,492	673	9,165
Total				$141,129	$462,627	$603,756

Source: Ted Miller, Mark Cohen, and Brian Wiersema, *Victim Costs and Consequences: A New Look*, Washington, D.C.: National Institute of Justice, January 1996, Table 2, 9, and Table 5, 17.

*1993 data adjusted for inflation based on CPI inflation calculator, the U.S. Bureau of Labor Statistics, www.bls.gov.

There are building inspectors who make certain contractors are following the safety requirements for building homes, apartments and businesses, and government regulators who oversee the operations of various financial institutions like banks. The cost of transfers is the other type of cost included in this study but not included in the NIJ study. These are goods and services, often in the form of money, involuntarily taken from one person and given to another. For example, the ownership of a car that is stolen, or its parts, is simply transferred from one person, the legal owner, to another. Other examples of crimes that impose significant transfer costs on individuals are unpaid taxes, fraud of all types, robbery and most property crimes. It should be noted that some researchers exclude these costs because they do not represent a use of resources or a lost opportunity to produce goods and services, but simply a reallocation from the victim to the criminal or the customer of the criminal.

Table 2–2 provides information from this report on the costs of crime by types of cost. The author aggregates costs into four categories: crime induced production, opportunity costs, implicit costs and transfer costs. The crime induced production costs are the costs of the resources used in the production and the reaction to crime. This would include the criminal justice system costs along with the costs of things like burglar alarms. The opportunity costs are the value of time foregone by the criminals, victims and their families, and in preventing crime. The implicit costs are the costs to the victim associated with risks to life and health. It is the transfer costs that are the largest cost. They account for 35 percent of estimated total costs. Excluding these costs still provides an estimate of $1.3 trillion for the annual cost of crime in the U.S. for 1997 in 2005 dollars.

There are costs that even this study is unable to include some of which have been examined by other researchers. Some of these are: the cost of crime on property values in a neighborhood, which is an example of a negative ex-

TABLE 2–2

COST OF CRIME BY SOURCE—2005* (IN BILLIONS)

Crime-induced production	$481
Opportunity costs	158
Risks	696
Transfers	731
Total	$2,065

Source: D. Anderson, "The Aggregate Burden of Crime," *Journal of Law and Economics,* October 1999, Table 7, 629.
*1997 data adjusted for inflation based on CPI inlation calculator, the U.S. Bureau of Labor Statistics, www.bls.gov.

ternality; the cost of migration from crime riddled neighborhoods and the difficulties employers might have in attracting workers to such areas; the costs of unreported crimes and the value of the lost taxes associated with activity in the underground economy. Therefore it is likely that the actual cost to society is greater than the $1.7 trillion ($2.1 trillion in 2005 dollars) estimated by this report, but how much greater is not known.

Using an entirely different approach to estimate the cost of crime, known as contingent valuation, a recent study of the social costs of crime estimates total costs for certain crimes to be 1.5 to 10 times higher than previous estimates. The study focuses on community-wide crime reduction based on individuals' willingness-to-pay for reducing crime by ten percent. This approach is thought to be more representative of social costs as opposed to studies based on costs to individual victims. The estimates are that the social costs are: $25,000 per burglary, $70,000 per serious assault, $232,000 per armed robbery, $237,000 per rape and sexual assault, and $9.7 million per murder.[6]

A relatively new area of criminal activity that is not likely to be included in either estimate is the cost of computer crime or cybercrime. A survey undertaken in 1999 by the Computer Security Institute and the San Francisco office of the FBI of almost 650 major corporations and public agencies estimated the cost of computer crime to be approximately $10 billion ($11.7 billion in 2005 dollars), double what it was estimated to be in 1998. The primary reason for the growth is the increased accessibility to the Internet. The losses are primarily from financial fraud and the theft of proprietary information over the Internet.[7] The Business Software Alliance estimated that in 1998 software theft over the Internet cost approximately 109,000 jobs in the U.S. and lost tax revenues of more than $990 million ($1.2 billion in 2005 dollars). Additionally, the Recording Industry Association of America estimates an income loss of more than $4.2 billion annually worldwide due to all forms of piracy.[8] It is expected that the cost of computer crime will continue to increase with the boom in **email** and **ecommerce.**

ANALYZING IMPACTS

From an economic point of view some crimes are more serious than others because they have a greater impact on the economy and on our well-being, or economic welfare. It is useful to consider exactly how each kind of crime affects economic welfare. To simplify, we will consider three broad classes of crime: crimes against persons, crimes against property, and illegal goods and services, or "victimless" crimes. In each case we will consider the impact on the economy or society as a whole, not the impact on a particular individual.

Crimes Against Persons

How can we begin to assess the economic impact of a crime against a person, such as assault? First, if the victim is injured and requires medical attention, there is the cost of that medical care. Society as a whole expends scarce medical resources, including land, labor, and machinery and buildings, in caring for the victim. This use of resources would not be required if the crime had not been committed. Thus, society is worse off by the amount of medical resources used up.

Second, if the individual is incapacitated either temporarily or permanently, there is a loss of output, i.e., the goods and services the individual would have produced. This cost can be evaluated by estimating the output's value. Generally, this is accomplished by estimating what the person would have earned during the period that she or he is incapacitated. In the case of murder, the income loss would be calculated for the number of working years remaining had the crime not occurred.[9] In order to evaluate correctly a loss in earnings that occurs over time, it is necessary to adjust the dollars lost in different time periods; that is, it is necessary to discount future dollars to their present value. This procedure is described in the appendix to this chapter.[10]

Additional costs to society due to crimes against persons include the psychic costs suffered by the victim and the victim's family, friends, and community. These may be severe, though difficult to assess. In some instances psychic losses may be demonstrated in measurable ways, such as when a family member is unable to work or seeks counseling because of mourning or grief.

There are other impacts on society when one of its members is injured or killed. An economic evaluation of the loss focuses on the loss of a productive member of the economy—a unit of economic resources. But beyond being a productive input and member of the economy, the individual is also a member of social groups—family, community, and so forth. The contributions lost by these groups are not considered here, although admittedly they may be just as important as lost earnings. An approach which estimates the value of reduced risk of death would be preferable because it would include more than the value of anticipated income.

Finally, costs to society from crimes against persons include costs incurred by the public sector to enforce the laws forbidding these crimes and to punish those who break the laws. Included are **expenditures for police, courts, and prisons.** Private expenditures by households and business firms or as a result of victimization by these crimes to avoid being victimized or are also a cost to society.

Crimes Against Property

Crimes against property, such as burglary, affect society in a very different way. In some property crimes (e.g., arson) real property is damaged and destroyed, and this represents a net loss to society; real assets are lost forever. But in a large number of property crimes property is not destroyed and therefore is not lost to society. It is simply transferred from one person or group to another. An economist would refer to this as an involuntary transfer: money or goods are transferred from one group to another, but the victim(s) did not agree to the transfer.

In the simplest case a burglar steals a television set for her or his own use. Here, while one individual loses a TV, another gains one. The net loss to society is zero. More typically, the burglar steals property for the purpose of fencing the merchandise to obtain cash. However, the television is ultimately sold to a customer at its market value. Again the television is not lost or destroyed and the net impact is zero.

There are, however, some real costs to society associated with crimes against property. First, there are the costs of having some people working to produce economic "bads" instead of goods. That is, some people work as burglars, fences, and the like rather than being employed in legitimate jobs producing something that people value. People do not value involuntary transfers. The valuable goods and services which these individuals do not produce because they devote their time and other resources to producing crime are a cost to society. This is referred to as an opportunity cost: society loses the opportunity to produce goods and services that are of value. The value of property stolen may over- or underestimate this opportunity cost component.[11]

Additional costs to society include psychic costs to victims and others, such as anger or fear. There is also the cost to society of having property rights threatened. The U.S. economy is a system of **mixed capitalism.** Capitalism relies on the institution of privately owned property. To the extent that we cannot guarantee protection of private property, we diminish the ability of a capitalist economy to function. This may, of course, be one reason why some people commit certain property crimes. We will discuss this in the next chapter, where we present an economic explanation of criminal behavior. For now, it is sufficient to note that this threat to the economic system does impose a cost, assuming that we believe a capitalist system is desirable.[12]

The final category of costs consists of private expenditures to protect property and public expenditures in the criminal justice system.

Victimless Crimes

Crimes without victims affect society in still another way. The kinds of costs imposed by these activities vary from one crime to another, but they fall into one or more categories. The largest, possibly not in terms of dollars but in terms of emotional input and vocal output, is the impact on the moral climate of society. Some would argue, for example, that prostitution encourages immoral behavior. It may also create urban areas that are objectionable to look at, such as the Combat Zone in Boston.[13] Economists refer to these kinds of costs as **negative externalities:** costs, even if only psychic, are imposed involuntarily on some people by the consumption and/or production decision of others.[14] Negative externalities are difficult to identify and measure. Some people may experience the negative externalities that victimless crimes create only if the activity is visible to them, like streetwalking by prostitutes or drunks lying in gutters. For others, visibility does not matter; rather, merely knowing that the activity exists is harmful.

Victimless crimes may also create net losses to society, losses measured by the amount of economic resources used up as an indirect result of the criminal activity. For example, purchase of the services of a prostitute may lead to venereal disease, which may mean lost work time and hospital resources which would not otherwise be needed, or AIDS, which eventually leads to the use of medical resources and lost output due to the premature death of the victim. These outcomes are possible, but are not necessarily costs of prostitution. Similarly for drug use, the addict who is unable to work or dies prematurely represents potentially productive labor which is lost.

Some would argue that the economic resources used directly in the production of illegal goods and services also represent a net loss to society in that the resources are being used to produce economic "bads" rather than "goods" and that therefore we as a society sacrifice some output. This is the opportunity cost concept again: by using scarce resources to produce "bads," we sacrifice the opportunity to produce "goods."

However, resources used directly in the production of victimless crimes are not losses to society the way those used directly in the production of burglary are. In the case of victimless crimes the illegal output is obviously valued by at least some members of society. If no one valued the output, there would be no demand for the product and there would, therefore, be no production and use of resources.

In addition, victimless crimes may result in transfers of income or wealth from some individuals to others. From society's point of view there is no net change, but from the individual viewpoint some people gain while others lose. Several kinds of transfers can result. One example is property stolen by drug addicts to support their expensive habits. Robbery committed by prostitutes against their customers is another.

The final cost category is the **criminal justice expenditures** that we make each year in an effort to police these activities and punish those who break the law.

THE DISTRIBUTION OF THE COSTS OF CRIME: IMPACTS ON INDIVIDUALS

In the preceding section we were concerned with analyzing the impact of various crimes on the economy or society as a whole, not the impact on particular individuals or groups of individuals. In this section we change the focus of our analysis and try to assess ways in which individuals are hurt by crime. We will also attempt to develop a framework for determining which individuals are hurt more or less than others. To emphasize the difference, consider the TV which is burglarized. We argued that for the economy as a whole, which is the summation of the individuals within it, the TV is not lost. From the point of view of the individual, however, there is a net loss to the person from whom it is burglarized.

Before developing a framework for determining the distribution of the costs of crime among individuals, it is necessary to identify the ways in which an individual can be hurt, or helped, by crime. It is important to realize that while some individuals lose as a result of crime, others gain, and these gains do not include criminal gains. Individuals can be affected by crime in the following ways:

Losses of property or productive assets
Psychic costs
Price effects
Employment effects
Tax effects

Losses of property or productive assets include those losses which represent net losses to society (e.g., a building destroyed by arson) and those which represent transfers from the viewpoint of society (e.g., the burglarized TV). Losses are experienced directly by victims and indirectly by nonvictims: for example, if a productive asset is destroyed, all individuals are affected to the extent that the productive capacity of the economy is reduced.

Psychic costs were explained earlier in the chapter. These costs are imposed directly on victims and, in many cases, indirectly on nonvictims. For example, a burglary will most likely create anxiety and anger in the victim, but neighbors of the victim are also likely to experience the same feelings, although their reactions will be less severe.

Price effects refer to the effects that criminal activities have on the demand for and/or supply of various goods and services, and therefore on various prices; that is, prices are different from what they would be if there were no crime. All consumers of the affected products bear the price effects, whether they are victims or not. Later we will present, in detail, an example of a price effect.

Associated with price effects are quantity effects; that is, the price and output of some goods and services are affected. If the output of a product is increased or decreased, the amount of resources used in the production of that product must be increased or decreased to realize the change in output. The individuals who employ their resources in the affected industries are the ones who experience the employment effects. While the employment effects can affect the use of all productive resources, including land and capital, the immediate impact is most likely to be on labor, which we assume is more variable than the other factors; however, returns to capital, or profits, may also be altered.[15] Later we illustrate an employment effect.

The final way in which an individual can be affected by crime is via a tax effect. Because of criminal activity certain expenditures on the criminal justice system are necessary. These expenditures by the public sector at the federal, state, and local levels are financed by taxes, which are paid by individuals. The tax effects are imposed on all taxpayers in the affected political jurisdiction, whether they are victims or not. It should be noted that the criminal justice system is financed and provided primarily at the local level and therefore is financed primarily from the local property tax. Table 2–3 illustrates the distribution of expenditures over the various levels of government.

From the table we can see that local governments (county and municipal) spend 50.2 percent of the total. State and local governments combined spend 84.1 percent of the total. Whether or not this distribution of financial responsibility is appropriate is a good topic for further discussion. It is an important consideration because it affects not only the geographic area which contributes, and at what rate, but also the type and incidence of the tax.

Another way to examine the impact of crime on taxes, and therefore, on the individual taxpayer, is to determine the sources of tax revenues used to finance the components of the criminal justice system. This information will enable us to answer questions such as what taxes are likely to increase if the number of incarcerated criminals were to increase, or what taxes are likely to

TABLE 2–3

DIRECT CRIMINAL JUSTICE EXPENDITURES, FISCAL YEAR 2002

	Amount (Billions)	Percentage
Federal	$28.55	15.9%
State	60.91	33.9
County	44.05	24.5
Municipal	46.07	25.7
Total	$179.58	100.0%

Source: U.S. Department of Justice, Bureau of Justice Statistics, *Expenditure and Employment Extracts Program* (www.ojp.usdoj.gov/bjs/eande.html#selected), Tables 1 and 3.

increase in order to put more police on the street to fight increased crime. The information in Table 2–4 will provide answers to these and similar questions.

From the table we can see that the tax revenues collected by state governments are the primary source of revenues for the corrections system in the U.S. In fact more than 61 percent of what was spent on corrections in fiscal year 2002 came from state governments. Therefore, if more criminals are to be incarcerated, leading to an increased need for prisons, then state taxes are likely to increase. How that impacts the individual taxpayer depends on what taxes are used by the state to raise revenues. States use a variety of taxes to raise revenues that include **personal and corporate income taxes, sales tax, "sin" taxes** (e.g., taxes on alcohol and tobacco), and inheritance taxes. The answer to the question concerning the increased cost of police is left to the student.

TABLE 2–4

DISTRIBUTION OF CRIMINAL JUSTICE SYSTEM EXPENDITURES, FISCAL YEAR 2002

	Police (%)	Courts* (%)	Corrections (%)
Federal	18.4	22.6	8.0
State	12.3	35.8	61.5
County	20.0	31.8	25.5
Municipal	49.3	9.8	5.0
	100.0%	100.0%	100.0%

Source: U.S. Department of Justice, Bureau of Justice Statistics, *Expenditure and Employment Extracts Program* (www.ojp.usdoj.gov/bjs/eande.html#selected), Tables 1 and 3.
*Includes courts, prosecution and legal services, and public defense.

ANALYZING THE DISTRIBUTION
OF COSTS TO INDIVIDUALS

Once we have determined the ways in which individuals can be affected by crime, we can analyze the distribution of those effects, or costs, among various population groups. For example, the distribution of costs can be analyzed by geographic area (i.e., central city vs. suburb vs. rural area). To do this, it is necessary to consider each of the types of costs which crime can impose on individuals and then determine the geographic distribution of that cost category. It is easier and more meaningful to consider particular crimes rather than crimes as a group, since different crimes have different impacts, particularly price and employment effects.

Consider the crime of burglary. This crime imposes a loss of property directly on the victim. To analyze the geographic distribution of this part of the cost, it is necessary to look at the geographic distribution of the victims. Since burglary rates are highest in central cities, we can conclude that direct property losses are felt more by central-city residents than by suburbanites. Direct and indirect psychic costs are also borne more by central-city residents than by suburbanites.

What about price and employment effects? To answer this, we must first determine which markets are likely to be affected and in what way. We must then determine the geographic distribution of consumers (in order to analyze the price effect) and the geographic distribution of workers in the industries (in order to determine the geographic distribution of the employment effect). As you can see, doing this completely would require a great deal of data that may not be available. However, we can get some idea of the geographic impact of burglary using available data.

One market that is likely to be affected by burglary is the market for security equipment, including locks and alarms. Figure 2–1 illustrates the **demand** for and **supply** of security equipment before an increase in burglary rates. Market demand is labeled D. Few units of the product are demanded at relatively high prices. As price decreases, quantity demanded increases. The supply of security equipment is labeled S. As price increases, quantity supplied increases. The **equilibrium price** of security equipment and the quantity bought and sold are determined by the interaction between demand and supply, and represented by the intersection of the demand and supply curves. P_1 represents the equilibrium price established by the market, Q_1 the equilibrium quantity. Associated with the output of Q_1 units of goods is a certain level of employment of labor and other resources in the industry.[16]

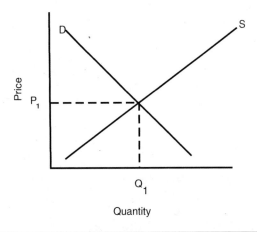

Figure 2–1 The Market for Security Equipment

The demand for security equipment, and the demand curve's position in the graph, is affected by the usual determinants: consumers' tastes and income, prices of substitute goods, and prices of complements. A change in one or more of these determinants will cause the consumers' demand to change and the entire demand curve to shift, which will therefore affect market price, quantity, and employment of resources.

An increase in burglary rates is likely to increase consumers' desire, or tastes, for security equipment. Other things being equal, this will cause the demand for security equipment to increase, a fact that is illustrated by an upward shift in the demand curve from D to D′ in Figure 2–2. Along D′, at every price people are willing to buy more security equipment than they were before. Tastes for the product are stronger.

Because demand has increased and the curve has moved to D′, P_1 and Q_1 no longer represent the market outcome. The price and quantity will be established where the new demand curve and supply curve intersect. This intersection has moved to P_2, Q_2. The equilibrium price for security equipment has increased to P_2, and the amount of equipment purchased by the market as a whole has increased to Q_2. Employment in the industry has also increased in order to produce the increased output.

In order to analyze the geographic distribution of the price effect, it is necessary to determine the geographic distribution of consumers of the product, that is, to determine which people buy the product and where they live. While answering this question completely would require a detailed market

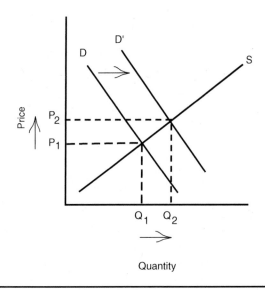

Figure 2–2 The Market for Security Equipment

analysis, we can get a rough idea by using some generalizations based on observation. It is probably correct to argue that central-city residents spend a
larger percentage of their incomes on security devices than suburbanites and
that, therefore, central-city residents are going to be hurt more by the price
increase than residents of other geographic areas.

The employment effect is more difficult to determine. To the extent that
the security equipment industry is a manufacturing industry which requires
medium or high skill levels, we might expect such firms to be located in the
suburbs and to hire primarily middle-income blue-collar workers, who tend to
live in the suburbs. Therefore, this group benefits from the employment effect.

Another market that is likely to be affected by an increase in burglary
rates is the market for insurance. Two things are likely to happen. First, with
increased incidents, the demand for insurance will increase as tastes for insurance increase. Second, as claims by victims go up, the costs of doing business
increase for insurance companies. This means that, for any level of output,
costs of production are higher; that is, the supply price is higher at every
quantity, or level of output. The supply curve, therefore, shifts to the left, indicating a decrease in supply. The combined effect of a demand increase and
a supply decrease is illustrated in Figure 2–3.

Before the increase in burglaries, the demand for insurance was represented by D and the supply of insurance by S. The interaction of supply and

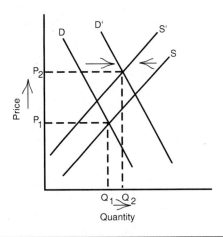

Figure 2–3 The Market for Insurance

demand, represented by the intersection of the two curves, determines market price and quantity bought and sold. This intersection occurs at price P_1 and quantity Q_1. A certain level of employment is associated with the production of Q_1 units of output.

Because of the increase in burglaries, demand for insurance increases (i.e., the curve shifts to D') and the supply decreases (i.e., the curve shifts to S'). A new price and quantity are determined. The price of insurance increases to P_2, and the quantity bought and sold increases to Q_2. Employment in the industry also increases.

To the extent that the price increase is passed on to all consumers of insurance, residents of all geographic areas could bear the price increase in proportion to the amount of insurance they buy, which, of course, increases with income and with the value of insured property. If, however, insurance rates vary from one insurance rating area to another, the price increase will be passed on primarily, if not exclusively, to residents of the insurance rating area(s) experiencing the increase in burglaries; in other words, to central-city residents.

Finally, there is a positive employment effect, which means that some individuals will gain jobs in the insurance industry. If clerical positions are more closely related to output than sales or executive positions, then the employment effect will consist primarily of low-skilled jobs, which are likely to be filled by central-city residents.

In the insurance market example, demand increased and supply decreased, illustrated by the shifts in the respective curves, causing price and quantity increases. The quantity increase, which was relatively small, was due to the fact that the supply decrease was less than the demand increase. Had the reverse been the case, quantity bought and sold would have dropped, employment would have dropped, and central-city residents would have lost jobs. Regardless of the relative magnitude of the changes, however, price will rise, since both changes are in a direction which puts upward pressure on prices.

There are probably some additional markets where prices and employment are affected; they could be analyzed in the same way, by determining whether prices and outputs rise or fall and then determining the geographic distribution of consumers and owners of resources employed in the industry.

In the two examples presented here, we made a simplifying assumption—we assumed that what happened in one market had no impact on what happened in the other. That assumption was all right to begin the analysis, but at this point we must recognize possible interactions. For example, as the price of insurance goes up there is likely to be an increase in the demand for security equipment. Why? Because, at least to some extent, security equipment and property insurance are likely to be substitute goods. A household, or perhaps more realistically, a business firm, may buy more security equipment to reduce the chances of burglary, and therefore may buy less property insurance, or vice versa.[17]

If this is so, and if the price of insurance increases relative to that of security equipment,[18] the demand for security equipment will experience an additional increase beyond that depicted in Figure 2–2. As the price of a substitute good (insurance) increases relative to that of security equipment, the demand for security equipment increases. At every price consumers are willing and able to buy more security equipment because they are substituting this equipment for the relatively more expensive insurance. This increase in demand will result in still higher prices for the equipment and additional increases in output and employment.

It is clear that the analysis of price and employment effects can be complicated, for impacts in one market are likely to cause impacts in related markets. Our analysis here suggests only the basis for understanding how individuals can be affected by changes in prices and outputs due to criminal activity.

The last way in which individuals can be affected by crime is via a tax effect. Other things equal, if burglary rates increase and cause the public sector to respond by spending more on police protection, property tax rates will have to increase to accommodate the increased expenditure. This increase in tax rates is paid by all residents of the geographic area experiencing the rise in crime rates. Since burglary rates are highest in central cities, central-city residents experience more of this kind of tax effect than suburban or rural dwellers. In 2003, cities with over a million residents spent almost $245 per resident on police department personnel alone, and cities with between one-half a million and a million residents spent approximately $250 per resident, while cities with between ten and twenty-five thousand residents only spent $154 per resident.[19]

This completes our discussion of how to analyze the distribution of the costs of crime among individuals. We showed how to assess the distribution of the costs (and benefits) of burglary by geographic area. Similar analyses can be done for other crimes and for other population groups. For example, the distribution of the costs of crime can be assessed by racial or income group. The same categories of impacts must be evaluated, but rather than focusing on the geographic area of impact, one must look at the impact by racial or income group. Different kinds of data would be necessary to implement this kind of study.

So much for the economic impact of crime. We have seen how crime hurts us as a society and as individuals within a society. We have also seen the different ways in which various crimes can affect us. All of this information is necessary for us to understand what it is worth to fight crime. In the next chapter we focus on another economic aspect of criminal activity—an economic explanation of why individuals commit criminal acts.

REVIEW TERMS AND CONCEPTS

Blue-collar workers	Discount rate
Complements	Discounting
Compliance enforcement costs	E-commerce
Consumers' tastes	Economic "bads"
Contingent valuation	Economic impact
Corporate income tax	Economic welfare
Crimes against persons	Employment effects
Crimes against property	Equilibrium price
Cybercrime	Equilibrium quantity
Demand	Future Value
Direct costs	Implicit costs
Direct monetary loss	Inheritance tax
Discounting future dollars	Involuntary transfer

Market equilibrium

Mixed capitalism

Negative externalities

Net loss

Opportunity cost

Organized crime

Personal income tax

Present value

Price Effects

Productivity cost

Property tax

Psychic costs

Public sector

Quality of life costs

Quantity demanded

Quantity effects

Quantity supplied

Real assets

Resources

Sales tax

Sin taxes

Substitute goods

Supply

Tangible costs

Tax effects

Transfer costs

Victimless crime

Willingness to pay

END OF CHAPTER QUESTIONS

1. Why is it that economists find it so difficult to measure the economic impact of crime to society? If it is so hard, why are there continued attempts to do so?

2. If your bicycle is stolen from in front of your dorm, from society's perspective this is simply an example of an involuntary transfer and does not impose a cost on society. Explain. Does this mean that crimes against property are costless to society?

3. Based on economic theory, how will an increase in the number of cyber attacks on the Web site of Amazon.com impact the price for the products they sell and the price of the products sold by their non-Web competitors? Explain.

4. In the state where you live, if a "three strikes you're out" law was passed by the legislature what taxes that you pay are likely to increase? What information do you need to know, if you don't already know it, to answer this question?

NOTES

1. David Anderson, "The Aggregate Burden of Crime," *Journal of Law and Economics,* October 1999, Table 1.

2. Dollar amounts adjusted for increases in the CPI through April 2005 here and throughout the book. (U.S. Bureau of Labor Statistics, "Inflation Calculator," www.bls.gov).

3. Ted Miller, Mark Cohen, and Brian Wiersema, *Victim Costs and Consequences: A New Look,* Washington, D.C.: National Institute of Justice, January 1996.

4. David Anderson, *op. cit.,* Table 7, 629.

5. *Ibid,* 624.

6. Mark A. Cohen, Roland T. Rust, Sara Steen, Simon T. Tidd; "Willingness-to-Pay for Crime Control Programs"; Criminology; Vol 42; Number 1; February, 2004.

7. Charles Piller, "Cyber-Crime Loss at Firms Doubles to $10 Billion," *The Los Angeles Times,* Part C, March 22, 2000, 1.

8. RIAA, "Issues: Anti-Piracy" (www.riaa.com).

9. In this case it might be more appropriate to evaluate the loss of a member of the economy as the difference between income and consumption expenditures lost, i.e., to consider the individual as both a producer and a consumer of goods.

10. Lee R. McPheters, "Measuring the Costs of Homicide," in Charles M. Gray, ed., *The Costs of Crime* (Beverly Hills, Ca.: Sage Publications, 1979), for an example of this type of economic study.

11. For a discussion of this point, see R. W. Anderson, "Towards a Cost-Benefit Analysis of Police Activity," *Public Finance,* 29, no. 1 (1974), 1–18.

12. If one argues that capitalism is undesirable, then the diminution of its workings, while imposing short-term costs, may ultimately lead to long-term benefits in the form of an alternative system.

13. The Combat Zone is an area of several blocks in downtown Boston zoned for adult entertainment establishments.

14. For a definition of all crime in terms of activities which generate negative externalities, see Robert G. Hann, "Crime and the Cost of Crime: An Economic Approach," *Journal of Research in Crime and Delinquency,* 9, no. 1 (January 1972), 12–30.

15. In the short run, defined to be that period during which at least one factor is fixed, we assume that labor is variable while land and capital are

fixed. In the long run all factors are variable, and therefore, all factors will experience an employment effect.

16. This is determined by the production function for the product(s).

17. For an advanced discussion of the relationship between market insurance and self-protection, see Isaac Ehrlich and Gary S. Becker, "Market Insurance, Self-Insurance and Self-Protection," *Journal of Political Economy,* 80; no. 4 (July–August 1972), 623–648. The authors conclude that market insurance and self-protection may be substitutes or complements, depending on the structure of the insurance scheme.

18. Notice that it is relative prices which are important.

19. U.S. Department of Justice, Bureau of Justice Statistics, *Sourcebook of Criminal Justice Statistics—Online* (www.albany.edu/sourcebook/pdf/t159.pdf), Table 1.59, 41. Four cities with populations more than one million, 2 cities with populations of 500,000 to 1,000,000, and 534 cities with populations between 10,000 and 25,000 were used to calculate the per capita police department personnel expenditures.

APPENDIX TO CHAPTER 2

Discounting to Present Value

The rationale for discounting is that a dollar in the future is not worth a dollar today. Perhaps it is easier to comprehend the argument in reverse: a dollar today is worth more than a dollar in the future, since that dollar can be invested so that it earns interest. For example, if the rate of interest is 10 percent per year, at the end of one year $1.00 is worth $1.10:

$$\$1 \times 1.10 = \$1.10 \tag{2–1}$$

or

$$PV \times (1+i) = FV \tag{2–2}$$

where   PV = present value or present stock
        i = the annual rate of interest
        FV = future value.

We have just solved for the future value, FV, knowing the present value, PV, and the interest rate, i. If we reverse the process, as in discounting, we know the future value (or values) and the interest rate, but not what that future value is worth today. Therefore, we would solve equation 2–2 for PV, knowing i and FV:

$$PV = \frac{FV}{(1+i)} \tag{2–3}$$

If we complicate the process by considering more than one future value, as in a stream of future earnings which are lost for a number of years due to incarceration, the calculation is extended:

$$PV = \frac{FV_1}{(1+i)} + \frac{FV_2}{(1+i)^2} + \ldots + \frac{FV_n}{(1+i)^n} \tag{2–4}$$

$$PV = \sum_{t=1}^{n} \frac{FV_t}{(1+i)^t} \tag{2–5}$$

Notice that as a dollar of future value or lost earnings becomes more and more distant in time, its value in the present becomes lower and lower. This is because in each year the future-value figure is divided by one plus the rate of interest, raised to a power, where the power increases with each year.

Therefore, the denominator is increasing, and at an increasing rate, making the value of the fraction smaller and smaller.

To illustrate this process, let us calculate the present value of $10,000 of lost income over a ten-year period. That is, for each of ten years in the future, $10,000 of income is lost. What is that worth today? We will use 10 percent as the annual rate of interest, or discount rate. Following equation 2–4, we have the following:

$$PV = \frac{\$10,000}{(1+.10)} + \frac{\$10,000}{(1+.10)^2} + \frac{\$10,000}{(1+.10)^3} + \frac{\$10,000}{(1+.10)^4} + \frac{\$10,000}{(1+.10)^5}$$

$$+ \frac{\$10,000}{(1+.10)^6} + \frac{\$10,000}{(1+.10)^7} + \frac{\$10,000}{(1+.10)^8} + \frac{\$10,000}{(1+.10)^9} + \frac{\$10,000}{(1+.10)^{10}}$$

or

$$PV = \frac{\$10,000}{(1.1)} + \frac{\$10,000}{(1.21)} + \frac{\$10,000}{(1.331)} + \frac{\$10,000}{(1.4641)} + \frac{\$10,000}{(1.6105)}$$

$$+ \frac{\$10,000}{(1.7716)} + \frac{\$10,000}{(1.9487)} + \frac{\$10,000}{(2.1436)} + \frac{\$10,000}{(2.3579)} + \frac{\$10,000}{(2.5937)}$$

or

$$PV = \$9090.91 + \$8264.46 + \$7513.15 + \$6830.13 + \$6209.25$$
$$+ \$5644.62 + \$5131.63 + \$4665.05 + \$4241.06 + \$3855.50$$

or

$$PV = \$61,445.76 \tag{2-6}$$

Notice from the calculations in equation 2–6 how the denominator grows and the present value in each year gets smaller. The present value of $10,000 ten years from now is only $3,855.50 if the rate of discount is 10 percent. And the present value of $10,000 for each of ten years in the future is only $61,445.76.

3

An Economic Model of Criminal Behavior

In this chapter we will try to explain criminal behavior in economic terms. To be useful, the explanation should be as simple as possible and as general as possible without being incomplete. That is, we would like a model of behavior which abstracts and simplifies reality without losing the essential ingredients of the explanation.

A TRADITIONAL ECONOMIC MODEL

We begin with a standard economic model of criminal behavior. At the end of the chapter we will look briefly at another, not completely inconsistent variety of economic explanation: a Marxian model of criminal behavior.

The standard model begins with an assumption about behavior. We will assume that criminals behave rationally. This does not mean that you or we necessarily approve of their behavior or share their value systems. All it means is that in making choices, the criminal takes account of expected gains and costs from various actions, where gains and costs include all kinds of psychic possibilities, including a taste or distaste for crime based on moral considerations.[1] There are several categories of gains and costs to be considered. As we review these it is necessary to keep in mind that the importance of various ingredients in the criminal choice, as well as the applicability of the assumption of rationality, varies from one individual to another and from one crime to another.

Gains from Criminal Behavior

The kinds of gains that can be derived from a criminal act vary, depending on the type of crime and the individual criminal. The most obvious form of gain is a monetary one. Stealing property yields monetary gains; murdering for insurance money also yields monetary gains. For some crimes, the exact value of the monetary gain is known; for example, the potential thief may know that there is $50,000 in the safe. In other cases, only the expected value or average monetary value to be gained is known. As an example, on the average a thief may expect to take $700 worth of property in a burglary in Boston's Back Bay neighborhood.

The second category of gains is psychic gains. This is a very general category and includes lots of possibilities—the thrill of danger or value of risk, a feeling of "getting back at the system," peer approval, a sense of accomplishment, and so forth. The importance of psychic gains depends on the crime; the psychic gains derived from a rape are different from those derived from burglary. Psychic gains also depend on the individual committing the crime. The psychic gains to a juvenile from auto theft are likely to be larger than those to an adult professional.

Costs of Criminal Behavior

The costs of engaging in criminal behavior are more varied and complicated. First, there are material costs. These include tools and equipment. A gun, a mask, and a counterfeiting press are examples. Materials costs obviously vary for different crimes.

Time costs are another category. Rather than committing an illegal act, the criminal could be doing something else, such as earning a legal wage or salary. This is the opportunity cost concept again. The value of the time used in planning and executing a crime must be considered a cost. Note that for an unemployed person time costs are reduced. However, at a minimum, opportunity costs are the value of leisure time.

The third type of cost is psychic cost. As with psychic gains, there are a large number of possible psychic costs which will vary with the crime and the individual. Fear, anxiety, dislike of risk, and guilt are examples.

The final type of cost is somewhat more complicated and requires more explanation. This is expected-punishment cost.

Expected-Punishment Cost

Expected-punishment costs are included to account for the possibility that the criminal will be caught and punished. If this were to happen, it would impose costs on the individual in the form of fines, a prison term, or both. Punishment is not certain to happen, but there is some probability of it. For this reason a cost must be included to compensate for the risk involved in criminal acts. The question is, how do we evaluate the risk?

To do this, we employ the statistical concept of expected value. Assume that if a criminal is caught for a particular crime he or she will have to pay a fine of $100. If the criminal is not caught, the punishment cost to the criminal is zero. Assume also that there is a fifty-fifty chance of the criminal being caught. While for a particular crime the criminal either is caught, and pays $100, or is not, and pays nothing, neither of these figures is a correct evaluation of the risk involved. A value of zero would underestimate the risk and assume no possibility of a fine. On the other hand, $100 overestimates the risk because the fine, or punishment, is not certain to be imposed. The best estimate of the value of the punishment is the "expected value" of the punishment. This is calculated as a weighted average of all possible values, where the weights are equal to the probability of occurrence:

$$\bar{V} = p_1 \cdot V_1 + p_2 \cdot V_2 + \ldots + p_n \cdot V_n \qquad (3\text{--}1)$$

where $\bar{V}$ = expected value
p_i = probability of outcome i
V_i = value of outcome i.

In our example the expected value of the punishment would be calculated as follows:

$$\bar{V} = 0.5\ (\$\ 100) + 0.5\ (\$0) \qquad (3\text{--}2)$$
$$= \$50.$$

There are only two outcomes. The value, or cost, of being caught is $100, with a probability of occurrence of 0.5, or 50 percent. The value, or cost, of not being caught is zero, with a probability of 0.5. With these possibilities, the expected value of the punishment is $50. On the average, this is the punishment cost to the criminal.

If we look at equation 3–1, we see that it can be simplified when it is used to calculate expected-punishment cost. Since there are only two outcomes, and the value of the one is always zero, expected-punishment cost can be calculated as follows:

$$\bar{V} = p \cdot P \qquad (3\text{--}3)$$

where $\bar{V}$ = expected value of the punishment
p = probability of punishment
P = value of the punishment.

In actuality, the value of the punishment to the criminal is not always so easily calculated, and the probability of punishment is the joint probability of being caught, convicted, and punished. In the following section we illustrate, in a somewhat simplified example, the calculation of expected-punishment cost and the comparison of gains and costs for a particular crime for two different individuals.

Numerical Illustration

We have argued that if a potential criminal behaves rationally, he or she compares the anticipated gains from a crime with the anticipated costs. If the gains exceed the costs, then it is rational to commit the crime. That is, if the monetary and psychic gains are sufficient to cover the material and psychic costs, as well as what the criminal's time is worth (time costs), and a compensation for risk (expected-punishment costs), then the rational crime will be committed. In order to illustrate this kind of comparison, we will consider two individuals facing the possibility of robbing a steak house.

Table 3–1 summarizes the gains and costs of the crime to individual A in the first column and to individual B in the second column. Gains are listed first. To both individuals the monetary gain is the $50,000 in the cash register.[2] In addition, for individual A there are $2,000 worth of psychic gains from "ripping off" this particular steak house. For individual B there are no psychic gains. Thus, the potential gains from the crime are somewhat different for each of the two people.

The costs are even more disparate. For both, there is the cost of a small handgun, $400. For A, there are no psychic costs, or a value of zero. For B, however, there is $1,000 worth of anxiety. The time costs of the crime also vary for the two individuals. The total time involved in the planning and execution of the crime is assumed to be the same for both—one month.[3] However, the value of that time is considerably different. In one month's time A would earn only $900 working as a dishwasher. But B could earn $6,000 in the same amount of time selling real estate. Time is worth a lot more to B than to A.

For the same reason, expected-punishment costs are much higher for B than for A. The calculation of expected-punishment cost is illustrated at the bottom of Table 3–1. The figures necessary for the calculation are listed first. The probability of arrest is assumed to be the same for both individuals and equal to 0.5, or 50 percent; the probability of being convicted of the crime, should one be arrested for it, is also assumed to be the same for both individuals and equal to 0.6, or 60 percent; the expected sentence, should one be convicted, is assumed to be ten years.

TABLE 3–1
STEAK HOUSE ROBBERY: GAINS VS. COSTS

	Individual A	Individual B
Gains		
Monetary	$50,000	$50,000
Psychic	2,000	0
	$52,000	$50,000
Costs		
Materials (gun)	$ 400	$ 400
Psychic	0	1,000
Time (1 month)	900	6,000
Expected Punishment[a]	32,400	216,000
Total costs	$33,700	$223,400
Net (undiscounted)	+ $18,300	– $173,400

[a]Expected-punishment costs are calculated as follows:
  Probability of arrest = 0.5
  Probability of conviction, given arrest = 0.6
  Expected sentence = 10 years
  Annual earnings forgone: individual A = $10,800
                             individual B = $72,000

Probability of punishment = probability of arrest • probability of conviction/arrest = (0.5)(0.6) = 0.3

Value of punishment: individual A = (10)($10,800) = $108,000
                       individual B = (10)($72,000) = $720,000

Expected-punishment cost: individual A = 0.3($108,000) = $32,400
                            individual B = 0.3($720,000) = $216,000

Notice that these numbers need not be the same for any two individuals considering the same crime. Differences in capability, or productivity, may cause the probability of arrest to vary. Differences in resources available or in financial or social status may cause the probability of conviction or the expected sentence to vary. Finally, while the actual probabilities and sentences may be identical, the perceived values may differ. For example, one person may overestimate the values while another may underestimate them. Whether or not differences in such perceptions are related to class, age, sex, race, or other socioeconomic variables would be interesting to explore, since they could help explain different levels of participation in criminal activities by various groups.[4]

The final figure required for calculating expected-punishment cost is the annual earnings for each individual if each were to work in the legal sector. For individual A, the figure is $10,800 per year; for B, it is $72,000 per year.

We are now prepared to calculate the expected-punishment costs for each person. First it is necessary to calculate the probability of punishment, p. This probability depends on two things: the probability of arrest, p_a, and the probability of being convicted of the crime if arrested, $p_{c/a}$.[5] To compute the probability of arrest and conviction, we multiply the probability of arrest times the probability of conviction, given that the person has been arrested:[6]

$$p = p_a \cdot p_{c/a} \qquad\qquad (3\text{--}4)$$
$$\text{or}$$
$$p = (0.5)(0.6)$$
$$= 0.3.$$

The probability of punishment is therefore 0.3—a 30 percent chance.

The next step is to calculate the value of the punishment to each person. Since the punishment involves a prison term of ten years, it is necessary to determine what ten years of prison are worth to each person. This is a rather difficult thing to determine. First we need to know what the person would be doing to earn income if he or she were not in prison. If we assume that the individual is trying to decide between breaking the law (robbing the steak house) and not breaking the law, then the alternative income is whatever the person could earn in the legal sector.

This is $10,800 a year for A and $72,000 a year for B. Since each would lose this for a period of ten years, we might assume that they would receive raises each year, and therefore we should increase the figure by some percentage each year. For simplicity we have not done this. Prison also costs some loss of freedom, as well as possible losses in dignity, privacy, or other things. What these are worth to each person is unknown, and we therefore omit them from the calculation; admittedly, this is a serious inadequacy.

Prison may impose additional costs beyond the term itself. Reduced earnings possibilities in the legal sector may be suffered by ex-convicts after release. Additional psychic costs, such as shame or ostracism, may be suffered. To include these, it would be necessary to evaluate their duration and worth to the individual.

Prison may not, however, be entirely without value. Free room and board are provided, for whatever it is worth, and there is the possibility that after release the individual's productivity, and therefore, earning potential in the illegal sector will be enhanced.[7] There is, also, often the opportunity for prisoners to learn skills that can increase their legal sector earnings potential through education[8] and vocational training programs. Technically, these should be included as gains if their values can be determined. They would make the (net) cost of punishment smaller than would otherwise be the case because they would be included as an expected gain to the robbery.

Finally, regardless of what is and is not included in the value of punishment to an individual each year, since the punishment occurs over a period of several years, each year's figure should be discounted to **present value** when computing the total value of punishment over that period. The reason for discounting and the way to do it were explained in the preceding chapter. Here we run into it again. However, in the illustration we cheated a little and did not discount. This was to make the illustration easy to understand. Rather than discounting each of the values for ten years and summing them, we simply multiplied each year's figure (assumed to be constant and equal to $10,800 for A and $72,000 for B) by 10. The value of the punishment is therefore $108,000 for A and $720,000 for B. To see whether you understand the numerical impact of discounting, try to figure out whether this shortcut overestimates or underestimates the value of punishment.

The final step in the calculation of expected-punishment cost is simply to multiply the probability of punishment times the value of the punishment. This follows equation 3–3, which we repeat here:[9]

$$\bar{V} = p\,V$$

or

$$\bar{V} = 0.3\ (\$108,000)$$
$$= \$32,400 \text{ for individual A} \qquad (3\text{–}5)$$

and

$$\bar{V} = 0.3\ (\$720,000)$$
$$= \$216,000 \text{ for individual B.}$$

These figures appear in the appropriate cost column for each person.

We are finally in a position to draw some conclusions from Table 3–1. For individual A, the rotbbery has gains worth $52,000, costs evaluated at $33,700, and a net gain, therefore, of $18,300. For A, it is rational to commit the crime.[10] In fact, it would be rational if the gains were worth only $34,000. For B, the gains are worth $50,000 and the costs are calculated at $223,400. For B, then, there is a net loss of $173,400 associated with the crime. For B, it is better not to commit the robbery. B would commit the crime only if the gains were equal to or slightly greater than $233,400.

A SUPPLY CURVE FOR CRIME

With an understanding of the elements involved in a rational decision to commit or not to commit a crime, we can proceed to develop the concept of a supply curve for crime. The supply curve will show, as any supply curve does, the relationship between the price of a good or service and the quantity that producers are willing to supply per time period. In our case the supply curve will show the number of crimes (quantity) per time period that criminals (producers) are willing to commit (produce) at various levels of average gain (price).

Before we proceed with the supply curve, however, it is important to review what we have learned so far. We have argued that criminals, or potential criminals, behave rationally. That is, they compare the gains from criminal activity with the costs involved before choosing whether or not to commit a crime. Obviously, this argument holds up better as an explanation for some crimes than for others (e.g., crimes against property vs. crimes against persons). Whether or not an economic approach to crimes against persons makes any sense at all will be discussed in a later chapter. For now, let us accept the argument that, for at least some crimes and some offenders, the economic model we have developed here is a good predictor of behavior.

The model, then, describes how an individual decides whether or not to be criminal. The next question is, how criminal will the person be? How many crimes will the person commit per time period (e.g., in a year)? Once an individual has decided to work in the illegal sector (i.e., to be a criminal), the number of crimes he or she commits depends on what economists refer to as the work/leisure choice.[11] This will determine how many crimes the person commits, as well as his or her annual illegal income.

The Choice Between Work and Leisure

The **work/leisure choice** is exactly what the name suggests—it is the choice that a person must make about how to spend the limited time available in a day, a week, or a year. How much of the time should be spent working and how much not working (leisure)? For many people working in the legal sector of the economy, their choice is somewhat limited; they work 40 hours per week, as required by their employer, and therefore have leisure for 128 hours per week. For many criminals, like the self-employed and part-time workers in the legal sector, there is a great deal more flexibility in the number of hours worked during a week, and therefore the work/leisure choice is a very real one.

Without going into all of the ingredients involved in the choice between work and leisure, it is important for us to consider what impact an increase in the average gain or price from a crime, would have on the work/leisure choice. What if, for example, the average gain from a burglary increased from $700 per crime to $800? If none of the costs of committing the crime increased, then the *net* gain from the crime increased by $100. Let us assume that for a particular individual a burglary requires one day. Now, every time that person decides to take the day off instead of burglarizing, it costs her or him $100 more than it did before. Leisure has gotten more expensive! The person may decide to take less of it. Economists call this the **"substitution effect"** of an increase in the average gain from crime. It refers to a change in behavior caused by a change in relative prices. Here, leisure has become relatively more expensive.

On the other hand, each day the person does work yields $100 more than it did before, so that working the same number of days, or committing the same number of burglaries, yields a higher income. With more income, the person is likely to want (or buy) more leisure. Economists call this the **"income effect"** of an increase in the average gain from crime. It refers to a change in behavior caused by a change in real income.

Whether or not the criminal takes more or less leisure as the average gain increases depends on whether the income effect or substitution effect is stronger.[12] It may be that, up to a point, the person will work more as average gain increases. That is, as the price (average gain) for a crime increases, an individual criminal will be willing to produce more crimes per time period. As the price (average gain) increases further, the person may start to work less, producing fewer crimes.[13]

Graphing the Supply Curve for Crime

We are now ready to try to see what a supply curve for crime would look like. In Chapter 2 we saw a few examples of typical supply curves. Each one showed a positive relationship between price and quantity supplied; as price increases, quantity supplied increases. Graphically, such a supply curve is represented by a line with a positive slope, as in Figure 3–1.

Would a supply curve for crime be similar? Remember, the supply curve would show the number of crimes per time period that criminals as a group are willing to commit at various levels of average gain (price). It describes the relationship between the price and the quantity of crime.

For any one criminal, the direction of the relationship between price and quantity is not immediately clear. As average gain (price) increases, the individual may commit more crime or less. This depends on the work/leisure choice just discussed. In describing that choice we assumed that all the costs

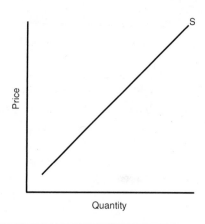

Figure 3–1 A Typical Supply Curve

of committing crimes remained constant. However, it is possible that as a criminal produces more crime per time period, the probability of punishment or the magnitude of the punishment may increase. If this happens, the criminal would have to be able to realize a larger gain from crime to be induced to commit more crime per time period. This means that the criminal would supply more crime only if the gain increased. The individual's supply curve would look like Figure 3–1.[14]

When we consider criminals as a group—that is, when we consider the supply curve for the industry—the case for a positively sloped supply curve is even stronger.[15] As the gain from crime increases, not only will some individuals, or firms, be induced to commit more crimes, but additional individuals, or firms, will be induced to enter the illegal industry. Remember individuals A and B considering the steak house robbery? With a gain of $50,000, only A would commit the crime. But if the gain were to increase to in excess of $223,400, B would commit this kind of crime, too. That means that as the average gain from crime increases, additional firms are encouraged to enter the industry and produce crimes. As the price goes up, the quantity suppliers are willing to produce per time period increases. The supply curve for crime therefore looks like Figure 3–2.[16]

Shifting the Supply Curve for Crime

The supply curve depicted in Figure 3–2 shows us that as the average gain from crime increases we can expect to see more crimes committed, assuming that other relevant things do not change. What are these other things, and what would happen if they did change? In what manner would we want

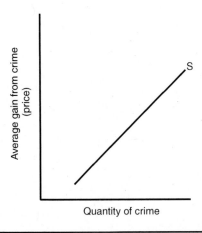

Figure 3–2 The Supply Curve for Crime

them to change? In which direction would it be desirable for supply to change and the supply curve to shift from the standpoint of public policy?

The supply curve in Figure 3–2 does not tell us how many crimes will be committed. That depends on the average gain which actually prevails at any particular time. Figure 3–2 simply shows us a series of possible quantities that would occur at various possible prices. In Figure 3–3 we reproduce the supply curve in Figure 3–2 and examine one point on that curve, $P_1 Q_1$.

The supply curve in Figure 3–3 indicates that if, for example, the average gain from a crime were equal to P_1, then Q_1 crimes would be committed per

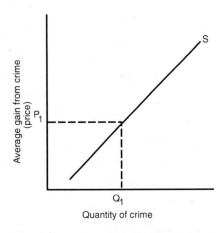

Figure 3–3 The Supply Curve for Crime

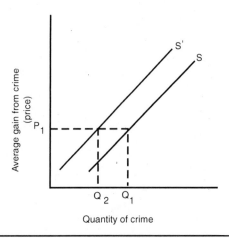

Figure 3–4 Comparing Supply Curves for Crime

time period. But what if there were different supply curves from the one drawn in Figure 3–3? In Figure 3–4 we show two different possible supply curves. The original one is labeled S. Another possibility, to the left of S, is labeled S′.

Which supply curve would be more desirable for society? To answer this, let us assume that the average gain from crime is P_1. If so, and if S were the supply curve, then Q_1 crimes would be committed. However, if S′ were the supply curve, only Q_2 crimes would occur during the same period. Clearly, S′ is preferable. Whatever the price, fewer crimes are produced along S′ than along S. A lesser supply, represented by a curve to the left of S′, would be even better. From a public policy viewpoint, we would like to know whether changes in public policy can affect supply and the position of the crime supply curve. Can we cause the supply of crime to decrease and the curve, wherever it is, to shift to the left? This would result in less crime.

PUBLIC POLICY OPTIONS

In this section we will discuss some general kinds of public policies which could change the supply of crime and shift the supply curve to the left. Specific kinds of policies to deal with particular kinds of crime will be discussed in later chapters. Here we are concerned only with general approaches. Another warning is appropriate. We are not yet prepared to recommend any of the options we are examining. Whether or not it is worth implementing any of these suggestions requires a detailed assessment of all the costs of any one of these options in comparison to all its benefits. The details of applying **cost-benefit analysis,** as this approach is known, are found in the appendix to this chapter and the next chapter. Right now we are concerned only with what we could do if we chose to.

As with supply of any good or service, an increase in the costs of doing business will cause the supply to decrease and the entire crime supply curve to shift up and to the left. Any level of output will require a higher price to cover the increased costs. If this is so, we simply have to identify the costs of doing business in the criminal industry and determine how to make them increase. To identify the costs of engaging in crime, we can refer back to our model of criminal behavior.

The costs associated with committing a criminal act are material costs, time costs, psychic costs, and expected-punishment costs. Public policy can be used to affect each, although some policies may be more effective than others.

Material costs may at first appear to be immune to public policy, but they are not. We may affect the materials required to perform a particular crime by altering the circumstances surrounding the typical crime. For example, making our paper currency more complicated in design would increase the material costs of **counterfeiting.**[17] Laws which require certain types of security devices in homes would increase the kinds of materials required in a typical burglary. The latter could occur without a public law, but legislation would be an incentive for such crime prevention behavior. Education would also have this effect. There are other examples of this type in which public policy in the form of education, legislation, or subsidy can be used to increase the material costs of crime, decrease the supply of crime, and therefore shift the crime supply curve in the appropriate direction.[18]

Time costs can also be affected by public policy. There are two basic approaches: (1) increase the time required to commit crime and (2) increase the value of time. The first approach is in some ways similar to increasing material costs. Requiring security devices on homes may force burglars to use additional equipment to commit the crime in the same amount of time as before, or to take longer to complete the crime if they use the same materials as before.

The second way to increase time costs is to make time worth more to potential criminals. The obvious way to do this is to increase legal income opportunities, either through programs to promote full employment or by increased training and other investments in "human capital." An interesting question is whether an across-the-board increase in average income would be effective. While it would increase costs to potential criminals, it would also increase the potential gains from crime, since with higher incomes there are likely to be more valuable assets to steal. In addition, a general increase in average income levels is unlikely to alter the psychic elements in criminal behavior. A redistribution of income in favor of the lower income classes is therefore likely to be more effective. Such a program would increase time costs to lower income individuals and, as we will see, would increase expected-punishment costs. It may also serve to increase "allegiance to the social contract"[19] and thus, the psychic costs of criminal behavior.[20]

How public policy can be used to increase psychic costs to potential offenders is an interesting question. Public information and advertisement could be used to increase feelings of guilt or fear. Whether or not such programs would be effective is unclear.[21] If they could be effective, there is the danger of potential misuse of this kind of technique by the public sector (i.e., "mind control").

Expected-punishment costs can be increased in a number of ways. Let us first consider how we might increase the value of the punishment. One possibility is to increase the magnitude of the punishment, that is, increase the value of fines and the length of prison terms. The latter appears to be a simple and inexpensive thing to do. If, however, increased prison terms are not effective deterrents to crime, an increase in the time spent in prison by inmates can be very expensive to society. In addition, the structure of penalties must remain rational, or else increasing penalties may have the effect of shifting crime to more serious offenses. This and other issues will be discussed in the following chapter. Another problem with increasing the length of prison terms is that, because of the discounting process, additional costs far in the future do not add much to the present value of the total cost of the punishment.

Another way to increase the value of the punishment is to increase the value of time lost in prison. Increasing legal income opportunities would therefore work to increase expected-punishment costs, as well as time costs. Effective **rehabilitation programs within prisons** and correctional institutions would serve to increase legal income opportunities after release. This would increase the time costs of crime for those who are released, decrease their willingness to commit crimes, i.e., decrease the supply of crime, and would therefore shift the crime supply curve for potential repeat offenders. Other things equal, such programs should reduce recidivism.

Expected-punishment costs can also be increased by increasing the probability of punishment. How this can be done effectively is a rather complicated question; some of the problems will be examined in the next chapter. Basically, there are three potential ways to increase punishment probability: (1) increase the quantity and/or quality of resources available to the criminal justice system; (2) increase the efficiency with which resources are used by the system; and (3) reduce the existing constraints which may hinder the effectiveness of the criminal justice system. Reducing constraints on the system may serve to reduce crime but is likely to reduce personal freedoms and civil liberties as well. The question then is whether the benefits of reduced crime are sufficient to compensate for the loss of freedoms. We are not in a position to answer that question here, but we can show that, as with many other social issues, there is an economic aspect to it—one social goal can be reached only at the cost of another.

In the appendix to this chapter and in the next chapter we will develop a general framework for making choices within the criminal justice system and for deciding between criminal justice and other public programs. Before moving to that, we will examine one additional factor that impacts the supply of crime and then look briefly at some additional economic explanations of criminal behavior.

TECHNOLOGICAL CHANGE AND THE SUPPLY OF CRIME

Many believe that technology is changing at a much more rapid pace than ever before and is having an ever-increasing impact on human behavior, including criminal behavior. While the pace may be increasing, its impact on behavior, non-criminal and criminal, has existed for thousands of years. Gutenberg's invention of moveable type in the middle of the 15th century, first used to print the Bible, enhanced the ability of law enforcement to track down criminals and increased the likelihood of their being arrested by making the posting of "wanted posters" quicker and less costly. Henry Ford's introduction of the assembly line in 1913 for the production of automobiles (the Model T) made them more accessible to both law enforcement for use as tools to catch criminals and criminals as tools to be used to commit crime. The personal computer is today's moveable type and assembly line. It, in conjunction with the Internet and the World Wide Web, can be utilized by both the criminal and law enforcement in ways that impact the supply of crime.

Generally, economists think of technological change as increasing the supply of goods and services since it increases the **efficiency** of the production process and lowers the costs of production. Increased efficiency in production means that it is possible to produce more goods or services with the same amount of inputs. For example, with the Internet (developed in the early 1960s), the World Wide Web (developed in 1989) and the web browser (developed in 1993) child pornographers can decrease the costs of distributing their products to their customers. They can reach more customers much more easily with the Internet and at a lower risk of being caught since they can more easily hide their place of business by constantly changing the location of

Figure 3–5 Increase in Supply of Crime (Child Pornography)

their web sites, i.e., the **IP (Internet protocol) addresses.** This would cause the supply of crime, i.e., child pornography, to increase and the supply curve to shift down and to the right as seen in Figure 3–5.

One thing about technological change and its impact on the supply of crime is that it also enhances the productivity of law enforcement efforts. The use of automobiles as patrol cars increased the amount of area that could be patrolled by police in a given period of time and decreased the time it took them to respond to a crime. The development of small portable personal computers and terminals, along with enhanced communications capabilities, has enabled police departments to install computers directly in patrol cars so that now a routine traffic stop may lead to the arrest of a person wanted in some other jurisdiction, thus increasing the criminal's probability of arrest. **DNA testing,** another technological change, has certainly made it easier to associate criminals with a victim or a crime scene, thus increasing the probability of being convicted. Both lead to increases in criminals' expected punishment costs, a decrease in their willingness to commit crime and a decrease in the supply of crime. A decrease in the supply of crime is reflected in a shift of the supply of crime curve up to the left as illustrated in Figure 3–6.

For the most part technological change does not add to the types of crime that can be supplied, but it provides "a new medium through which traditional crimes can now be committed."[22] The introduction of the automobile added automobile theft to the list of crimes, but it is simply another

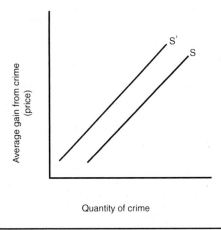

Figure 3–6 Decrease in the Supply of Crime

form of larceny, which was already a crime. The Internet and the World Wide Web have added cybercrime or computer crime but, like automobile theft, it essentially is a name for crimes that already exist. Computer break-ins that destroy information, such as what was accomplished by the "Melissa" virus, is the same crime as breaking into any business or residence and destroying property. Downloading software, i.e., **software piracy,** or music from the Internet without paying for it is the same as shoplifting the software or music CD from the store, which is already a crime. But, just as the automobile added the opportunity for criminals to commit a new crime, e.g., driving under the influence (DUI), the Internet and the World Wide Web will certainly add new crimes, too. Perhaps one will be "denial of service" an action that was recently accomplished by a hacker against Amazon.com and eBay.com when access to these e-commerce sites was blocked electronically. New crimes generated by technological change will increase the supply of crime as well.

Finally, technological change will affect the skill level required for criminals to participate in certain crimes. An increased level of skills requires an increased investment in education and training, thus increasing the costs of committing the crime and decreasing the supply of potential criminals and crime. For example, as banking continues to move out of the branch bank office and onto the Internet, bank robbers will need to develop the skills that will enable them to steal money electronically rather than with a ski mask, a note and a weapon.

SOME MACROECONOMIC EXPLANATIONS
OF CRIMINAL BEHAVIOR

The economic model and public policies discussed up to this point comprise the fundamentals of the economists' traditional model of behavior for the individual criminal. This is what economists call the microeconomic foundations of criminal behavior. It is also true that the overall health of the economy, what economists call macroeconomic conditions, influences criminal activity.[23]

Macroeconomic health generally relates to the growth or decline in economic activity throughout the economy. It is generally measured by changes in the total value of the goods and services produced by residents and businesses in an economy, known as **gross domestic product (GDP)**,[24] and by the level or **rate of unemployment.** Typically when an economy is healthy, i.e., growing, GDP is increasing and unemployment is decreasing. This means more goods and services are being produced, people's incomes are rising, and employment opportunities in the legal sector are improving. All of this is likely to have an impact on criminal activity.

Improved economic conditions will increase the value of time in the legal sector. With employment opportunities improving and unemployment decreasing, wages in the legal sector will be increasing. As discussed above, this increases the opportunity cost of participating in crime and increases expected punishment costs. Decreases in income related to a deterioration in the health of the economy may lead to increases in criminal activity. People may no longer have sufficient income from legal sources to purchase the goods needed for survival, so they may be more likely to turn to illegal activities to obtain the income necessary to purchase what they need or to obtain them directly.

Economic growth provides individuals with more income. On the one hand this income can be used to purchase increased amounts of private protection services, such as burglar alarms. This may increase a number of the costs of committing crime, such as the amount of time needed to commit an offense. On the other hand, placing more income in consumers' pockets increases the expected benefits from certain illegal activities. There are likely to be more tourists with more money in their pockets and cameras in their cars for thieves to steal. There would probably be an increase in expected benefits to thieves and pickpockets during the holiday season, too. Consumers are also likely to purchase more expensive items for home use, such as stereo equipment and television sets, increasing the expected benefits to a burglar.

Changes in income are also likely to affect consumers' demand for illegal goods and services. Increased income related to economic growth may increase consumers' interest in illegal goods and services, especially those used for leisure time activities. Examples of this might be illegal gambling or increased consumption of illegal drugs for "recreational" purposes.

A slowdown in economic activity generally leads to decreased employment opportunities in the legal sector. This is often associated with increased levels of frustration among the newly unemployed and those already unemployed. As an escape, the people who are directly affected and those who are indirectly affected, such as a spouse, may increase their consumption of alcohol and illegal drugs. This often leads to increases in alcohol and drug related crime, including assault and crimes related to the operation of motor vehicles.

Government expenditures on the criminal justice system used to combat criminal activity are also directly influenced by economic growth. Tax revenues at all levels of government will increase with economic growth. Personal income, corporate profits, and property values will all be increasing and generating increased tax revenues. Governments at all levels will be able to increase their criminal justice system expenditures. This may increase expected punishment costs by influencing the probability of arrest, if the additional expenditures go to hiring more police, or the severity of the punishment, if additional resources are used to expand prison capacity. The increased revenues may also be utilized for increased public crime prevention activities.

It should be apparent from this theoretical discussion that no conclusive statement can be made about the relationship between the overall health of the economy and criminal activity. There are reasons to believe that economic growth would be associated with decreases in overall criminal activity, because of increased expected punishment costs and public and private crime prevention activities. There are also reasons to believe that economic growth would be associated with increases in criminal activity, because of increases in the expected benefits from crime. The relationship is likely to vary by type of crime and by the distribution of growth across sectors of the economy.

In order to better understand the relationship between the business cycle and crime, economists are also interested in whether there is a symmetry in the rate of growth in criminal activity during a period of decline in the economy and the rate of decline in criminal activity when the economy returns to a period of growth.[25] In theory a person's crime skills and knowledge, his/her criminal human capital, is likely to increase as he/she spends more time committing crimes. At the same time the person's skills and knowledge that are valued in the legal labor market, his/her legal human capital, are likely to depreciate. Therefore, the incentives that criminals have to give up criminal activity during a period of economic growth are diminished and therefore we should expect to see a slower decrease in criminal activity in comparison to the increase that occurred during the recession.

We are only going to be able to determine whether the economic environment actually affects criminal activity by direct observation over a period of time. Several economists have done empirical studies of the relationship between the health of the economy and criminal activity.[26] They will be examined later in the book when we discuss, in more detail, crimes against persons, crimes against property, and crimes without victims.

A MARXIAN EXPLANATION OF CRIMINAL BEHAVIOR

The bulk of this chapter has been devoted to the development of a traditional economic model of criminal behavior. A Marxian explanation of criminal behavior is not completely inconsistent with the model we have developed, but it emphasizes the structure of the economic system as the root cause of at least some crimes.[27] It links crime to the structure of **monopoly capitalism** and to the capitalist competition which is inherent in the economic model of behavior described so far. In a capitalist society, the argument goes, property crime is inevitable. Capitalism is the product of class antagonism. The lower classes will always commit crimes against the property owned by the upper classes. The true property crime, however, is the capitalistic exploitation of lower-class labor by the upper classes. This is inevitable and necessary for the perpetuation of capitalism. Since the upper classes require the lower classes to perpetuate the system, a certain amount of lower-class crime is tolerated as the price of maintaining the system and the advantages it provides for the upper classes. This explanation would predict, for example, that robbery, burglary, larceny, and auto theft would be committed primarily by individuals from lower economic classes and that the victims would be primarily from the middle and upper classes.[28]

The Marxian approach also addresses such crimes as embezzlement, fraud, and violations of antitrust regulations and fair business practices. The reason such crimes are committed, according to the theory, is that capitalist competition forces the middle and upper classes to steal, cheat, and do anything else necessary to survive in the marketplace. These kinds of crime would be committed primarily by members of the middle and upper classes. They commit the crimes in order to retain their position in the marketplace, for losing in the market means losing all economic and social status. Therefore, it is essential to succeed.

Violent crimes may also be explained as the outgrowth of economic desperation. If humans are governed by material needs, hostility and aggression must be due to physical deprivation brought about by the unequal distribution of income and wealth inherent in capitalism.

Finally, we must note what the policy implications of this theory of criminal behavior must be. If it is correct, public efforts will not necessarily reduce crime but may only serve to protect the upper classes from excessive victimization by the lower classes. Crimes committed by upper classes against lower classes, however, would not be diligently investigated or punished or even considered criminal. Who gets victimized, and therefore who, at least in part, bears the cost of crime, depends on where and how the law enforcement resources are spent. This depends on the class bias of the state. Therefore, to eliminate crime, including the exploitation of lower-class labor, an alternative economic system would have to be instituted.

In the following chapter we return to a discussion of the kinds of decisions which must be made concerning the spending of law enforcement resources. We will also discuss how economically efficient decisions should be made. In doing so, we gloss over considerations of equity and return to a more conventional economic approach. The social welfare model which underlies much of this analysis is based on a state which is assumed to be a pure democracy.

REVIEW TERMS AND CONCEPTS

Average gain
Benefits (A)
Business cycle
Capitalism
Cost-benefit analysis (A)
Cost-benefit ratio (A)
Costs of doing business
Criminal behavior
Decrease in supply
Discount rate (A)
Discounted
DNA testing
Economic efficiency (A)
Economic growth
Efficiency
Equity (A)
Expected costs

Expected gains
Expected punishment costs
Expected value
External benefits (A)
External costs (A)
Gross domestic product (GDP)
Human capital (criminal/legal)
Income effect
Joint costs (A)
Legal income opportunities
Macroeconomic explanation of
    criminal behavior
Marginal benefits (A)
Marginal costs (A)
Marxian model of criminal
    behavior
Material costs

Microeconomic foundations of
   criminal behavior
Monetary gains
Monopoly capitalism
Negative externalities (A)
Net benefit
Net gain
Opportunity costs
Present value
Private discount rate (A)
Probability of arrest
Probability of conviction
Productivity
Program objectives
Psychic costs
Psychic gains/benefits

Public policy
Public sector (A)
Rational behavior
Real income
Recession
Recidivism
Redistribution of income
Social discount rate (A)
Social welfare (A)
Substitution effect
Supply curve
Technological change
Time costs
Unemployment
Work/leisure choice

(A) = from chapter appendix

END OF CHAPTER QUESTIONS

1. What are some public policies that society might be able to implement if it wants to increase the potential criminal's opportunity cost of committing a crime? What impact would this have on the supply of crime?

2. An increase in the price that a motor vehicle thief can obtain from selling a car will always entice the thief to steal more cars. Is this a correct statement?

3. What are examples of recent technological changes that have the potential to increase the supply of crime? Explain why they should have this impact on criminals' behavior.

4. At mid-year 2000 the national unemployment rate was at 3.9 percent, a thirty year low. In 1992, the rate was 7.5 percent. Based on this what would you expect to be happening to crime nationwide and why? How does this compare to what's actually happened (see Chapter 1)?

NOTES

1. It is actually not important whether the assumption is correct or not as long as it permits us to make predictions which are consistent with observation. This is similar to the assumption that pool players make

calculations based on the laws of physics in deciding which shots to take and how to execute them. There have been several empirical studies with results that are consistent with the economic rationality argument, including studies of the deterrent effect of punishment. For a review, see Gordon Tullock, "Does Punishment Deter Crime?" *The Public Interest*, no. 36 (Summer 1974), 103–111, also reprinted in Neil O. Alper and Daryl A. Hellman, *The Economics of Crime: A Reader* (Needham, Ma.: Simon & Schuster, 1997). A confirmation can be found in Iljoong Kim, Bruce Benson, David Rasmussen, and Thomas Zuehlke, "An Economic Analysis of Recidivism Among Drug Offenders" (Tallahassee, Fl.: Florida State University, Department of Economics Working Paper, no. 91-02-10, May 1991).

2. Throughout the comparison we assume that a dollar is worth the same thing to both individuals. A more sophisticated version of the model would be expressed in terms of utility rather than dollars. Cf. Gary S. Becker, "Crime and Punishment: An Economic Approach," *Journal of Political Economy*, 72, no. 2 (March–April 1968), 169–217, also reprinted in Neil O. Alper and Daryl A. Hellman, *op.cit.*

3. It is possible that the two individuals would require different amounts of time for the crime. This would mean that their productivity is different. To keep the example simple, we assume that the individuals are equally productive in the production of steak house robberies.

4. Charles Tittle, "Punishment and Deterrence of Deviance," in Simon Rottenberg, ed., *The Economics of Crime and Punishment* (Washington, D.C.: American Enterprise Institute for Public Policy Research, 1973).

5. Not every person arrested for a crime is convicted of that crime. The person may be found innocent, or guilty of a lesser crime. We will discuss these possibilities, and whether or not they make any economic sense, in the next chapter.

6. For those who are familiar with statistical jargon, the joint probability of arrest and conviction is equal to the marginal probability of arrest times the conditional probability of conviction, given arrest.

7. This is Avio's negative training effect. See Kenneth L. Avio, "An Economic Analysis of Criminal Correction: The Canadian Case," *Canadian Journal of Economics*, 6, no. 2 (May 1973), 164–178.

8. In 2000 almost every state prison and all the federal prisons provided education programs to assist inmates. More than 80 percent of the state prisons and more than 90 percent of the federal prisons provided basic adult education and secondary education programs. More than 25 percent of the state prisons and 80 percent of the federal prisons provided the opportunity to take college courses. See U.S. Department of Justice, Bureau of Justice Statistics, *Sourcebook of Criminal Justice Statistics—2002* (Washington, D.C.), Table 1.107, 101, for details.

9. Notice that additional forms of punishment, or harm, are possible. For example, the criminal may be wounded during the crime. These possibilities can be included by using the same approach— probability of punishment times value of punishment gives the expected punishment cost.

10. We could also say that in one month's time, A can earn $18,300 net of costs illegally and only $900 legally.

11. Strictly speaking, these decisions are made simultaneously. Time is allocated among leisure (or consumption time), legitimate work, and illegitimate work. This permits the individual to participate in all three activities; in other words, legitimate and illegitimate participation are not mutually exclusive. For an advanced presentation of this model, see Isaac Ehrlich, "Participation in Illegitimate Activities: A Theoretical and Empirical Investigation," *Journal of Political Economy*, 81, no. 3 (May–June 1973), 521–564.

12. We are assuming that leisure is a normal good. In such a case the net impact of an increase in average gain depends on the strength of the substitution effect vs. that of the income effect. If leisure is an inferior good, then the effect will definitely be to increase the time spent "working" at crime.

13. This would result in a "backward-bending" supply curve.

14. Strictly speaking, the positively sloped supply curve is being described by a series of shifting functions.

15. For simplicity we assume no positive externalities in production among firms. This is not unrealistic, except perhaps when dealing with organized crime. This is discussed in Chapter 9.

16. For an advanced defense of a positively sloped supply function, see Ehrlich, *op.cit.,* 534–536.

17. This is suggested by George Stigler in "The Optimum Enforcement of Laws," *Journal of Political Economy,* 78, no. 3 (May–June 1970), 526–536.

18. There is, of course, the problem of crime displacement if the policy does not affect a substantial proportion of crime targets. For a discussion of these and other incentives to crime prevention behavior, see Daryl Hellman, Joel Naroff, Susan Beaton, and Barbara Ianziti, *Incentives and Disincentives to Crime Prevention Behavior,* U.S. Department of Justice, Law Enforcement Assistance Administration, National Institute of Law Enforcement and Criminal Justice (Washington, D.C., 1978).

19. This term comes from S. Danziner and D. Wheeler, "The Economics of Crime: Punishment or Income Redistribution," *Review of Social Economy,* 33, no. 2 (October 1975), 113–131.

20. For a detailed discussion of the policy-relevant issues surrounding the relationships between crime and employment, see American University Law School, Institute for Advanced Studies in Justice, Employment and Crime Project, "Crime and Employment Issues" (Washington, D.C., June 1978).

21. A state-sponsored TV advertisement campaign to warn Massachusetts residents against illegal purchase and transportation of cheaper liquor in neighboring New Hampshire reportedly stimulated border sales to Massachusetts residents who had been unaware of the illegal opportunity.

22. President's Working Group on Unlawful Conduct on the Internet, *The Electronic Frontier: The Challenge of Unlawful Conduct Involving the Use of the Internet,* Washington, D.C., March 2000, 1.

23. For more detailed discussion of these theoretical issues and empirical analysis see Philip Cook and Gary Zarkin, "Crimes and the Business Cycle," *The Journal of Legal Studies,* vol. XIV(1) (January 1985), 115–128, also reprinted in Neil O. Alper and Daryl A. Hellman, *op.cit.*; Richard Freeman, "Crime and Unemployment," *Crime and Public Policy,* 89 (James Q. Wilson, ed., 1983); Sharon Long and Ann Witte, "Current Economic Trends: Implications for Crime and Criminal Justice in a Declining Economy," (K. N. Wright, ed., 1981); Gloria Lessan, "Macroeconomic Determinants of Penal Policy: Estimating the Unemployment and Inflation Influences on Imprisonment Rate Changes in the United States,

1948–1985," *Crime, Law, and Social Choice,* vol. 16, no. 2 (September 1991), 177–198; and H. Naci Mocan and Turan Bali, "Asymmetric Crime Cycles," (www.aeaweb.org/annual-mtg-papers/2005/0108-1430-1303.pdf) December 2004.

24. Until 1992 the U.S. used gross national product (GNP) to measure aggregate output. The difference is that GDP measures economic activity within a country while GNP measures it for all the people and businesses of a country, whether or not the activity occurs within the geographic boundaries of the country.

25. A detailed discussion on the asymmetry in criminal behavior can be found in H. Naci Mocan and Turan G. Bali, "Asymmetric Crime Cycles," *op.cit.*

26. Cook and Zarkin, *op.cit.* and Mocan and Bali, *op.cit.*

27. Cf. John Keracher, *Crime—Its Causes and Consequences* (Chicago: Charles H. Kerr, 1937); David M. Gordon, "Class and the Economics of Crime," *Review of Radical Political Economics,* 3, no. 3 (1971), 50–75; Edwin H. Sutherland, *On Analyzing Crime* (Chicago: University of Chicago Press, 1973); Richard Quinney, *Class, State, and Crime* (New York: David McKay, 1977). A detailed review of the radical and orthodox literature with respect to the relationships among crime, law enforcement, and the structure of U.S. capitalism is provided by Harold C. Barnett in "Wealth, Crime, and Capital Accumulation," *Contemporary Crises,* 3 (1979), 171–186.

28. For more on this see Barnett, "Wealth, Crime, and Capital Accumulation" and "The Distribution of Crime and Punishment," papers presented at the Western Economics Association Meeting, San Francisco, Ca., June 24, 1976.

Appendix to Chapter 3

Cost-Benefit Analysis

Cost-benefit analysis provides a technique for evaluating public programs or policy changes from an economic perspective by comparing the benefits of the program or policy with its costs, where both benefits and costs should be measured in marginal, or incremental, terms. Thus, it is basically a technique for evaluating the marginal or additional benefits of a particular program or policy compared with the marginal or additional costs. Such a comparison is necessary in the public sector if economically efficient resource allocation decisions are to be made.

The Fundamentals of Cost-Benefit Analysis[a]

Cost-benefit analysis dates back to the water project evaluation studies done by the U.S. Army Corps of Engineers in the 1930s. Since that time, particularly in the last twenty-five or thirty years, it has become widely known and used as an evaluation tool by various agencies and departments in the public sector.[b]

Basically, cost-benefit analysis involves adding up all the benefits, or potential benefits, generated by a program, adding up all the costs, and then constructing a ratio of benefits to costs. Because in grouping and comparing benefits and costs a common denominator is required, benefits and costs are measured in dollars. This, as we will see, leads to some difficulties. If the ratio of benefits to costs is greater than one, it indicates that the program is economically feasible; that is, the program will yield benefits in excess of costs and will therefore improve economic efficiency and social welfare, i.e., make society better off. The cost-benefit ratio also permits comparison and ranking of alternative programs.[c]

Measurement Problems

While some costs and benefits (e.g., salaries) are easily measured in dollars, others (e.g., the value to an inmate of working in the community vs. a prison shop) are more difficult, if not impossible, to measure. Several problems may be encountered in measuring the benefits of a program or policy change. A basic one is determining what outcomes are the result of the program or policy change and what would have happened anyway. Since it is impossible to hold everything else in the world constant when a new program or policy is introduced, it is sometimes difficult to determine what results occurred because of some other influence. For example, if a police department increases the number of patrol officers on the beat and a decrease in crime is observed, can we attribute the reduction in crime to the increase in patrol officers? The answer is no, unless adequate account has been taken of other factors which influence the crime rate, such as unemployment rates or legal income opportunities.

A second basic problem in measuring benefits is to count only net gains, or net benefits, and not transfers. A net gain means that, overall, society is better off. A transfer means that a gain in one place is offset by a loss somewhere else. A reduction in welfare payments, for example, represents a transfer, not a net benefit to society, i.e., less money is transferred from the taxpayer to the welfare recipient.

Some benefits may be long-range benefits. For example, the "community service" approach to police patrol is intended, among other things, to reduce fear of crime on the part of the community and increase cooperation between the police and the community. However, thus far the evidence suggests that, if this does happen, it happens only after a certain period of time. If the benefit is long term, how can it be predicted? In this particular case, of course, the problem is compounded by the fact that the benefits are difficult to count in dollars, even if they were known. Finally, if benefits occur in the future, they must be discounted to present value in evaluating what they are worth today. (We first discussed discounting in Chapter 2. The appendix to that chapter describes the process.) This reduces the feasibility of introducing programs which cost money to implement today but yield benefits primarily in the distant future.

There are also problems involved in measuring costs. First, there are joint-cost problems. This occurs when some of the costs of the program or project being evaluated are shared by other programs. The difficulty is in allocating the appropriate portion of these costs (e.g., administrative personnel, electricity, etc.) to each program. The appropriate method depends on the type of cost and its relationship to the program being evaluated. Percentage of work time devoted to the program and percentage of floor space used are examples of methods of allocating joint costs.

There is also a tendency for agencies to ignore costs which are outside their domain or area of responsibility (e.g., the costs of obtaining legal advice from the legal department when that department is budgeted separately). In a real sense, use of the resources of outside agencies or departments has a cost and must be included in the cost figures whether the cost is borne directly by the evaluating agency or only indirectly.

A final problem in measuring costs is evaluating opportunity costs. Generally, in cost-benefit analysis we are trying to evaluate the cost of using resources in one particular program as opposed to using them somewhere else. Thus, the whole problem of measuring costs is concerned with measuring opportunity costs. In most cases we use the price of a resource as a measure of its opportunity cost—of what the resource would be worth if it were used somewhere else. This, of course, is not always true. The various problems involved in using prices as measures are discussed later.

In some cases, however, direct prices are not even available. For example, one cost of incarcerating individuals is the opportunity cost of their labor. Rather than sitting in prison, those individuals could be working in the legal sector of the economy producing something of value. How can this opportunity cost be evaluated? To look at the person's employment and earnings prior to incarceration as an indication of opportunity cost may reflect the individual's choice to earn illegally. An alternative is to look at the person's age, training, and so forth and attribute earnings by similar individuals. This procedure is more complicated and obviously is not necessarily correct.

There are other problems in measuring costs and benefits. As mentioned earlier, prices do not always reflect true opportunity costs. In assessing costs and/or benefits which accrue in the future, the magnitudes must be discounted to present value using an appropriate rate of discount. The discount rate selected should reflect the opportunity cost of the funds used, which, in part, depends on where the funds to finance the project came from. Did consumers sacrifice consumption opportunities in order to pay taxes to finance it, or were alternative investment opportunities in the public or private sectors sacrificed? Should a private or a social rate of discount be used? Again, opportunity costs are often difficult to assess. In many cost-benefit studies several different discount rates are used to assess costs and benefits in order to get around this particular problem.[d]

Some costs and benefits are not reflected in prices and therefore are difficult to include in the calculations, although they can be included in the analysis and discussion. Examples are psychic costs and benefits and positive or negative externalities. We encountered the concept of negative externalities in Chapter 2. These occur when costs are imposed involuntarily on some people by the consumption and/or production decisions of others. Because the costs are imposed involuntarily, no "transaction" takes place and no prices are charged or received. Air pollution is an example. In a similar way positive externalities can be generated by consumption and production activities. Again, since there is no transaction, prices are not charged for the external benefits.

External costs and benefits and psychic costs and benefits are underestimated (and sometimes ignored altogether) in cost-benefit studies.

A final problem in using prices to reflect costs and benefits is that the program or project being evaluated may affect or distort prices. Any significant increase or decrease in the supply of or demand for a product or factor of production will affect the market for that product or factor, and therefore, its price. Relatively large programs with impacts concentrated in particular market areas can change prices. Program purchase prices may be underestimated, or output benefits overestimated, as a result.

Broader Problems

Beyond measurement problems, there are some broader problems with using cost-benefit analysis. The first concerns program objectives. To evaluate the benefits of a program accurately, it is first necessary to understand its objectives. However, program objectives are often vaguely defined. This, of course, can lead to misunderstanding and incorrect evaluation of program effectiveness and feasibility. Evaluation results can therefore be challenged if the evaluation results are not "politically" popular. Political goals and agency bias may get in the way of economically efficient decision-making.

In addition to vague or missing objectives, multiple objectives can be a problem. The difficulty then is in weighting the various objectives of a program. In some cases objectives may be inconsistent. For example, some programs aimed at reducing juvenile crime may aim to increase the employability of participants as well as to keep them "off the streets" and out of trouble. The difficulty is that the most effective ways of doing the latter (e.g., providing recreational activities) may not necessarily be consistent with the former. This is not to say that both cannot be accomplished, but some of one is sacrificed to get the other. The weights associated with this trade-off should be made clear.

A final problem with cost-benefit analysis concerns its focus. It is a tool designed to evaluate economic efficiency, that is, to evaluate how well we are using our scarce economic resources. It therefore measures costs and benefits and compares them. However, it does not include an evaluation of equity considerations. Cost-benefit analysis does not measure or evaluate the distribution of the benefits or costs of a program. It does not contain an assessment of who gains and who loses. Thus, programs are judged on the basis of efficiency, not equity. Economically inefficient programs (those in which costs exceed benefits) which appear equitable—for example, programs that benefit the needy at the expense of the non-needy—would not be selected on the basis of cost-benefit analysis alone. Of course, cost-benefit analysis can always be supplemented with a distributional analysis so that equity considerations can be added to considerations of efficiency in making policy decisions.

NOTES

a. For good reviews of cost-benefit analysis, see A.R. Prest and R. Turvey, "Cost-Benefit Analysis: A Survey," *The Economic Journal,* 75, no. 300 (December 1965), 683–735; Richard A. Musgrave, "Cost-Benefit Analysis and the Theory of Public Finance," *Journal of Economic Literature,* 7, no. 3 (September 1969), 797–806; for a guide to cost-benefit analysis and applications in criminal justice, see Jeffrey I. Chapman and Carl W. Nelson, *Handbook of Cost-Benefit Techniques and Applications* (Washington, D.C.: American Bar Association, Correctional Economics Center, July 1975).

b. For a sample theoretical application of this kind of approach to the criminal justice system, see P. L. Szanton, "Program Budgeting for Criminal Justice Systems," Appendix A, President's Crime Commission, *Task Force Report: Science and Technology* (Washington, D.C.: U.S. Government Printing Office, 1967).

c. Although this ratio is widely referred to as the "cost-benefit ratio," in constructing the ratio, benefits are placed in the numerator and costs in the denominator. Alternative measures, e.g., benefits net of costs, or the ratio of net benefits to net costs, can also be calculated and can be useful in program evaluation.

d. The choice of the appropriate discount rate is an important question which has received a good deal of attention in the literature. For a good summary of the issues, see Richard A. Musgrave and Peggy B. Musgrave, *Public Finance in Theory and Practice,* 4th ed. (New York: McGraw-Hill, 1984), 179–182, and 185–187.

4

Optimum Allocation of Criminal Justice Resources

In this chapter we will develop a general framework for making choices within the criminal justice system and for deciding between the provision of criminal justice and other public and private goods. We focus, for the most part, on **crime prevention,** or **deterrence,** as the primary output of the criminal justice system.[1] Up to this point we have considered two basic economic aspects of crime: the economic impact of criminal activity and economic explanations of criminal behavior. We now turn to a third and related aspect: the costs of law enforcement and crime prevention, and knowing these costs and recognizing the ways in which criminal activity hurts society, the amount we should spend to prevent crime. How much should we spend on criminal justice? In addition, given a particular budget for criminal justice, how should those dollars be spent? Which crimes should we concentrate on? Should we fight crime with more patrol officers or more patrol vehicles? In which neighborhoods? How much should be spent on police? On courts? On corrections? These are all questions concerning the best use of scarce economic resources within the criminal justice system—questions concerning the optimum allocation of resources. While we cannot answer all of these questions within the space of one chapter, we will focus on a few of them.

We begin with the most basic question—the optimum amount for society to spend on crime prevention. As we will see, this will define the optimum amount of crime for society to tolerate. We then elaborate on this question by defining the optimum "mix" of crime and the optimum allocation of crime prevention resources among neighborhoods within a city. Finally, we look briefly at the criminal justice system as a whole and consider optimum resource allocation within branches of the system.

DETERMINING THE OPTIMUM AMOUNT OF CRIME[2]

As discussed in Chapter 2, criminal activity imposes various kinds of costs on society. Because of this, crime prevention creates benefits in the form of harm avoided. However, crime prevention must be produced, like any other good or service, with scarce economic resources. There are economic costs associated with the production of crime prevention either by the public sector (police, etc.) or by the private sector (burglar alarms, security guards, etc.). In this chapter we begin by discussing the production of crime prevention in general, by either the public or the private sector, but then focus on public crime prevention. A similar kind of analysis can be applied to private crime prevention activity.[3]

Because there are costs associated with producing crime prevention, society cannot afford to prevent all crimes. Society values other public and private goods in addition to crime prevention and does not wish to devote all of its scarce resources to the production of only one of them. Society must therefore choose how many of its scarce resources to devote to crime prevention. By doing so, society also chooses the amount of crime that it will tolerate.

Choices concerning the amount of resources to expend are reflected in budgets. A given budget will buy only a certain amount of resources. Crime prevention budgets thus reflect decisions concerning how many resources will be spent on crime prevention, and therefore, how much crime to tolerate. For example, in 2003 one could argue that the Boston City Council voted to tolerate 39 murders, 262 rapes, 4,113 assaults, 4,344 burglaries, and so forth.[4] That is, it approved a budget of approximately $214 million for the Boston Police Department for that period.[5] Whether or not this was too much or too little to spend cannot be determined without additional information. We turn now to the way that decision can be made.

The Optimum Size for Any Industry

The optimum amount of crime prevention for society to produce can be defined by applying the general economic rule for the optimum size of any industry: units of output should be produced up to the point at which the marginal benefits from the last unit of output produced are equal to the marginal costs of production. By producing this amount in each industry, no more and no less, society will be maximizing the happiness it derives from the production and consumption of goods and services; it will be maximizing what is called its "social welfare."

To understand this rule, let us take a moment to define some terms and relationships. First we assume that the objective of society as an economic unit is to maximize its social welfare, that is, to maximize the happiness it gets from the goods and services it produces. Let us define social welfare as the total benefits that society derives from using all of its products minus the total costs of producing those products:

$$\text{Social welfare = total benefits – total costs} \qquad (4\text{–}1)$$

or, symbolically,

$$SW = TB - TC.$$

Marginal benefits, MB, are defined as the change in total benefits, TB, with an additional unit of output produced, Q. Therefore, marginal benefits can be expressed as follows:

$$MB = \frac{\Delta TB}{\Delta Q} \qquad (4\text{–}2)$$

where the symbol Δ means "change in." The marginal benefits of an additional unit of output are the increase in benefits that society derives from one more unit of product, whatever the product is. We assume, in general, that marginal benefits are positive: that is, increases in output will increase total benefits. However, while the marginal benefits from producing more of any product are positive, they get smaller and smaller as we produce more and more of the same thing. We value each extra unit less and less. Therefore, if we graph the relationship between marginal benefits, MB, and the amount of output, Q, it looks like Figure 4–1. Marginal benefits, in dollars, are measured on the vertical axis. Output is measured on the

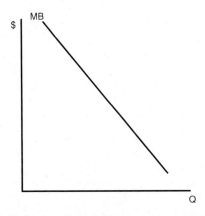

Figure 4–1 The Marginal Benefit Function

horizontal axis. As output increases, marginal benefits decrease. As Q increases, MB decreases. The marginal benefit function has a negative slope.

Marginal costs, MC, are defined as the change in total costs, TC, with an additional unit of output. Marginal costs can be expressed as follows:

$$MC = \frac{\Delta TC}{\Delta Q}. \qquad (4\text{–}3)$$

The marginal costs of an additional unit of output are the increase in costs caused by the increase in output. Marginal costs are positive—producing more will cause total costs to increase. In addition, the increase in total costs will get larger and larger; that is, marginal costs are positive and increase with increases in output.[6] If we graph the relationship between marginal costs, MC, and the amount of output, Q, it looks like Figure 4–2. As output (Q) increases, marginal costs (MC) also increase. The marginal cost function has a positive slope.

With this understanding of the marginal benefits and marginal costs of additional units of output, let us look again at equation 4–1, which defines social welfare. From the equation we see that social welfare will increase as total benefits increase but will decrease as total costs go up. As output increases, we know that both total benefits and total costs go up. Whether or not social welfare increases, then, depends on which increases more, total benefits or total costs.

The increase in total benefits is measured by marginal benefits. The increase in total costs is measured by marginal costs. If the marginal benefits of an additional unit of output exceed the marginal costs of producing that output, then social welfare will increase if we produce that additional unit. The

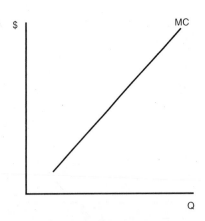

Figure 4–2 The Marginal Cost Function

increase in total benefits will exceed the increase in total costs, and therefore the difference between them, social welfare, will increase.

The opposite would happen if marginal benefits were less than marginal costs. In this case the increase in total benefits with an additional unit of output would be less than the increase in total costs, so that the difference between total benefits and total costs would actually get smaller, thereby diminishing social welfare. Therefore, since social welfare increases when marginal benefits are greater than marginal costs and decreases when marginal benefits are less than marginal costs, social welfare is maximized when marginal benefits are equal to marginal costs of producing an additional unit of output. These relationships are summarized in Table 4–1.

TABLE 4–1

MARGINAL BENEFITS, MARGINAL COSTS, AND SOCIAL WELFARE	
Marginal Benefits vs. Marginal Costs	*Social Welfare*
MB > MC	SW ↑'s as Q↑'s
MB < MC	SW ↓'s as Q↑'s
MB = MC	SW maximized at that Q

Social welfare is maximized by producing up to the point at which the marginal benefits of the additional unit of output equal the marginal costs. This is the optimum output level—the optimum size for any industry. Combining Figure 4–1 with Figure 4–2, we can define the optimum size of an industry graphically, as in Figure 4–3. Optimum size, or output level, is defined as that Q

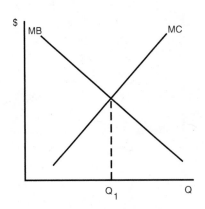

Figure 4–3 Optimum Industry Size

at which marginal benefits, MB, equal marginal costs, MC. This occurs at that output level at which the marginal benefit function intersects the marginal cost function. In Figure 4–3 this occurs at output Q_1.

The Optimum Amount of Crime Prevention

The optimum amount of crime prevention for society to produce can now be defined: society should produce units of crime prevention up to the point at which the marginal benefit of the last unit of crime prevention equals the marginal costs of producing it. The marginal benefit of preventing one more crime is the harm avoided. The marginal cost is the additional cost of producing one more unit of prevention. Figure 4–4 describes the relationship between both marginal benefits and marginal costs and quantity of crime prevention, $\overline{Q}$. The optimum amount of crime prevention is $\overline{Q}_1$, where marginal benefits of prevention equal the marginal costs.

The Optimum Amount of Crime

Having defined the optimum number of crimes to be prevented, it is easy to define the optimum amount of crime. It is simply the amount of crime left after the correct, or optimum amount, has been prevented. Let us call the amount of crime that society would have if it did not try to prevent any crime at all the amount of "laissez-faire crime." The amount of laissez-faire crime minus the optimum amount of crime prevented leaves, as a

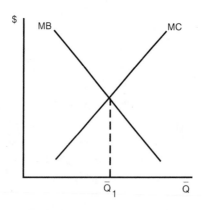

Figure 4–4 Optimum Amount of Crime Prevention

residual, the optimum amount of crime. This relationship is summarized in equation 4–4:

$$Q^* = Q - \overline{Q}_1 \tag{4–4}$$

where Q = laissez-faire crime
$\overline{Q}_1$ = optimum amount of crime prevented
Q^* = optimum amount of crime.

The optimum amount of crime for any society to tolerate at any given time depends on two things: its laissez-faire crime and its optimum amount of crime to be prevented. Changes in either of these will change the optimum amount of crime. The optimum amount of crime to be prevented will change if either the marginal benefit function or the marginal cost function shifts. For example, let us assume that initially society's marginal benefits and marginal costs of prevention are as in Figure 4–4, so that the optimum amount of crime prevention is $\overline{Q}_1$. Given Q, the amount of laissez-faire crime, the optimum amount of crime, Q^*, is defined by equation 4–4. Now let us assume that police salaries increase more than police productivity, so that the costs of preventing crime have increased. The marginal cost function of Figure 4–4 will shift to the left, to MC′, thereby changing the optimum amount of crime prevention. This impact is illustrated in Figure 4–5.

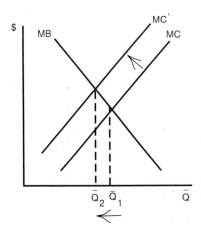

Figure 4–5 Optimum Amount of Crime Prevention

Now, with higher marginal costs for producing any amount of crime prevention, the optimum amount to prevent has been reduced from $\overline{Q}_1$ to $\overline{Q}_2$. With no change in laissez-faire crime, the optimum amount of crime for society to tolerate has increased.[7] Crime prevention has become more expensive, so that, with no change in society's valuation of crime prevention, society should buy less of it.

DETERMINING THE OPTIMUM MIX OF CRIME

In the preceding section we discussed the prevention of units of crime, without making any distinction among the various kinds of crimes. Now we must recognize that some types of crimes (e.g., murder) are more harmful than others (e.g., burglary). Therefore, the marginal benefit to society of preventing a murder is greater than the marginal benefit of preventing a burglary. Remember that the marginal benefit of preventing any crime is the value of the harm to society which is avoided through prevention. Because crimes are not equally harmful, when deciding how many crimes to prevent (optimum amount of crime prevention) society must also decide which crimes to prevent. Given the crime prevention budget, society should select, or tolerate, that crime "mix" which minimizes the harm done to society.

Accomplishing this is not as simple as it may seem. Initially, one's reaction to the problem would be to argue that we should prevent the most harmful or serious crimes first, then the next most harmful, and so on down the scale. The total number of crimes prevented and the point on the scale of seriousness to which prevention would extend would depend on the total crime prevention budget. However, not only do the marginal benefits of preventing different crimes vary, but the marginal costs of preventing different crimes also vary. Therefore, the problem of the optimum mix of crime must be solved by considering both the marginal benefits and the marginal costs of preventing each type of crime. The rule, then, for defining the optimum mix of crime is that society should derive the same marginal benefit per dollar of marginal cost from the prevention of all crimes. Thus, we consider marginal benefits relative to marginal costs. The rule is summarized in equation 4–5:

$$\frac{MB_1}{MC_1} = \frac{MB_2}{MC_2} = \cdots = \frac{MB_n}{MC_n}. \qquad (4\text{--}5)$$

The numerator, MB, measures the marginal benefit of preventing each type of crime, where there are n different types of crime. MC measures the marginal cost of preventing each type. The ratio, MB/MC, measures marginal benefits per dollar of marginal cost. This ratio must be equal for all crimes. If it is not, society could gain from shifting resources toward prevention of those crimes with higher marginal benefits per dollar of cost.[8] Let us look at a simplified example to see why.

Assume that we have a certain amount of crime prevention resources which we are currently using to prevent two different types of crime—burglary and aggravated assault. Given the number of each we are currently preventing, assume that we know the following:

1. the marginal benefit of preventing an additional assault is $3,500;
2. the marginal benefit of preventing an additional burglary is $1,100; and
3. per time period (whether it is per day, week, or month is immaterial), crime prevention resources can be used to prevent one assault or three burglaries.

Given this information, should more resources be allocated to the prevention of assault? This, of course, means preventing fewer burglaries, so the question is, "Should the optimum mix of crime prevention contain more assaults prevented and fewer burglaries prevented?" According to equation 4–5, we should consider marginal benefits and marginal costs before deciding. Marginal benefit information is given, but marginal cost information is not. However, productivity information is, and the costs of production depend on the productivity of economic resources. Maybe we can use the productivity information to get cost information. If we think about it, we can.

In order to prevent an additional assault, resources would have to be shifted from burglary prevention. Given the productivity information listed earlier, we know that preventing one more assault would mean preventing three fewer burglaries. Therefore, the marginal cost of preventing an additional assault is three more burglaries. To measure this in dollars, we simply ask what three burglaries cost. Since an additional burglary costs $1,100, three would cost $3,300.[9] So the marginal cost of preventing one more assault is $3,300.

Now, should resources be shifted? The answer is "yes," because shifting to the prevention of more assaults provides a net gain to society. The marginal cost of preventing an additional assault is $3,300. The marginal benefit of preventing an additional assault is $3,500. There is, therefore, a net gain equivalent to $200 if we shift resources.

In using equation 4–5 to get our answer, we must keep in mind that we have measured the costs of preventing assault in terms of burglary production (i.e., one assault costs three burglaries). Therefore, we must measure the costs of producing burglary in the same way. Under these circumstances the cost of producing one burglary is one burglary. We can now use equation 4–5, substituting the following marginal benefit and marginal cost information:

$$MB_{assault} = \$3,500 \qquad\qquad MB_{burglary} = \$1,100$$
$$MC_{assault} = 3 \text{ burglaries} = \$3,300 \qquad MC_{burglary} = \$1,100.$$

So marginal benefits per dollar of marginal cost are as follows:

$$\frac{\$3,500}{\$3,300} > \frac{\$1,100.}{\$1,100} \qquad\qquad (4\text{–}6)$$
$$\text{(Assault)} \quad \text{(Burglary)}$$

According to equation 4–5, we must get the same marginal benefit per dollar of cost from preventing each crime. But equation 4–6 shows that the marginal benefit per dollar of cost is higher for assaults than for burglaries. Therefore, we should shift resources from burglary prevention to assault prevention. We gain more per dollar of cost when preventing assaults.[10]

Does this mean that all resources should be devoted to assault prevention? The answer is no, because as more assaults are prevented (and fewer burglaries), the marginal benefit of assault prevention will decrease while the marginal costs of assault prevention will rise. (The opposite will be happening to the marginal benefits and marginal costs of burglary prevention.) We should shift resources to assault prevention and away from burglary prevention only up to the point at which we get the same marginal benefit per dollar of marginal cost from preventing each. We should allocate resources to the prevention of each crime so that the rule defined in equation 4–5 holds. This will give us the optimum mix of crime prevention and, as a leftover, the optimum mix of crime.

Measuring Marginal Benefits and Marginal Costs

In order to implement the rules for defining the optimum amount of crime prevention and the optimum mix of crime, it is necessary to obtain marginal benefit and marginal cost information. Where does this information come from? How do we know what the marginal benefit of preventing an additional crime is? How do we measure marginal costs of prevention? We cannot answer these questions completely here, but we can give some indication of how it can or should be done so that the reader knows that the theoretical material we have presented can be put into practice.

Marginal benefits can be measured in three ways. First, it is possible to measure benefits by calculating the marginal harm to society from the commission of a particular crime. The kinds of harm, and the value of the harm done, would depend on the type of crime. These costs of crime to society were discussed in detail in Chapter 2. If, for example, we were to measure the marginal benefits of assault prevention, we would measure the medical costs saved, the lost labor saved, and so forth. There are two problems with this approach. First, it may not be possible to include all types of harm (e.g., the psychic harm from crime). Second, while we may know the average harm done by a particular kind of assault, we do not necessarily know the harm that would be done by the next assault that would happen. Within particular kinds of assaults (characterized by time and place of occurrence, choice of weapon, age/sex of victim, etc.), we could assume that the potential harm done by the next crime is equal to the average for that kind of crime.[11]

The second way to measure marginal benefits is to obtain information on relative benefits rather than absolute figures. This can be useful when trying to make choices concerning the optimum mix of crimes. Relative marginal benefits can be compared with relative marginal costs to determine the best mixes of crime prevention and crime.[12] Relative marginal benefits can be obtained through **community polling.** It would be possible to inform the community of its current chances of victimization by assault and theft, and ask by how much they would be willing to increase the risk of one in order to decrease the risk of the other. This gives a measure of relative marginal benefits. For example, assume that the current chances of victimization are as follows:

Chances of assault = 8 in 1,000
Chances of burglary = 65 in 1,000.

The question is, by how much is the community willing to let the risk of burglary increase in order to decrease the risk of assault to 7 in 1,000? Assume that residents indicate that they are willing to permit the burglary risk to increase to 70 in 1,000. What does this tell us? It tells us that, given the amount of each crime going on now, the community considers one assault prevention to be equal in harm, or seriousness, to five burglaries. Therefore,

$$\frac{MB_{assault}}{MB_{burglary}} = 5. \qquad (4\text{--}7)$$

In 1977 the U.S. Department of Justice completed an extensive "community" poll to determine how people ranked the severity of crimes in the U.S.[13]

The National Survey of Crime Severity was conducted as a supplement to the National Crime Victimization Survey, which was described in Chapter 1. A national sample of 60,000 households was asked to rank the severity of more than 200 actions, each of which was illegal in at least one state.

Each person surveyed was asked to rank the severity of each crime in comparison to their evaluation of the severity of a person stealing a bicycle parked on the street. This bicycle theft was to be rated 10; a crime rated 20 was to be considered twice as serious, while a crime rated 5 was to be considered only half as serious. The average rating for each crime was used to determine the ranking of the severity of the 200 crimes. The scores were then re-scaled.

The scores, after re-scaling, ranged from 72.1 for planting a bomb that explodes in a public building killing twenty people, to 0.2 for a person under 16 years old playing hooky from school. Table 4–2 provides a summary of the ranking of the severity of crime. The overall pattern of the scores indicates that violent crimes are regarded as more serious than property crimes. Some interesting findings are that running a narcotics ring (with a score of 33.8) was viewed as a more serious crime than skyjacking (with a score of 32.7), while selling heroin for resale (with a 20.6 score) was more serious than rape if the woman did not require hospitalization (with a 20.1 score). Smuggling heroin (19.5) is about twice as serious as smuggling marijuana (10.5). Keep in mind that this survey was completed in 1977.

Community polling, regardless of the form it takes, can give us relative benefit information. One advantage of this approach is that it permits inclusion of psychic costs, since residents will consider these kinds of impacts when they vote or rank the severity of criminal activity. There is also the interesting possibility of converting severity scores, or relative rankings, into dollar amounts by defining the relationship between severity scores and dollar costs.[14]

Contingent valuation, the third method, also requires community polling but it asks people how much of their own money they are willing to pay to reduce crime by a specified amount. This is certainly a measure of the marginal benefit an individual expects to receive from not being victimized. Contingent valuation can estimate a monetary value based on consumers' stated preferences for something that cannot be directly observed by consumers' purchases such as preventing a crime from being committed. It is believed that these estimates are more likely to be more comprehensive than attempting to directly measure the marginal harm to society because they incorporate the social costs of crime such

TABLE 4–2
SEVERITY OF CRIME

Offense	Severity Score
Bombing a public building causing 20 deaths	72.1
Forcibly raping a woman resulting in her death	52.8
Stabbing a victim to death	35.7
Running a narcotics ring	33.8
Skyjacking	32.7
Child beating requiring hospitalization	22.9
Intentionally burning a building causing $500,000 worth of damage	22.3
Selling heroin	20.6
Rape not requiring hospitalization	20.1
Smuggling heroin	19.5
Killing a victim by recklessly driving a car	19.5
Armed robbery of a bank of $100,000 during business hours	17.7
Theft of a locked car and selling it	10.8
Smuggling marijuana for resale	10.5
Hindering a criminal investigation by a government official	10.0
Breaking into a home and stealing $1,000	9.6
Stealing $1,000 worth of merchandise from a department store counter	7.6
Assaulting a person with your fists with the victim requiring hospitalization	6.9
Cheating on your federal income tax return	4.5
Prostitution by a woman	2.1
Stealing $10 from a parking meter	1.6
Public drunkenness	0.8

Source: U.S. Department of Justice, Bureau of Justice Statistics, "The Severity of Crime," (Washington, D.C.: January 1984), 2–4.

as concerns about community safety. As discussed in Chapter 2, a recent study estimated the value of preventing five crimes (burglary, armed robbery, serious assaults, rape and sexual assaults, and murder) using this approach. The estimates are that society places a value of $25,000 on preventing a burglary; $70,000 on preventing a serious assault; $232,000 on preventing an armed robbery; $237,000 on preventing a rape and sexual assault, and $9.7 million on preventing a murder.[15]

Measuring Marginal Costs

The marginal costs of crime prevention depend basically on two things: how much it costs to hire an additional resource to produce more crime prevention (i.e., prices) and how many additional resources have to be hired to prevent one more crime. The latter piece of information is based on productivity. Price information is fairly easy to obtain, but what about productivity data? Where does this come from? In the earlier example we saw that, per time period, crime prevention resources could prevent one assault or three burglaries. How do we know this?

This kind of information comes from knowing the relationship between inputs of economic resources and output of a product called crime prevention. The relationship between inputs and output is described in what is known as a **production function.** In general, a production function is described as follows:

$$\text{Output} = f(\text{inputs}) \tag{4–8}$$

where the symbol, or operator, f, reads "is a function of." Output is a function of inputs. The problem, of course, is describing that function—getting measures of the relationship between inputs and outputs. If all inputs are increased by one, by how much will output increase? If an additional patrol officer is hired, how many additional crimes will be prevented? This measure of the change in output (or product) associated with a change in an input is called the marginal product of the input. In order to measure marginal costs, then, what we really need are measures of the marginal products of all inputs—estimates of the crime prevention production function.

This kind of information can be obtained by direct observation. Of course, there are difficulties in measuring the number of crimes prevented, and it would be necessary to adjust for factors other than the increase in inputs that might cause crime to go up or down. Because of the need to correct for other factors in measuring marginal products, it is sometimes useful to use sophisticated statistical techniques to estimate crime prevention production functions. There are several examples of this kind of approach, most of which focus on police production functions.[16] Without describing these studies here, we should note that each has to face the difficulties involved in measuring police outputs and inputs, for the police provide many different outputs, including noncriminal activities like giving traffic directions, and some inputs may simultaneously produce different outputs (e.g., the police officer directing traffic who deters a crime in the area). The studies must also correct for other factors that affect crime rates. Regardless of the manner in which police production functions have been estimated, we still do not know very much about police productivity. Some statistical studies suggest that the marginal productivity of police is zero.[17] This means that an additional unit of police resources leads to no reduction in crime. One reason for this may be that the police are just one part of the criminal justice system. We will return to this question later in the chapter. Another reason may be the difficulty of measuring the number of crimes prevented by police.

Other studies have found a perverse relationship between police presence and crime—an increase in police is associated with increases in crime. Partly, this may be because reported crime may increase as more police are hired and more crime is detected. That is, police produce detection, as well as deterrence. Partly, too, this may be because when crime rates are high, cities increase the number of police; that is, the causal direction of the relationship is reversed. Some studies take these possibilities into account in their estimation techniques, and often use measures of police productivity such as probability of punishment rather than number of crimes prevented. When these corrections are made, the results concerning police productivity are not so discouraging.[18] Finally, the strategies that police employ may have a greater impact on crime rates than the number of police.[19] In order to answer all of these questions concerning police productivity, a lot more research is needed.

OPTIMUM ALLOCATION OVER NEIGHBORHOODS[20]

So far we have discussed two aspects of the optimum allocation of crime prevention resources question: the optimum amount of crime and the optimum mix of crime. We now turn to the question of how to distribute scarce crime prevention resources geographically within a city. Given a particular crime prevention budget for the city, how much of that budget should be spent in each neighborhood? Some expenditures (e.g., upper-level administrative personnel) benefit all neighborhoods more or less equally. But other expenditures (e.g., for patrol officers or vehicles) benefit only particular areas. For these kinds of expenditures, how much is the right amount to allocate to each neighborhood? The answer depends on the objective of the decision maker. We will discuss several alternatives, but first one point should be made. Increased police efforts in one neighborhood may be reflected in increased crime in another (i.e., crime may be displaced). In the following discussion we assume that while reduced law enforcement efforts in one neighborhood may increase crime there, increased law enforcement in other

neighborhoods need not shift crime to other areas. This is a somewhat simplifying assumption.

Perhaps the most equitable objective would be to equalize crime rates in
all neighborhoods. To illustrate how this is accomplished, and the implications of achieving this objective, let us consider a situation in which there are
only two neighborhoods. Assume that the population of each is equal, so that
the same number of crimes would mean the same crime rate per person. This
makes our analysis easier. Let us also assume that the costs of crime prevention
differ in the two neighborhoods, perhaps because one neighborhood is more
cooperative with the police. Figure 4–6 illustrates the marginal costs of crime
prevention in each neighborhood. Neighborhood 1 is the high-prevention-
cost neighborhood, and neighborhood 2 is the low-prevention-cost area.

Number of crimes prevented, $\overline{Q}$, is measured on the horizontal axis.
Both marginal costs of prevention increase as more crimes are prevented.
Equalizing crime rates in the two neighborhoods means having the same
amount of crime in each. If we assume that laissez-faire crime is equal in the
two neighborhoods, then equalizing crime rates means preventing the same
number of crimes in each. This means going out the same distance on the
horizontal axis for each neighborhood. The total number of crimes prevented will depend on the size of the city's budget. Given this budget, the
same number of crimes should be prevented in each neighborhood. This is
illustrated in Figure 4–7. $\overline{Q}_1{}^*$ measures the number of crimes prevented in
neighborhood 1, and $\overline{Q}_2{}^*$ measures the number of crimes prevented in
neighborhood 2. The number prevented in each is equal: $\overline{Q}_1{}^* = \overline{Q}_2{}^*$.

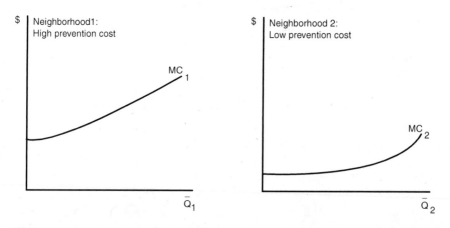

Figure 4–6 Marginal Costs of Crime Prevention: Two Neighborhoods

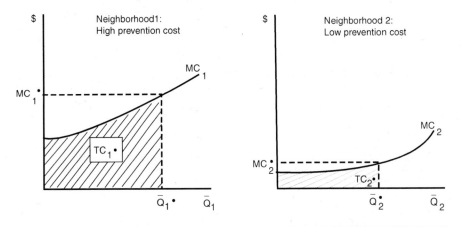

Figure 4–7 Equalizing Crime Rates: Two Neighborhoods

While this may be the fairest solution, it is interesting to consider its implications. First, the marginal costs of preventing an additional crime in neighborhood 1, MC_1^*, far exceed the marginal costs of preventing an additional crime in neighborhood 2, MC_2^*. This means that resources are not equally efficient in both neighborhoods. Second, the total costs of prevention in each neighborhood also differ widely. Total costs of prevention are measured by the area of the shaded section under each MC curve. TC_1^* measures the total costs of prevention in neighborhood 1, and TC_2^* measures the total costs of prevention in neighborhood 2. It is clear from the figure that a substantial percentage of total costs (and therefore of the budget) is attributed to neighborhood 1.

The discrepancy between marginal and total costs between the two neighborhoods would be aggravated if the amount of laissez-faire crime in neighborhood 1 exceeded the amount of such crime in neighborhood 2, for then it would be necessary to prevent more crimes in 1 than in 2 by moving out further on the horizontal axis in 1 and increasing the marginal and total costs there, while moving to the left in 2 and reducing marginal and total costs there. In fact, if the amount of laissez-faire crime in one neighborhood greatly exceeds the amount of such crime in the other, and if prevention costs are also higher in the high-crime area, it may not be possible to equalize crime rates even if all resources are assigned to the high-crime-high-cost area. Finally, while equalizing crime rates by neighborhood may be equitable, it is not necessarily efficient. That is, it may not minimize the city's overall crime rate.

Minimizing the overall, or aggregate, crime rate for the city is a second possible objective. To the extent that media coverage focuses on city crime rates, this may be a politically attractive objective. To fulfill this objective, it is necessary to allocate crime prevention resources to each neighborhood so that the marginal cost of prevention is equal in both areas. This solution is illustrated in Figure 4–8.

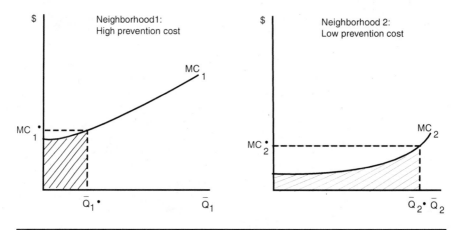

Figure 4–8 Minimizing the Aggregate Crime Rate: Two Neighborhoods

Again, the total number of crimes prevented will depend on the overall prevention budget. Given that budget, the city crime rate will be minimized by preventing $\overline{Q}_1^*$ crimes in neighborhood 1 and $\overline{Q}_2^*$ crimes in neighborhood 2. The marginal costs of prevention in each neighborhood are equalized. If marginal costs were not equal, as in Figure 4–7, it would be possible to shift resources from the high-marginal-cost area to the low-marginal-cost area and have the overall crime rate go down. This is because, when resources are removed from neighborhood 1 the crime rate there goes up, and when they are shifted to neighborhood 2 the same resources will prevent more crimes than they did in neighborhood 1, since resources can prevent crime more cheaply in neighborhood 2. Resources are more efficient, or productive, in neighborhood 2. Therefore, the reduction in crime in neighborhood 2 more than offsets the increase in crime in neighborhood 1. The city crime rate goes down overall. This phenomenon would occur until marginal costs of prevention were the same in each area.

What are the implications of minimizing the city crime rate? The obvious one is that while overall the city may have the lowest crime rate possible given its budget, crime rates are likely to differ widely across neighborhoods.

The discrepancy will depend on how large the differences in laissez-faire crime are, how large the differences in costs of prevention are, and whether the high-crime areas are also the high-prevention-cost areas. Finally, minimizing the crime rate is not the same as minimizing the harm done to the city, for, as we argued before, different kinds of crime create different amounts of harm. In our analysis we have made no distinction between the benefits of preventing different crimes in different neighborhoods.

It is obvious, then, that more sophisticated objectives are possible, such as minimizing the harm done to the city as a result of crime or equalizing the harm done in each neighborhood. Meeting these objectives would require not only marginal cost information by neighborhood, but also marginal benefit data by neighborhood. It is also possible to have less sophisticated objectives which focus not on output but on inputs. Examples are the provision of equal numbers of patrol officers or vehicles per person or per square mile, or provision of the same average response time to all calls for police help. The latter would involve predicting the frequency and location of calls.[21] Finally, it may be necessary to combine equity and efficiency considerations and attempt to fulfill some combination of objectives; for example, minimizing the aggregate crime rate while at the same time guaranteeing a minimum level of inputs allocated to each neighborhood.[22]

Optimum Allocation Within Courts and Corrections

There are other questions concerning the optimum use of resources within the criminal justice system. We have focused on crime prevention, primarily by police.[23] We have argued that, owing to scarce resources, society cannot prevent all crimes; the police cannot enforce all laws completely. Just as the police must make choices, so must decision-makers within the rest of the criminal justice system—the courts and correctional institutions. For example, prosecutors cannot afford to prosecute all offenders who have been charged. In making choices about which cases to prepare for prosecution, the same principles apply: the marginal benefits and marginal costs of successful prosecution should be considered.

Currently, choices are made about the allocation of scarce court resources. In the United States in 2001–2002 about 95 percent of felony criminal charges at both the federal and state levels are settled without a trial.[24] This is because of the process of **plea bargaining** which typically precedes the trial, usually ending in a pretrial settlement. A settlement would be a plea of guilty to a less serious offense than the one charged, or dismissal of the charge. Plea bargaining, therefore, saves scarce court resources. It would be impossible to bring all charged offenders to trial without a tremendous increase in the resources allocated to criminal justice, particularly the court system. Therefore, choices must be made. Whether or not plea bargaining is used efficiently to make these choices is not clear.[25]

The other question, of course, is whether or not more resources should be allocated to the courts, either at the expense of other areas within criminal justice or at the expense of other public or private goods. This decision requires a comparison of marginal benefits and marginal costs. A cost-benefit study was done of criminal courts in the District of Columbia.[26] It was determined that each additional dollar spent on expanding the capacity of the courts to process criminal cases would benefit society by between $5 and $11 ($11.72 and $25.82 in 2005 dollars) in the value of the resultant reduction in crime. The study was limited to the four FBI index property crimes so this result may not extend to all the courts' activities. It also assumes that congestion exists in the courts' processing of these cases. Without congestion, the benefits of spending additional resources on the courts would certainly be reduced.

Recent technological advances have made inroads into improving the courts efficient utilization of their resources.[27] Video evidence presentation during trials decreases the time for a trial and therefore decreases the related court costs. The use of video conferencing decreases the need for all parties to be in the same physical location at the same time decreasing time and travel costs; increasing accessibility to judges; and decreasing the security risk associated with transporting criminals to and from the courthouse. Increased use of the Internet decreases the costs to the judiciary of providing information. The costs of phone inquiries decreases as do the associated mailing and printing costs. Also, the use of various remote supervision technologies to monitor the behavior of defendants and offenders on probation reduces judicial costs. Remote alcohol and drug detection devices and the use of GPS (global positioning satellite) technology allowing for real-time monitoring of an offender's location decreases probation and pre-trial incarceration costs. A recent study found a $40 ($46.05 in 2005 dollars) per day per offender savings in the incarceration costs of offenders awaiting trial.[28]

Resource allocation decisions must be made within the system of prisons and corrections as well. Here there are several important questions that should be addressed, such as: What is the rational structure of punishments? What is the optimum magnitude of punishment? What is the optimal form of punishment, and what, if any, is the appropriate role of the private sector in corrections?

The first question concerns the relationship of the punishment for one crime to the punishments for others. Regardless of the absolute magnitude of each punishment, how do the punishments compare with one another? The focus is therefore on relative size. The argument is that, for the structure of punishments to be rational, more serious crimes must have larger penalties. For example, in order to have marginal deterrence, a more serious crime must have a stiffer penalty. If not, there is nothing to deter commission of the more serious act. If we invoke the death penalty with equal probability for a theft as for a murder, what is there to deter a robber from killing the victim? It is interesting to note that an examination of the probability of conviction and the average length of prison term for each of the FBI index crimes, excluding arson, in 1960 suggested that the structure of penalties was rational.[29] A more recent study of the same crimes for Georgia and North Carolina also indicates rationality in the structure of penalties.[30]

The growing concern with drug use and drug related crime in the 1970s led to a significant increase in the severity of punishment for drug crimes and the growth in the use of mandatory sentences that took sentencing out of the hands of prosecutors and judges and into the hands of Congress and state legislators. Once the implication of these new laws became clear many people, including several Supreme Court justices in 2002, have suggested that the structure of these penalties is far from rational.[31]

Beyond the structure of penalties is the question of the optimum magnitude of the penalty. Assume for the moment that all punishments take the form of prison terms. How long should each sentence be? What is the optimum magnitude of punishment for aggravated assault? for burglary? The appropriate prison term depends on our objective(s). Four different, and sometimes inconsistent, **objectives of prisons** have been identified: deterrence, incapacitation, rehabilitation, and retribution. At different times in our history we have tended to emphasize one or another of these objectives.[32]

Using prisons for deterrence means incarcerating criminals in order to provide an example for potential criminals and thus deter them from crime. In choosing prison terms for this purpose, we should consider the marginal social costs of imprisonment (which include the marginal costs of maintaining an additional prisoner plus the potential lost income of the prisoner) and compare these social costs with the social benefits of reducing the harm done by potential offenders. If the marginal social costs of imprisonment exceed the marginal benefits, the prison term is too long.

Incapacitation means incarcerating criminals in order to prevent them from committing additional criminal acts. In choosing prison terms for this purpose, we should compare the marginal social costs of imprisonment with the marginal social benefits of a reduction in the amount of crime committed by that offender. If, for example, an offender typically commits crimes which cost society $8,000 per year, we should not spend more than $8,000 a year to incapacitate this offender. To do so is to waste resources.

If prisons are used primarily for rehabilitation, the questions of whether to use prison and, if it is used, how long the sentence should be are answered differently. In fact, if rehabilitation is the goal, prison terms are indeterminate—the prisoner is released when he or she is rehabilitated. This is when the costs expended exceed the discounted value of any possible future benefits.

Using prisons for retribution means punishing the offender because he or she deserves it. In this case we attempt to use prison to extract a "payment" from the offender equal to the harm he or she has done to society. Of course, while prison costs the offender (as well as society), lost income, and so forth, no payment is made to society. In fact, society loses, since it costs a considerable amount of money to keep the offender incarcerated. If prison is used for retribution, society loses twice: we are hurt by the crime and again by the punishment for the crime. The benefit to society is the psychic value of knowing that the offender has received "just desserts."

This suggests that other forms of punishment might be substituted for imprisonment, for a net gain to society. Possibilities include fines and sentencing offenders to appropriate work within the legal sector. Whether or not these are appropriate alternatives depends, again, on our objectives. As retribution, they make sense. For incapacitation, they do not. They can be effective deterrents, depending on the probability of punishment, and may provide rehabilitation at lower cost. On balance, the most appropriate thing to do to increase **economic efficiency,** as well as **equity,** might be to reduce the construction and use of prisons.[33] Money saved within the prison system could be reallocated to the courts to increase the probabilities of punishment. This conclusion is, of course, premature without a careful evaluation of the costs and benefits involved, which in part depends on a clear delineation of the objectives of punishment.[34]

The public sector is increasingly under pressure to allocate resources efficiently within corrections. This has been brought about by rapid increases in the prison population due both to demographic factors and changes in the certainty and the severity of punishment. From 1985 through June 2004, the **U.S. prison population** has increased by almost three times (744,208 prisoners in 1985 and 2,131,180 as of June 30, 2004). This represents an incarceration rate of 726 inmates per 100,000 people in the U.S., currently the highest in the world (with Russia second), and an increase from 140 per 100,000 barely 30 years ago (1972).[35] In addition, the courts have become concerned with overcrowding and prisoners' rights, providing pressures for the expansion of corrections facilities.[36] Also, legislative and other restrictions have been placed on many states' abilities to raise the revenues needed to meet these increased demands. Public reluctance to approve bond issues for prison construction, and siting problems, have made the provision of increased prison space extremely difficult.

In response, state governments are examining various alternatives, including the private sector, to provide the desired level of corrections services more efficiently. Private industry has been involved in corrections for some time. It has primarily provided a limited number of specialized services that include: education, training and placement programs; counseling and other mental health services; drug treatment programs; prison industries programs; community treatment centers; and food services for the inmates. Recently there has been an expansion of the private sector's role in the financing, ownership, and operation of prisons.[37] In 1995 private firms were operating more than 110 adult correctional facilities in the U.S. and in 2000 they were operating 264 prisons. In 2004 private prisons housed 98,791 inmates, or almost seven percent of all state and federal inmates.[38]

It has been suggested that increased utilization of the private sector in corrections will lead to improvements in the efficient use of resources allocated to corrections. It is believed these gains can be obtained from several sources. The profit motive, which does not exist in the public sector, provides the motivation for the provision of required services utilizing cost minimizing behavior. The private sector may well provide greater flexibility in raising capital to finance construction or expansion because it is not constrained by legislated limitations on the amount of debt it can hold, nor does it need voter approval to raise funds. There may be flexibility in operating in terms of the allocation of personnel because the private sector is not constrained by civil service regulations. The private sector is also likely to have a greater incentive to adjust its programs more rapidly to meet the changing needs of the inmates as the inmate population changes or as labor market and other conditions change.

On the other hand, some economists have suggested that while increased **privatization** may well increase the efficiency in the provision of correctional services, it may harm the **allocative efficiency** of the criminal justice system. In part, this may be a result of having a single contracting firm providing services, and therefore behaving as a monopolist.[39]

There are concerns about the appropriateness of increased privatization of corrections that are essentially noneconomic, but not unimportant. For many people the administration of justice is an essential reason for the existence of government, and delegating a significant portion of this activity, corrections, to the private sector is, therefore, inappropriate. Another concern is that private providers will unduly influence public policy to improve their profits at the expense of the public interest or the well being of the inmate population. There are the administrative concerns of maintaining quality and the accountability of private sector providers. Legal concerns exist over whether a state can turn over management of prisons to private sector providers and whether the state can give them the right to use force, especially deadly force, to maintain security.

There are also some financial and economic issues. It is possible for the private provider to become bankrupt and be unable to operate the prisons. The state would then have to find the resources and expertise to step in to operate the prison on short notice. Probably most important for the economist is whether the expected benefits in efficiency and cost savings from privatization offset the expected costs. With many of the possible costs being non-economic or difficult to quantify, it is almost impossible to know whether privatization will actually lead to a more efficient allocation of resources in corrections.

There are other issues concerning resource allocation within the prison system which we could examine,[40] as well as other aspects of the resource allocation problem within the criminal justice system as a whole. In this chapter we have tried to show the kinds of questions that can and should be asked, and the basic approach that should be used to answer the questions— a comparison of marginal benefits with marginal costs. Before turning to the next chapter, we will briefly discuss the role of private security.

There is evidence that the public criminal justice system is not leading to welfare maximization for society. Newspaper stories report on community dissatisfaction with policing, the courts, and corrections. At the same time it is equally clear that society is hesitant to allocate more resources to the public sector.[41] As we have already discussed, governments are trying to reallocate resources in a number of ways, including privatization. The private sector is also trying to increase its welfare through direct expenditures on private security. It is estimated that approximately $103 billion (almost $115 billion in 2005 dollars) will be spent on private security goods and services in 2000. Included in this estimate are the **costs of proprietary security** (e.g., university security who are employees of the university), guard and patrol services, alarm services, private investigators, armored car services, manufacturers of security equipment, locksmiths, and security consultants. More than one-third the amount will be spent on security equipment and another one-third for guard companies and proprietary security guards. A 2004 FBI study found that small firms (those with sales less than $10 million) spent more the $500 per employee just on computer security and large firms (those with sales of greater than $1 billion) spent almost $110 per employee.[42] The private security industry is expected to employ approximately 1.9 million people making it approximately the same size as the public criminal justice system.[43] The existence of such a large private system that regularly employs approximately one-quarter of local police officers[44] raises some interesting questions concerning the incentives in the public sector for economic efficiency and achieving welfare maximization.

This chapter completes our development of a theoretical framework within which to examine the various economic aspects of criminal activity. In the remainder of the book the theoretical approach that we have developed is applied to several classes of criminal activity and problems, beginning with crimes against property.

REVIEW TERMS AND CONCEPTS

Allocative efficiency
Community polling
Contingent valuation
Crime prevention
Crime prevention production
   function
Deterrence
Economic resources
Efficiency
Equity
Incapacitation
Incarceration costs
Iso-benefit function (A)
Laissez-faire crime
Marginal benefit function
Marginal benefits
Marginal cost function
Marginal costs
Marginal deterrence
Marginal product
Marginal social benefits
Marginal social costs
Minimizing crime
Monopolist
National Survey of Crime
   Severity

Net gain
Optimum allocation of resources
Optimum amount of crime
Optimum amount of crime prevention
Optimum form of punishment
Optimum industry size
Optimum magnitude of punishment
Optimum mix of crime
Plea bargaining
Point of tangency (A)
Police production function
Private goods
Privatization
Product transformation curve (A)
Productivity
Profits
Public goods
Rational structure of punishment
Rehabilitation
Retribution
Social benefits
Social costs
Social welfare
Total benefits
Total costs
Value of harm avoided

(A = from chapter appendix)

END OF CHAPTER QUESTIONS

1. From the economists' perspective it makes more sense for the criminal justice system to be provided by the government than by the private, for profit, sector. Why? Why isn't the same true for a Ricky Martin CD?

2. If the police chief knows that the benefit from preventing the next murder is $10,000 and the benefit from preventing the next bicycle theft is $200, but it costs $1,000 to prevent the next murder and only $100 to prevent the next bicycle theft, should the chief reallocate resources to prevent more murders or more thefts? Why?

3. New technology, such as computers, can enhance the productivity of police officers in the prevention of crime and court officials in the processing of criminals. What impact would the introduction of a productivity enhancing technology have on the optimum amount of crime committed in the city or town where you live? Why?

4. Privatization of corrections has been suggested as a means of improving the allocation of resources in corrections. What are some of the pros and cons in support of this?

NOTES

1. Technically, there is a distinction between prevention and deterrence. Little is known about the impact of the preventive activities of police or other agencies. Deterrence activities, which also prevent crimes, are efforts to convince criminals that the probability of being caught and punished is high.

2. For an advanced discussion of the optimum amounts of law enforcement and of crime, see Gary S. Becker, "Crime and Punishment: An Economic Approach," *Journal of Political Economy*, no. 2 (March–April 1968), 169–217. For a less mathematical discussion of a related issue, the definition of an optimum law, see Gordon Tullock, "An Economic Approach to Crime," *Social Science Quarterly*, 50, no. 1 (June–September 1969), 59–71. Both are reprinted in Neil O. Alper and Daryl A. Hellman, *The Economics of Crime: A Reader* (Needham, Ma.: Simon & Schuster, 1997).

3. For an advanced discussion of optimal private expenditures for crime prevention, see Gary Becker, *op.cit.* For an examination of the substitutability of public and private expenditures, see Charles T.

Clotfelter, "Public Services, Private Substitutes, and the Demand for Protection Against Crime," *American Economic Review*, 67, no. 5 (December 1977), 867–877, and Itzhak Goldberg, "Public and Private Protection: Substitutability or Complementarity?" Occasional Paper Series, Domestic Studies Program (Stanford, Ca.: Stanford University, Hoover Institution, Center for Econometric Studies of the Criminal Justice System, April 1977).

4. *Uniform Crime Reports for the United States*, 2003, U.S. Department of Justice, Federal Bureau of Investigation (Washington, D.C., 2004), Table 8, 147.

5. Since Boston's fiscal year (FY) runs from July 1 to June 30, the City Council actually voted on two budgets for the Police Department, and the reported budget is estimated from a FY 2003 appropriation of $217,405,619 and a FY 2004 appropriation of $211,363,261 (Summary Budget, www.cityofboston.gov/budget/pdfs/02-summary-budget.pdf).

6. This is because in the short run, when at least one factor of production is fixed, the law of diminishing returns holds. This means that as more of the variable factors are employed to increase output, the increases in output, called the "marginal product," get smaller and smaller. Diminishing marginal product means rising marginal costs.

7. From Figure 4–5, the optimum amount of crime initially is Q_1^* $(= Q - \overline{Q}_1)$. With higher marginal costs the optimum amount of crime becomes Q_2^* $(= Q - \overline{Q}_2)$. Since $\overline{Q}_1 > \overline{Q}_2$, then $Q_1^* < Q_2^*$ or the optimum amount of crime has increased.

8. An alternative and equivalent way of looking at this solution, using product transformation and iso-benefit functions, is described in the appendix.

9. For simplicity we assume the marginal benefit is the same for each of the three preventions. Theoretically, marginal benefits diminish with each additional prevention.

10. The same result can be obtained by using assault as the "base" crime. In this case we use the fact that preventing an additional burglary will cost one-third of an assault, so:

$MB_{assault}$ = \$3,500 $MB_{burglary}$ = \$1,100
$MC_{assault}$ = \$3,500 $MC_{burglary}$ = 1/3 assaults = \$1,167.

Therefore, marginal benefits per dollar of marginal cost are:

$$\frac{\$3,500}{\$3,500} > \frac{\$1,100}{\$1,167}.$$
$$\text{(Assault)} \quad \text{(Burglary)}$$

11. This does not mean that marginal benefits are constant. We are simply approximating the marginal figure by using the average. In addition, as we move from more serious assaults to less serious ones (characterized by time and place of occurrence, choice of weapon, age/sex of victim, etc.), average (and marginal) benefits decrease.

12. Assuming that there are only two types of crime, equation 4–5 can be rewritten in terms of relative marginal benefits and relative marginal costs:

$$\frac{MB_1}{MC_1} = \frac{MB_2}{MC_2}$$

or

$$\frac{MB_1}{MB_2} = \frac{MC_1}{MC_2}$$

Relative marginal benefits (the ratio of the marginal benefits from preventing crime 1 to the marginal benefits of preventing crime 2) must equal relative marginal costs. (See the appendix.)

13. See the U.S. Department of Justice, Bureau of Justice Statistics, *The National Survey of Crime Severity* (Washington, D.C.: June 1985).

14. See Llad Phillips and Harold L. Votey, Jr.; *The Economics of Crime Control,* (Beverly Hills, Ca.: Sage Publications, 1981), Chapter 4.

15. Cohen, Rust, Steen and Tidd, *op. cit.*

16. Werner Z. Hirsch, *Urban Economic Analysis* (New York: McGraw-Hill, 1973), Chap. 12, 356–362; J. M. Heineke, "An Econometric Investigation of Production Costs Functions for Law Enforcement Agencies," Occasional Paper Series, Domestic Studies Program (Stanford, Ca.: Stanford University, Hoover Institution, Center for Econometric Studies of the Criminal Justice System, August 1977).

17. For a review and summary of various efforts to measure police productivity, see James Q. Wilson, "Do the Police Prevent Crime?" *The New York Times Magazine,* October 6, 1974, 18–19, 96–101. For a bibliography on police productivity, see *Police Productivity,* compiled by Justus Freimund and Marjorie Kravitz (Washington, D.C.: U.S. Department of Justice, Law Enforcement Assistance Administration, National Institute of Law Enforcement and Criminal Justice, May 1978). This bibliography includes references which address problems in measuring productivity, approaches and experiments with improving productivity, and related management issues.

18. Thomas J. Orsagh, "The Determinants of Major Crime in California in 1960," Western Economics Association Meeting, August 1970; Llad Phillips and Harold L. Votey, Jr., "An Economic Analysis of the Deterrent Effect of Law Enforcement on Economic Activity," *Journal of Criminal Law, Criminology,* and *Police Science,* 63, no. 3 (September 1972), 330–342; and James Q. Wilson and Barbara Boland, "The Effect of the Police on Crime," *Law and Society Review,* 12, no. 3 (Spring 1978), 367–390.

19. For an empirical examination, see Wilson and Boland, *ibid.* They find that, other things equal, both increased numbers of patrol units and more aggressive strategies lead to increased arrest rates, which, in turn, reduce robbery rates.

20. This section is based on a similar discussion in Carl S. Shoup, "Standards for Distributing a Free Governmental Service: Crime Prevention," *Public Finance/Finances Publiques,* 19, no. 4 (1964), 383–394, reprinted in Neil O. Alper and Daryl A. Hellman, *op.cit.*

21. For a model designed to forecast calls for police assistance, see Nelson B. Heller and Robert E. Markland, "A Climatological Model for Forecasting the Demand for Police Service," *Journal of Research in Crime and Delinquency,* 12, no. 2 (July 1970), 167–176.

22. For a discussion of equity vs. efficiency considerations, see Lester C. Thurow, "Equity Versus Efficiency in Law Enforcement," Public Policy, 18, no. 4 (Summer 1970), 451–459. It is also interesting to consider the allocation of crime prevention resources by income class as well as by neighborhood. For an empirical examination see John C. Weicher, "The Allocation of Policy Protection by Income Class," *Urban Studies,* 8, no. 2 (October 1971), 207–220.

23. For a schematic which describes the relationships among activities of the public, criminals, and the police, as well as the resource allocation decisions which must be made within police departments, see Martin T. Katzman, "The Economics of Defense Against Crime in the Streets," *Land Economics,* 44, no. 4 (November 1968), 431–440. He illustrates choices among criminal and noncriminal activities, among crimes, among neighborhoods, among programs, and among inputs.

24. See "Federal Criminal Case Processing, 2001" (U.S. Department of Justice, Bureau of Justice Statistics, www.ojp.usdoj.gov/bjs/pub/pdf/fccp01.pdf), Table 5, 11 and "State Court Sentencing of Convicted Felons, 2002" (U.S. Department of Justice, Bureau of Justice Statistics, www.ojp.usdoj.gov/bjs/pub/pdf/scscf02.pdf), Table 4.2, 45.

25. For an advanced theoretical treatment of the choice between a trial and a pretrial settlement, see William M. Landes, "An Economic Analysis of the Courts," *The Journal of Law and Economics,* 14, no. 1 (April 1971), 61–107.

26. E. Noam, "A Cost-Benefit Model of Criminal Courts," *Research in Law and Economics,* vol. 3 (1981), 173–183.

27. United States Courts, *Report to Congress on the Optimal Utilization of Judicial Resources* (Washington, D.C.: United States Courts, Administrative Office), February 2000.

28. *Ibid.,* 35.

29. Gary Becker, "Crime and Punishment." For further discussion of the properties of a rational structure of punishments, see George Stigler, "The Optimum Enforcement of Laws," *Journal of Political Economy,* 78, no. 3 (May–June 1970).

30. Thomas Orsagh, *Judicial Response to Crime and the Criminal: Utilitarian Perspective,* Report to U.S. Department of Justice, Bureau of Justice Statistics (Washington, D.C., May 1982).

31. See, for example, "Drug Laws That Destroy Lives," *New York Times,* May 24, 2000, and P. Simon and D. Kopel, "Restore Flexibility to U.S. Sentencing," *National Law Journal,* Dec. 16, 1996.

32. For an economic analysis of various incarceration objectives, see Daryl A. Hellman, "Social Welfare Implications of Sentencing Policy: An Economic Perspective," *Legal Studies Forum,* vol. XII, no. 1, 1988.

33. The opposite conclusion is reached by James Q. Wilson in "Who Is in Prison?" *Commentary,* 62, no. 5 (November 1976), 55–58. For a bibliography see *Issues in Sentencing,* compiled by John Ferry and Marjorie Kravitz (Washington, D.C.: U.S. Department of Justice, National Institute for Law Enforcement and Criminal Justice, March 1978).

34. For more on the equity considerations involved in the use of jails see Ronald Goldfarb, *Jails* (New York: Twentieth Century Fund, 1975). The author describes jails as the "nation's dumping ground."

35. P. Harrison and A. Beck, *Prison and Jail Inmates at Midyear,* 2004, Washington, D.C., Bureau of Justice Statistics, Bulletin, April 2005, Table 1, 2; "U.S. Incarceration Rates Timeline" (www.angelfire.com/rnb/y/ratesusa.htm#years); and International Centre for Prison Studies, "Entire World—Prison Population Rates" (www.prisonstudies.org).

36. In 2003, the federal prison population was 139 percent of the rated capacity of the system's facilities; the states' prison population was estimated to be 116 percent of the rated capacity; and local jails were at 94 percent of the rated capacity. Approximately 60 percent of the states and the District of Columbia have been under court order or consent decree concerning overcrowding. Recent increases in local jail construction have led to excess capacity. P. Harrison and A. Beck *op.cit.,* p.1. (April 2005) *Prison and Jail Inmates at Midyear 2004.*

37. A summary of the issues related to privatization in corrections can be found in U.S. Department of Justice, National Institute of Justice, *Research in Brief: Corrections and the Private Sector* (Washington, D.C., March 1985).

38. J. Stephan and J. Karberg, "Census of State and Federal Correctional Facilities, 2000," U.S. Department of Justice, Bureau of Justice Statistics, August 2003, p. iv; and Harrison and Beck, *op.cit.,* Table 3, 4.

39. Bruce L. Benson, "Do We Want the Production of Prison Services to Be More 'Efficient'?" Tallahassee, Fl.: Florida State University, Department of Economics Working Paper Series, no. 91–06–6.

40. Kenneth Avio, "An Economic Analysis of Criminal Corrections: The Canadian Case," *Canadian Journal of Economics,* 6, no. 2

(May 1973), 164–178, and "Recidivism in the Economic Model of Crime," *Economic Inquiry*, 13, no. 3 (September 1975), 450–456.

41. The tax "revolts" in a number of states are certainly indications of the public's lack of trust in that sector's ability to allocate resources in a manner that maximizes social welfare. Two early examples of this revolt were California's Proposition 13 and Massachusetts' Proposition "2½," both of which led to initial cutbacks in government expenditures and placed restrictions on future expenditures.

42. L. Gordon, M. Loeb, W. Lucyshyn and R. Richardson, "2004 CSI/FBI Computer Crime and Security Survey," Computer Security Institute, www.gocsi.com, 2004, 5.

43. "Economic Crime Cost Reaches $200 Billion in 2000," Security Industry Association Research Update, Report for 1st Quarter 2000; and Bureau of Justice Statistics, "Justice Expenditure and Employment in the United States, 1995" (Washington, D.C.: U.S. Department of Justice, November 1999), Table 6, 6.

44. William C. Cunningham, et al., "Private Security: Patterns and Trends," U.S. Department of Justice, National Institute of Justice, *Research in Brief,* August 1991, 3.

APPENDIX TO CHAPTER 4

The Optimum Mix of Crime

An alternative and equivalent way of defining the optimum mix of crime is in terms of product transformation and iso-benefit functions.

Assuming only two different types of crime, these functions can be presented graphically:

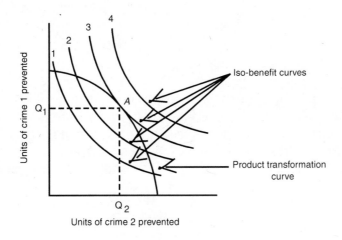

The product transformation curve shows all possible combinations of units of crime 1 and crime 2 prevented, given the crime prevention budget and existing technology. The slope of the product transformation curve is equal to the ratio of the marginal costs of preventing each crime at that point:

$$\text{Slope of product transformation curve} = -\frac{MC_2}{MC_1}$$

The slope (absolute value) increases as more of crime 2 (and less of crime 1) is prevented, assuming that marginal costs increase.

The iso-benefit curves show a set of possible benefit levels. Along each curve, the benefits to society from crime prevention are equal. The slope of the curve is equal to the ratio of the marginal benefits of preventing each crime at that point:

$$\text{Slope of iso-benefit curve} = -\frac{MB_2}{MB_1}$$

The slope (absolute value) decreases as more of crime 2 (and less of crime 1) is prevented, assuming that marginal benefits decrease.

The product transformation curve summarizes the crime prevention possibilities if all available resources are used. Defining the optimum mix of crime prevention and, therefore, of crime involves finding the best point on the product transformation curve at which to operate. Since society's objective is to attain the highest possible level of benefits, the optimum mix of crime prevention is that point on the product transformation curve which is on the highest possible iso-benefit curve. This occurs at point A, where the product transformation curve is tangent to iso-benefit curve 3. Society should prevent Q_1 units of crime 1 and Q_2 units of crime 2 to minimize the amount of harm done, given its crime prevention budget. This will determine the optimum mix of crime for society.

Notice that the optimum point is the point of tangency of the two curves. At a point of tangency, such as A, the slopes of the two functions are equal. Therefore, the optimum mix of crime prevention is defined as that point at which the slope of the product transformation curve equals the slope of the iso-benefit curve, or:

$$\frac{MC_2}{MC_1} = \frac{MB_2}{MB_1}$$

This equation can be rearranged as follows:

$$\frac{MB_1}{MC_1} = \frac{MB_2}{MC_2}$$

which is equivalent to equation 4–5 when there are only two different classes of crime.

5

Crimes Against Property

Crimes against property include the FBI index crimes of **robbery, burglary, larceny, arson,** and **auto theft.** Robbery, while classified as a "violent" crime, is similar to burglary in an economic sense in that it represents an attempt to obtain property from a victim. Although not index crimes, white-collar crimes are also generally viewed as property crimes. **White-collar crimes** are nonviolent crimes typically committed for financial gain by individuals in white collar occupations.[1] Included among the crimes that are often classified as white-collar crimes are theft, fraud, and embezzlement. Additional non index property crimes that have increased significantly along with the use of personal computers and the Internet are identity theft and illegal file-swapping of copyrighted material, e.g., movies, music, games and software.

In this chapter we start by reviewing the kinds of economic costs generated by crimes against property. We will then focus on the impact of such crimes on various markets in terms of altered prices and outputs. In Chapter 2 we discussed the ways in which individuals can be affected by crime via price and employment effects. Here we examine that phenomenon again with reference to crimes against property. Then we will examine the market for stolen property and see whether public policy can be used to reduce the size of that market. Finally, we will summarize a few empirical studies of crimes against property.

ECONOMIC COSTS

While in some property crimes (e.g., arson) real property is damaged and destroyed, in a large number of property crimes property is not destroyed and therefore is not lost to society. It is simply transferred from one member, or group, to another. The crime represents an involuntary transfer; money or goods are transferred from one group to another, but the victim(s) did not agree to the transfer.

In the simplest case, a burglar steals a television set for his or her own use. Here, one individual loses a TV and another gains one. The net loss to society is zero. More typically, the burglar steals property but for the purpose of fencing the merchandise to obtain cash. However, the television is ultimately sold to a customer at its market value. Again the television is not lost or destroyed, so the net impact is zero.

There are, however, some real costs to society associated with crimes against property. First, there are the costs of having some people working in our economy as burglars, **fences,** and the like, rather than being employed in a legitimate job producing something that people value. People do not value involuntary transfers. The valuable goods and services which those individuals do not produce because they devote their time and other resources to producing crime are a cost to society. This is the "opportunity cost" of these crimes.

Additional costs to society include psychic costs to victims and others, such as anger or fear. There is also a cost to society, perhaps more remote. Mixed capitalism relies on the institution of privately owned property. To the extent that we cannot guarantee protection of private property ownership, we diminish the ability of our economy to function.

The final category of costs consists of private expenditures to protect property[2] and public expenditures in the criminal justice system.

IMPACTS ON MARKET PRICES AND OUTPUTS

While in the aggregate, crimes against property represent primarily transfers they nevertheless cause prices of various products in the legal marketplace, and therefore the pattern of output and employment, to be different from what would otherwise be the case. In order to summarize the kinds of impacts which these crimes have, we will first consider impacts on the supply side of various legal markets, then impacts on the demand side, and then impacts on the public sector.

Impacts on the Supply Side

To the extent that property crimes impose costs on producers of goods and services, their costs of doing business are increased;[3] therefore, assuming that nothing else has changed, these producers' supply has decreased and the curves shift to the left. As an example, consider the crime of shoplifting. Let us assume that in order to avoid shoplifting losses, retail store owners install mirrors and TV monitors. This costs money, so that any level of output is now going to have a higher price attached to it. The retailer's willingness to supply goods at the same prices has decreased and the supply curve has shifted to the left, as in Figure 5–1.

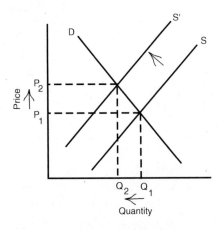

Figure 5–1 Supply and Demand for Retail Goods

Before the change in supply, the demand and supply curves intersected at P_1Q_1. The price of retail goods per unit was P_1 and the output of goods per time period was Q_1. Associated with this level of output was a certain employment level.

As the shoplifting problem developed, retailers took measures to avoid losses. This caused their willingness to supply goods to decrease and the supply curve to shift from S to S′. Any level of output now costs more. Since supply has decreased and the curve has shifted, a new equilibrium price and quantity are established. Price increases to P_2 and output drops to Q_2. Because output has gone down, employment in retail stores has also gone down.

This crime causes prices to consumers of retail goods to be higher than they would be otherwise,[4] and it causes employment in the retail industry to be lower than it would otherwise be. The burden of the crime is, therefore, shared by consumers of retail goods and by individuals who employ their resources in the production of retail goods. While the employment impact is on the use of all productive resources, including land and capital, the immediate impact is most likely to be on labor, which we assume to be more variable than the other factors.

The extent to which the burden falls on consumers or on producers depends on the **price elasticity of demand** for the product. Before seeing why, let us see what price elasticity of demand is. It is simply a measure of how responsive, or elastic, the quantity of a product demanded is to changes in the price of that product. It, therefore, compares the change in quantity demanded with the associated change in price, where both changes are measured in percentages. The comparison is made by taking the ratio of the two

percentage changes. The number that results is called the price elasticity coefficient:

$$\text{Price elasticity of demand coefficient} = \frac{\text{percentage change in quantity demanded}}{\text{percentage change in price}} = \frac{\% \Delta Q^D}{\% \Delta P}. \qquad (5\text{--}1)$$

It is interesting to consider the different values a price elasticity of demand coefficient could assume and how these might be related to the shape
of the demand curve. First consider the most typical case, a negatively sloped
demand curve such as the one in Figure 5–1. Without some actual numbers
on the axis, it is impossible to calculate the value of the coefficient; moreover,
the value will be different at different points along the demand curve.
However, one thing can be said about the coefficient. At every point along
the curve, regardless of the value of the number calculated, it will always have
a negative sign. The reason is that if a demand curve has a negative slope, it
means that price and quantity demanded change in opposite directions. If
price goes up, quantity demanded goes down, and vice versa. Therefore, the
numerator and denominator of equation 5–1 will always have opposite signs.

So much for the typical case. Now let us consider an extreme case. What
if, as price changed, quantity demanded did not change at all, that is, quantity demanded were completely unresponsive to price change? In such a case
the demand curve would be like the one in Figure 5–2.

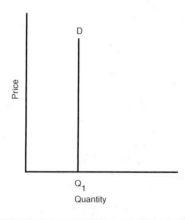

Figure 5–2 A Perfectly Inelastic Demand Curve

This is called a perfectly inelastic demand curve. If price changes, there is no change in quantity demanded. Quantity demanded is always Q_1 units per time period, regardless of price. The price elasticity coefficient is zero. We might wonder whether or not there are any products which have a demand curve like the one in Figure 5–2. While perfect price inelasticity may not exist, there are goods and services for which demand may be almost perfectly inelastic. Such products are characterized by a lack of adequate substitute goods, in terms of either strength or number, so that when price changes, consumers cannot change their consumption of the product very much. Heroin, which is discussed in a later chapter, may be an example.

If demand were perfectly price inelastic and an increase in crimes against property caused a change in supply and a shift in the curve, how would the outcome be different from that shown in Figure 5–1? The answer can be seen in Figure 5–3. Here we illustrate the same supply change as in Figure 5–1, but we have drawn a perfectly price-inelastic demand curve. What happens is clear. The entire burden of the crime falls on the consumers of the product in the form of higher prices. Price rises from P_1 to P_2. Output and employment in the industry are unchanged.

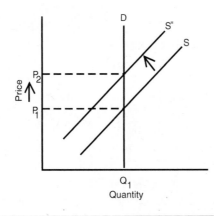

Figure 5–3 Supply Shift with a Perfectly Inelastic Demand Curve

Another extreme case is drawn in Figure 5–4. Here the demand curve illustrated is perfectly elastic, that is, completely responsive to price change. At a price higher than P_1, quantity demanded would be zero. At the same time, producers can sell as much as they like at price P_1; it is not necessary to lower the price to sell more. Therefore, the price is always P_1.[5]

When supply decreases and the curve shifts from S to S′ as a result of an increase in property crimes which cause the costs of doing business to go up,

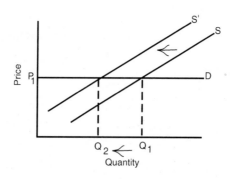

Figure 5–4 Supply Shift with a Perfectly Elastic Demand Curve

the change in the marketplace is completely reflected in a change in output and employment. Price stays the same. Output decreases from Q_1 to Q_2, and employment of resources in the industry falls along with it. What consumers pay for the produce is unaffected, but the amount consumed by them is less.

The extent to which the burden of increased costs caused by crime falls on consumers or on producers depends on the price elasticity of demand. If demand is highly price inelastic, consumers will be hurt most. If, however, demand is very sensitive to price (i.e., very elastic), it will be the workers in the industry who bear the burden.

Impacts on the Demand Side

Crimes against property can also cause demand in various legal markets to increase or decrease. This will also cause prices and outputs to be different from what they would be in the absence of crime.

Demand will change and the curves will shift if any of the determinants of demand change, that is, if there is a change in any of the following: consumers' tastes or income, prices of substitute goods, and prices of complements. In Chapter 2 we looked at the impact burglary might have on the insurance industry. We argued that an increase in burglary rates would cause the consumers' taste for insurance to increase, thereby increasing demand and shifting the demand curve for insurance upward and to the right. We also argued that, because of increased claims, costs would increase, causing supply to decrease and the supply curve to shift to the left. The combined effect is reproduced in Figure 5–5. Price increases from P_1 to P_2. Quantity bought and sold also increases, from Q_1 to Q_2. Employment in the industry increases.

In general, we would expect the demand for any kind of property protecting device or service to increase as property crimes increase and tastes for

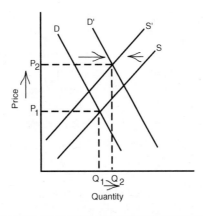

Figure 5–5 The Market for Insurance

such products therefore increase.[6] The result will typically mean higher prices for consumers of these products and increased employment in their production.

It is also possible for property crimes to cause demand for some products to decrease. For example, as insurance premiums go up, it would be expected that the demand for insurable property would drop. Why? Because insurance and valuable property are complementary goods—you tend to buy them together. If the price of a complementary good (insurance) goes up, demand for the product (valuable property) goes down. The impact is illustrated in Figure 5–6.

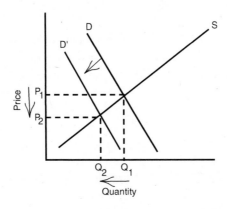

Figure 5–6 The Market for Valuable Property

Price drops from P_1 to P_2 and output drops from Q_1 to Q_2. Employment also goes down. The impact illustrated in Figure 5–6 is likely to be strengthened by a decrease in tastes for property that is likely to be a target of crime, regardless of changes in insurance prices. This is because insurance cannot eliminate psychic or nonmonetary losses from crime.

The extent to which changes in demand translate into price changes or into quantity changes depends on supply conditions, in particular, on the price elasticity of supply. The **price elasticity of supply** is analogous to the price elasticity of demand—it measures how responsive the quantity supplied is to changes in the price of the product. A price elasticity of supply coefficient is calculated as the ratio of percentage change in quantity supplied to the associated percentage change in price:

$$\text{Price elasticity of supply coefficient} = \frac{\text{percentage change in quantity supplied}}{\text{percentage change in price}} = \frac{\%\,\Delta\,Q^s}{\%\Delta\,P}. \qquad (5\text{–}2)$$

Typically, a supply price elasticity coefficient is positive, since quantity supplied and price are positively related. However, as with demand curves, it is possible to have unusual values for elasticity when supply curves have unusual shapes. A perfectly inelastic supply curve graphs as a vertical line—quantity supplied is the same regardless of price. The price elasticity coefficient is zero. At the other extreme, a perfectly elastic supply curve graphs as a horizontal line—supply is infinitely responsive. Producers are willing and able to produce any level of output at a constant price.

Let us take a look at what a demand decrease caused by increased property crime would mean if supply were perfectly inelastic. This situation is illustrated in Figure 5–7. The vertical supply curve shows that, regardless of price changes, output of this product will be Q_1 units per time period. As demand decreases from D to D', price drops from P_1 to P_2.

Figure 5–7 may describe the market for housing in an area where crime has increased recently. In such a market the supply of housing is likely to be almost perfectly inelastic, at least in the "short run." The short run is defined as a period during which at least one of the inputs required in the production of the good cannot be changed. Usually land and/or capital inputs are fixed for a while. If so, during that period the quantity of housing cannot be changed and the supply curve looks like Figure 5–7.

What happens, then, when demand drops because of a decrease in tastes for property in a neighborhood where property crime has recently increased

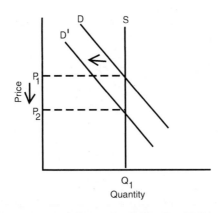

Figure 5–7 Demand Decrease with a Perfectly Inelastic Supply Curve

and property insurance premiums are going up?[7] With a perfectly inelastic supply, the entire impact is reflected in a decrease in the price of housing units; in other words, values go down. Profits to property owners drop (or losses increase). In the long run, when all productive inputs are variable, we would expect to see housing units removed from this neighborhood unless something can be done to stimulate demand for housing of this quality.

As an interesting exercise, the reader might try to analyze the impact of the same demand decrease if the supply curve were perfectly elastic.

IMPACTS ON THE PUBLIC SECTOR

In the preceding section we saw how property crimes cause prices, outputs, and employment of resources in various private markets to be different from those which would exist without the crimes.[8] In this section we look at the impact these crimes have on the public sector (i.e., government). In Figure 5–8 we show the supply and demand for crime prevention by the public sector. Here we lump all parts of the public sector together and ignore the distinctions among federal, state, and local governments. Realistically, as we saw in Chapter 2, the majority of public criminal justice services are provided at the local level.

The demand curve for public crime prevention is the marginal benefit curve (MB), as we saw in Chapter 4. The supply curve is the marginal cost curve (MC). Before the increase in property crimes the optimum output of public crime prevention is at the intersection of marginal benefits and marginal costs, or Q_1. On the price axis, price P_1 is indicated in parentheses since it is only a shadow price, or a price that does not really exist. Rather than paying a price for crime prevention, we pay for it via taxes.

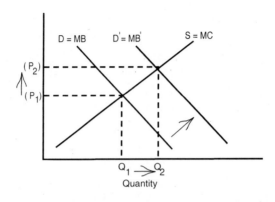

Figure 5–8 The Supply and Demand for Public Crime Prevention

As property crimes increase, the taste for public crime prevention increases; that is, we value any level of crime prevention more highly. Therefore, the demand, or marginal benefit, increases and the curve shifts from MB to MB′. The new optimum output of crime prevention has increased to Q_2. Employment in public crime prevention increases, and tax rates will have to increase to pay for it unless there are budget cuts elsewhere, or unless the tax base increases enough to produce the additional revenues needed.

An interesting situation would exist if the supply curve for public crime prevention were perfectly inelastic and demand for services increased. This situation is illustrated in Figure 5–9. Here, output does not increase although employment of resources does.[9] The public gets no more crime prevention, but it has to pay more for what it gets. We need to know more

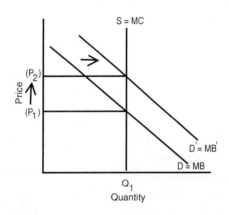

Figure 5–9 The Supply and Demand for Public Crime Prevention

about the productivity of inputs in the production of crime prevention before we can conclude whether or not this is the case.[10]

THE MARKET FOR STOLEN PROPERTY

In Chapter 3 we argued that a rational criminal will produce a crime if the gains from the crime exceed the costs, including opportunity costs; a criminal will commit a property crime if the monetary and psychic gains from the crime exceed the costs. While in some instances the monetary gains are cash or its equivalent, in most thefts the monetary gains are in the form of property which is converted into money via the **market for stolen property.**[11] The market for stolen goods determines the market prices of the various forms of stolen property. Thieves seldom sell directly to final customers. As we will see later, there are often several middle people, just as there are in legal markets. Thus, prices are determined at each of several stages of distribution. To simplify the analysis, however, we will collapse the market and discuss a single supply of and demand for stolen property.

The Demand for Stolen Goods

The demand for stolen goods is similar to that for nonstolen goods; that is, the relationship between price and quantity demanded is an inverse one and demand will change, the curve will shift, with a change in any of the determinants of demand—consumers' tastes and income, and prices of related goods. The negatively sloped demand curve for stolen property is illustrated in Figure 5–10.

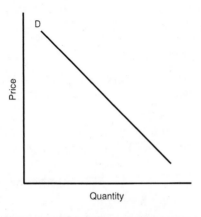

Figure 5–10 The Demand for Stolen Property

A change in consumers' tastes for stolen property would cause demand to change and the curve to shift. For example, a decrease in tastes, perhaps because of a drop in the thrill of owning stolen goods or because of an increase in guilt associated with participating in illegal markets, would cause demand to decrease and the curve to shift downward, as in Figure 5–11. The consumers in the market are willing and able to buy fewer units of stolen property at each price along demand curve D′ than along demand curve D.

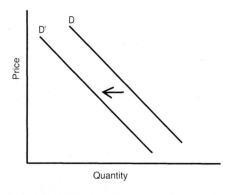

Figure 5–11 The Demand for Stolen Property

The effect of a change in income is less clear. If the penalty for purchasing stolen property is a prison term, then the value of the penalty increases as income increases, so stolen goods in general would be inferior goods. As income increases, demand for the product decreases, as in Figure 5–11. However, if there is no penalty, or a very unlikely penalty (i.e., a probability of punishment equal to zero), then the effect of a change in income is less certain. Some stolen products (e.g., Yugos) are likely to be inferior goods, while others (e.g., BMWs) are likely to be normal goods.

Analyzing the effect of a change in the price of related goods is more complicated. In the first place, the effect depends on whether the related good is a substitute or a complement. If the good is a substitute, a drop in its price will cause the demand for stolen property to decrease. An increase in its price will have the opposite effect. We might ask, what goods would be substitutes for stolen property? The answer is nonstolen property. A legally purchased good can always be substituted for an illegally purchased one. The important thing to remember here is that we are talking about relative prices. If, for example, the price of legally purchased cars are to decrease relative to that of illegally purchased ones, we would expect to see the demand for stolen cars decrease, as in Figure 5–11. Notice that we are not saying that the price of legally purchased cars drops below that of stolen cars, only that legally purchased cars become *relatively* cheaper. In fact, it is likely that just the opposite has been the case for many cars, particularly when we include insurance, taxes, and registration in the price of a legally purchased car. Other things equal, this increases the demand for stolen cars and means an increase in the quantity of stolen cars bought and sold in illegal markets.

Automobile insurance is an example of a product that is complementary to automobiles, at least legally purchased ones. You tend to buy the two products together. Changes in the prices of complementary goods can also shift demand curves. An increase in the price of a complementary good will decrease demand, while a decrease in price will increase demand. In the case of stolen property, there are at least three kinds of complementary goods (or services): information, transaction requirements, and the need to protect or maintain property rights after purchase. While each of these is complementary to the purchase of most products, they take on added importance in illegal markets.

In order to buy stolen property it is necessary to have information about what is available, where, and at what prices. If this kind of information becomes difficult to obtain—that is, if the price of information increases—the demand for stolen property will drop. Similarly, if the transaction requirements of dealing in stolen markets increase, demand will decrease. By transaction requirements we mean the time, trouble, and risk involved in buying.

Because of the importance of information and transaction costs in the market for stolen property, and because of the need to keep these costs down to avoid adverse impacts on demand, middle-people are required to facilitate the flow of information and to reduce transaction costs to buyers. The way these "fences" work is similar to the way wholesalers and retailers in legitimate markets work; they try to make the market operate more smoothly. In fact, at times the distinction between middle-people in the legitimate and illegitimate markets may be blurred, for a large portion of the property stolen in this country is ultimately handled, knowingly or unknowingly, by the legitimate marketing system. One researcher, after a three-year study of the distribution of stolen goods in a city in upstate New York, estimated that 67 percent of the market for stolen goods was provided by supposedly legitimate businesses.[12] In 2003 it was estimated that more than $13.2 billion worth of property was stolen in this country, with only $4.5 billion recovered; the remainder was redistributed by thieves. The recovery of stolen motor vehicles accounted for approximately 90 percent of what was recovered by the police while stolen motor vehicles accounted for less than half the value of what was stolen.[13]

The last category of goods or services that are complementary to stolen property consists of the goods or services needed to protect or maintain property rights after purchase, that is, to prove ownership or disprove the fact that the property has been stolen. Techniques to make stolen property more recognizable could therefore cause the demand for stolen property to drop, since the "price" of proving legal ownership would increase. **Operation Identification** programs, which involve engraving personal property such as TVs and stereos with identification numbers, are an example of such a technique. While on a small scale such programs may shift crime to easier targets, on a large scale, other things equal, they should reduce the market for stolen property. Of course, it is to the sellers' advantage to avoid such adverse impacts. This is one reason why sellers go to the trouble of assembling bicycles from the parts of several stolen bikes. While this may avoid impacts on the demand side, it increases time and materials costs to sellers, and therefore shifts the supply curve for stolen property to the left, reducing the size of the market. To see this, let us turn to the supply side of the market.

The Supply of Stolen Goods

The supply of stolen goods is simply one example of the supply-of-crime function which we discussed in Chapter 3. This function describes the relationship between price, or average gain from crime, and quantity of crime. More specifically, it describes the relationship between the price of stolen property and the quantity of stolen property supplied per time period. For the reasons discussed in Chapter 3, we would expect this relationship to be a positive one. When graphed, the supply curve would have a positive slope, as in Figure 5–12.

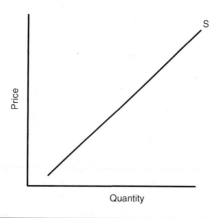

Figure 5–12 The Supply of Stolen Property

Supply will change, and the curve will shift, with a change in any of the costs of doing business. To review, for criminal activities such as stealing property, the costs of doing business are material costs, time costs, psychic costs, and expected-punishment costs. An increase in any one of these costs will cause supply to decrease and the supply function to shift to the left; any quantity of stolen property will now require a higher price. On the other hand, a decrease in any of the cost categories will cause supply to increase, shifting the supply curve to the right.

The Price of Stolen Goods

The actual price paid by buyers of stolen goods and received by sellers will be determined by the interaction of supply and demand forces. The equilibrium price of goods and the quantity bought and sold (and stolen) can be illustrated by the intersection of the supply and demand curves. The equilibrium price and quantity are illustrated in Figure 5–13. The price is P_1 per unit, and Q_1 units of stolen property are exchanged per time period.

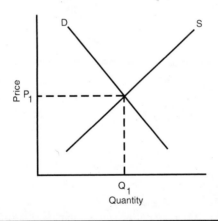

Figure 5–13 The Market for Stolen Property

PUBLIC POLICY TOWARD CRIMES AGAINST PROPERTY

Using Figure 5-13 for reference, we can see that a decrease in demand (a shift down to the left), supply (a shift up to the left), or both, will reduce the market for stolen property; that is, it will reduce the amount of stolen property exchanged during any given time period. Therefore, if we want to reduce the number of crimes against property we must design public policies which will change supply and demand in the proper direction.

One suggestion which has been made is to focus law enforcement efforts on apprehending and punishing fences. The idea is that, since fences are so important to the smooth working of the market, making life difficult for them will tend to disrupt the market for stolen property by reducing demand (because information and transaction costs will increase) and/or reducing supply (because the costs of doing business, particularly risk, or probability of punishment, will go up). Analytically, this is correct. The difficulty, of course is that "getting the goods" on fences may not be that easy. It is generally more difficult than catching thieves.[14]

Various policies which would increase the costs of doing business for criminals were discussed in Chapter 3. These include "target hardening" strategies, such as increased use of security devices to increase the time or material costs of burglary; Operation Identification, which would require thieves to spend time or money removing identification numbers which reduce the resale value of the stolen property; more legal employment opportunities and higher incomes for potential offenders, which would increase both time and expected punishment costs; and finally, increased probability of arrest and conviction. The latter could be accomplished in a variety of ways.[15]

Regardless of the policy chosen, it should be evaluated in terms of the costs of the program versus the benefits as measured by the anticipated decrease in property crimes. Notice that some policies (e.g., reduced unemployment in the legal sector) would produce additional benefits beyond crime reduction, and these should be included in the evaluation.

It is also possible to direct efforts toward the demand side of the market. One suggestion is to try to convince the public to pass up bargains which appear to be too good to be true. What this kind of campaign amounts to is an effort to reduce the taste for stolen property and thereby reduce demand for stolen goods. An interesting experiment in Portland, Oregon, sheds some light on whether or not this would be effective, although certainly the results are not conclusive. In the experiment, a nonuniformed policewoman loaded the trunk of her car with portable televisions and drove around the city looking for customers, purposely avoiding known outlets for stolen property. In her search for buyers she made no phony claims about where she had gotten the TVs; she said her boyfriend had stolen them. The response of the public to the stolen bargains she offered is interesting. "Some took them home. Some turned around and sold them. Some asked if she could get more. Only one person turned her down."[16]

WHITE COLLAR CRIME

White collar crimes cannot be easily categorized as either crimes against persons or property crimes. Some white collar crimes, such as the production of unsafe products that lead to the physical harm of consumers, are more like crimes against persons than property crimes. The victims are physically harmed by the criminal activity of the firm. Others, like **bribery, employee theft,** and **embezzlement,** are more like property crimes where the victim of the criminal act is the firm. Still others, like the **insider trading** of **Ivan Boesky** and **round-trip trading** of energy by **Dynergy Inc.** in 2002, simply involve the transfer of resources from the victim to the criminal and impose no direct costs on the production of any goods or services, nor do they physically harm anyone. To the extent that white collar crime is a property crime, much of its impact is on the cost of doing business in the victimized firm(s).

While there is no generally accepted definition of white collar crime, there are a number of elements that seem to be common to most of them.[17] White collar crimes are committed in the course of one's occupation and involve a violation of the trust associated with the job. The criminal act does not involve physical force and the primary goal is generally money, property, power or prestige. The act is committed intentionally, and the perpetrator of the crime attempts to conceal it. According to the FBI, the majority of white collar offenders are white males and there are a greater proportion of female white collar offenders than female property crime offenders.[18]

The difficulty in defining white collar crime also leads to difficulty in measuring the magnitude of the problem and the costs it generates. The FBI recently estimated that over the 1997–1999 period white collar crimes accounted for almost four percent of all reported crime and that the value of the property loss per incident was, on average, greater for white collar crimes than for property crimes.[19] Fraudulent billings for public and private health care programs are estimated to be between three and ten percent of total health care expenditures that were estimated to be $2.1 trillion in 2004.[20] According to the 2002 National Retail Security Survey, employee theft and internal fraud may cost up to $31.3 billion annually.[21] The Foundation for Taxpayer and Consumer Rights estimates the cost of corporate crime to be $1.5 trillion annually.[22] An Internal Revenue Service study found that the federal government lost about $127 billion in FY 1998 in tax revenues (about $150 billion in 2005 dollars) from individuals' and businesses' failure to report income and profits.[23] As these are only estimates for a limited number of crimes that would be included among white collar crimes, it is clear that these crimes impose a significant cost on society.

An example of a white collar crime that would be classified as a property crime would be employee theft. Employee theft of goods or services used in the production of some other good or service increases the firm's costs of doing business. For example, employees who take office supplies home for their personal use, or use computer resources for personal gain, force the firm to purchase more office supplies and more computer resources than actually needed. This leads to a decrease in the supply of whatever product the firm produces, or a shift in the supply curve to the left as depicted in Figure 5–1.

Another example would be embezzlement. Embezzlement of funds by a bank official, which imposes no real direct resource costs on society because it is simply a transfer of resources from the bank's depositors to the official, may also have an indirect effect on the cost of doing business. If the bank's loss is covered by its liability insurance, then its premiums are likely to increase to offset the insurance company's cost of replacing the funds. If the bank is self-insured, it will have to include as part of its costs of doing business the expected losses it may well incur due to the likelihood of one of its officials embezzling funds. In either case, the costs of doing business have increased, leading to a decrease in the supply of funds available to the bank's customers. This will probably raise the price at which the bank lends money to its customers so that it can recover the funds, if they are not directly recoverable from the embezzler, or pay the increased cost of its insurance premiums (see Figure 5–1).

Identity theft has become one of the most important white collar crimes of the 21st century, according to the FBI. It generally includes, though is not limited to, three types of fraud: credit card, check and/or mortgage fraud.[24] Not only does it impose significant costs to the monetary victims, like the financial institutions, it also may significantly limit the ability of the individual whose identify was stolen to obtain credit, purchase a home or simply cash checks. A Federal Trade Commission survey in 2002 found that almost five percent of consumers over 18 years old, or almost 10 million individuals, were victims of an identity theft during the year. The losses totaled almost $53 billion with the vast majority of them, almost $48 billion, incurred by businesses.

In 2002, the FBI created a Cyber Division to address the expansion of computer-based crimes, due to a rapid growth in computer technology, computer use, and e-commerce in recent years. Computer crimes include illegal hacking into other computers, "cyber terrorism," fraud, theft, illegal gambling and child pornography. [25]

COPYRIGHT INFRINGEMENT

Another property crime that has shown recent rapid growth due to technological change is copyright infringement. Copyright protects the ownership rights of authors of 'original works,' such as novels, music, plays and other forms of intellectual property. It was viewed as such an important right that the authors of the U.S. Constitution included the protection of it in Article I and the first federal law establishing copyright was signed by George Washington in 1790. The justification for copyright, and patents on inventions, is to create an incentive for authors/inventors to invest time and energy into the creation of something new. As stated in the Constitution the purpose of copyright is '...To promote the Progress of Science and useful Arts, by securing for limited Times to Authors and Inventors the exclusive Right to their respective Writings and Discoveries...' Today copyright law protects an author's control over her music for her lifetime plus an additional 70 years and if a person created something, like Mickey Mouse, while an employee for some firm, such as Disney Studios, then the firm can control the rights to that property for 95 years from its development.

Illegal file swapping over the Internet, a violation of U.S. and international copyright laws, may well be the most common property crime committed. In March 2005 in testimony before the U.S. Supreme Court a lawyer for the entertainment industry indicated that 2.6 billion files of music, film and other copyright protected material are stolen every month.[26] In the U.S. alone it has been estimated that more than four million people per day swap music files over the Internet in violation of the law.[27] The cost of all this illegal activity to the entertainment industry is difficult to measure. The music industry blames illegal file-sharing for a decrease of 22 percent in the sales of CDs over a five year period starting in the late 1990s. Recent estimates are that illegal file sharing cost the music industry $2.1 billion in 2004 and that more than one-third of file swappers purchase less music than they would have otherwise purchased.[28]

Like many policies copyright laws may impose costs along with the benefit of encouraging creativity. By providing the copyright holder with monopoly power and thus raising the price of the product above the competitive market price for a copy, it restricts legal access to those who can afford the higher price. Additionally, copyright may deter creating something new through building upon or borrowing from the inventions of others due to the price set by the copyright holder. For these reasons and others, there are some economists who advocate the elimination of copyright and related laws.[29] Not all artists support making file swapping illegal either because they believe that it is likely to make it more difficult for new artists to be heard or seen.[30]

EMPIRICAL STUDIES OF CRIMES AGAINST PROPERTY

In this final section, we summarize some empirical studies of crimes against property. Three basic kinds of studies are considered. In the first type the researcher collects data on the gains from crimes against property and the costs of engaging in crimes against property (including expected-punishment costs), and then compares the two. The purpose is to determine whether these crimes are profitable (i.e., yield a net positive return). Four such studies are summarized in Table 5–1.[31] Each uses a somewhat different methodology, and while each looks at burglary (Cobb also looks at grand larceny—see column 2), each looks at the crime in a different area (column 4) for somewhat different years (column 3). Sesnowitz and Cobb restrict their analysis to adult burglars, but Gunning makes no such distinction (column 5). The conclusions are contained in the final column. Sesnowitz finds that burglary by adults in Pennsylvania in 1967 was not profitable. Cobb concludes that adult theft in Norfolk, Virginia, in 1964 and 1966 was profitable. Krohm finds that burglary in Chicago in 1969 was very profitable for juveniles but not for adults unless they had very little aversion to risk or a low time-discount rate. The study by Gunning comes to no conclusion concerning burglary in Delaware in 1967.

The reader, too, should be cautioned against drawing any firm conclusions before carefully examining each of the studies summarized here. In each study various assumptions are made and data difficulties are encountered. This is typical of empirical studies and does not necessarily diminish their value, but it suggests that the results should be evaluated carefully with an eye to the methodological problems involved and the direction in which each compromise forces the results. The studies are mentioned here as evidence of the interest in an economic approach to an understanding of crimes against property.[32]

In the second type of study, the researcher again collects information on the gains and costs of crime, but this time there is an attempt to measure and test the relationship between the amount or rate of crime and its gains and costs. For this purpose data are collected from different places (e.g., cities or states at one point in time-cross-sectional data) or for one place (e.g., a city, state, or nation for a series of months or years—time series data). The data represent a series of observations on crime rates and the associated values for gains from crime and costs of committing crime. Using these observations it is possible to estimate with statistical techniques the "average" relationship between the amount of crime on the one hand (the dependent variable) and the gains and costs of committing crime on the other (independent variables). The estimated equation or equations which result from this kind of

TABLE 5–1

CRIMES AGAINST PROPERTY: STUDIES OF PROFITABILITY

Author (1)	Crime(s) Studied (2)	Year Studied (3)	Area Studied (4)	Criminal Group Studied (5)	Conclusion (6)
Sesnowitz	Burglary	1967	Pennsylvania	Adult burglars	Not profitable
Cobb	Burglary, grand larceny	1964, 1966	Norfolk, Va.	Adult thieves	Profitable
Krohm	Burglary	1969	Chicago	Adult and juvenile burglars	Profitable for juveniles but not for adults unless there is little aversion to risk or a low time-discount rate
Gunning	Burglary	1967	Delaware	All burglars	No conclusion

study describe the relationship between the amount or rate of crimes against property and the gains and costs of committing these crimes. Statistical tests of the reliability of the results can be performed.

A detailed description of these studies is beyond the scope of this book. Obviously, proxy measures are often used in measuring the gains and costs of crime, and such measures may be indirect. Other factors which affect the amount of property crime (e.g., the weather or the age distribution of the population) also must be accounted for by being measured and included in the equation.[33]

There are several examples of this kind of study.[34] Some are more sophisticated than others, and each is different with respect to data base, variables measured, and so forth. On the whole, however, the results of the studies are fairly consistent with the economic model of behavior. That is, while the results vary somewhat, the rate of property crime tends to be positively related to measures of the gains from the crimes and negatively related to measures of the costs associated with committing the crimes. This is what we would expect if thieves are rational. However, the results are mixed and have been criticized for not paying enough attention to the theoretical basis for the inclusion of "correcting" variables in the equations. The most severe criticism, however, is that these studies look at aggregate measures which reveal very little about individual criminal behavior. Because of this, some more recent studies have used individual level data with some success.[35]

In the third type of study, the researcher obtains information on criminal activity, usually the crime rate for specific crimes, and attempts to identify the relationships between them and measures of macroeconomic activity. A direct test of the relationship between crime and **business cycles** pretty much requires the use of time series data to at least identify the peaks and troughs of the cycle. The unemployment rate, or a similar measure of overall economic activity, such as the employment to population ratio, or gross domestic product, is utilized.

Studies by economists who have reviewed the research conclude that there is little evidence of a strong relationship between business cycles and criminal activity.[36] A study by two economists reaches a somewhat stronger conclusion with regard to the relationship between business cycles and three types of property crime.[37] They find a countercyclical pattern in the burglary rate and robbery rate in the United States over the period from 1935 to 1979. They also find evidence of a procyclical pattern in the motor vehicle theft rate over the period 1949–1979. Countercyclical means the level of criminal activity increases as the economy is declining, while procyclical means just the opposite.

Both these results are consistent with the economic model of crime. A decline in economic activity, as reflected in an increasing unemployment rate, is likely to create more people who cannot obtain the goods and services they need from income they can generate through legal activities. Therefore, they increasingly turn to illegal activities to directly obtain the needed goods or to obtain the income needed to purchase them. When the economy is growing, with increases in legal sector employment, the need to obtain goods and services through illegal means diminishes. This explains the countercyclical pattern observed for burglary and robbery rates.

It is also generally true that as consumers' incomes decrease during an economic slowdown, their demand for certain goods and services decreases. Luxury goods, i.e., goods with high income elasticity of demand such as expensive automobiles, are often the most affected. If consumers' demand decreases for expensive automobiles, then the price the auto thief can get for a stolen car, or the average gain, decreases. This is because the demand for stolen automobiles will decrease (recall our earlier discussion of how the stolen goods market works). With everything else being the same, i.e., no change in the costs of producing the stolen car, fewer cars will be stolen. When the economy is growing and incomes are rising, then consumers' demand will increase for items such as expensive automobiles. Thus, the observed procyclical pattern for automobile thefts is also explained by the economic model of crime.

Like the study about crime and the business cycle discussed above, a more recent study using data for the U.S. covering the period 1981 through 2000, found property crime rates to be countercyclical. It also found evidence that property crime rises "quickly" during periods of economic decline and declines more "gradually" during the following periods of economic recovery.[38] This lends support for the existence of asymmetry in criminal behavior with respect to property crime over the business cycle suggesting that the rise in property crime during an economic slowdown is more rapid than its decline during a period of economic growth.

In the next chapter, we turn to a discussion of crimes against persons.

REVIEW TERMS AND CONCEPTS

Business cycle
Change in supply
Complementary goods
Consumer's tastes
Copyright
Countercyclical
Demand for stolen goods
Embezzlement
Employee theft
Employment impact
Equilibrium
Fences
File swapping
Identity theft
Income
Income elasticity of demand
Inferior goods
Information costs
Involuntary transfer
Legal employment opportunities
Long run

Market for stolen goods
Normal goods
Patents
Perfectly elastic demand
Perfectly elastic supply
Perfectly inelastic demand
Perfectly inelastic supply
Price elasticity coefficient
Price elasticity of demand
Price elasticity of supply
Procyclical
Property rights
Public sector
Real property
Shadow price
Short run
Substitute goods
Supply of crime function
Target hardening
Transaction requirements
White-collar crime

End of Chapter Questions

1. If in a market for a good where the consumers' elasticity of demand is relatively inelastic there is an increase in shoplifting at the stores that sell this product, which is likely to be affected more, the product's price (the price effect) or the quantity of the product purchased (the output effect)? Which of these products is likely to have a more inelastic demand, salt or Cheerios?

2. Increased use of vehicle identification numbers on automobiles was encouraged by insurance companies because of their impact on the market for stolen cars. Which aspect of the market would this impact, the demand side, the supply side or both? Why?

3. Identify and describe a white-color crime that is a property crime. What makes it different than the more traditional property crimes of robbery, burglary and theft?

4. Identify several public policies that can be used to decrease the supply of property crime and several that can be used to decrease the demand.

Notes

1. It is generally agreed that white-collar occupations are those that use knowledge and skills in the manipulation of numbers and concepts, and include managerial, professional, and semi-professional occupations. It is also true that the occupation of the offender is less important in classifying the crime than the method used for committing the crime. Detailed discussions of white-collar crime can be found in Gilbert Geis and Robert F. Meier, eds., *White-Collar Crime* (New York: The Free Press, 1977), and James W. Coleman, *The Criminal Elite* (New York: St. Martin's Press, 1985).

2. It was estimated that businesses and private individuals would spend approximately $103 billion on private security goods and services in the year 2000 ($115 billion in 2005 dollars). (Security Industry Association, Research Update, "Economic Crime Cost Reaches $200 Billion in 2000," Issue 3, vol. 2.)

3. An estimate of the likely cost of crime to businesses for 2000 is $200 billion ($223 billion in 2005 dollars), *ibid.*

4. It has been estimated that 15 percent of the cost of goods in the U.S. is due to theft (William C. Cunningham, et al., *Private Security Trends* 1970 to 2000, Boston, Butterworth-Heinemann, 1990, endnote 1, 39).

5. Unless, of course, the demand were to change, which would be reflected in a shift in the demand curve to some price other than P_1.

6. As mentioned in Chapter 2, there are additional effects on demand as relative prices of substitutes are altered. Here, for simplicity, we omit such interactions, but the interested reader can refer to Chapter 2 for details.

7. Notice that an increase in crimes against persons or transactions in "victimless" crime markets may have similar impacts on property values. Perhaps different classes of property respond differently to each category of crime. For a model and estimates of this kind of effect, see Daryl Hellman and Joel Naroff, "The Impact of Crime on Urban Residential Property Values," *Urban Studies,* 16, no. 1 (February 1979), 105–112.

8. It is also possible that property crimes have an impact on market structure. If property crimes are concentrated in smaller firms in competitive industries, this leads to increased market power within those industries. There is some evidence of this. See Small Business Administration, *Crimes Against Small Business* (Washington, D.C., 1969).

9. This would be the case if the marginal productivity of the added resources were zero; i.e., if the additional output associated with additional input were zero.

10. For some studies of crime prevention production functions, see Werner Z. Hirsch, *Urban Economics* (New York: Macmillan, 1984), Chapter 10; J. M. Heineke, "An Econometric Investigation of Production Cost Functions for Law Enforcement Agencies," Occasional Paper Series, Domestic Studies Program, (Stanford, Ca: Stanford University, Hoover Institute, Center for Econometric Studies of the Criminal Justice System, August 1977). This paper also reviews the results of several cost and production function studies of law enforcement agencies. A more recent study is Amor Diez-Ticio and Maria-Jesus Mancebon, "The Efficiency of the Spanish Police Service: An Examination of the Multiactivity DEA Model," *Applied Economics,* February 2002.

11. *FBI Uniform Crime Report* figures for 2003 show that approximately seven percent of the monetary value of stolen property involved cash. (*Uniform Crime Report,* 2003; www.fbi.gov/ucr/03cius.htm, Table 24, 252).

12. Daniel Jack Chasen, "Good Fences Make Bad Neighbors," *The New York Times Magazine,* December 29, 1974, 12–17. For more details see Marilyn E. Walsh, *The Fence: A New Look at the World of Property Theft* (Westport, Ct.: Greenwood Press, 1977).

13. The estimate is from the U.S. Department of Justice, Federal Bureau of Investigation, *Uniform Crime Report,* 2003 (www.fbi.gov/ucr/03cius.htm), Table 24, 252. It is for robbery, burglary, larceny–theft, and motor vehicle theft. It is viewed as a conservative estimate since the majority of these crimes are not reported to the police, except for motor vehicle theft.

14. Chasen, *op.cit.*, 14.

15. Citizen patrol projects and citizen crime reporting projects are examples. The (then) National Institute of Law Enforcement and Criminal Justice of the Law Enforcement Assistance Administration, U.S. Department of Justice, has published a series of nationwide studies of these kinds of projects, and evaluations of them, in its National Evaluation Program: *Operation Identification Projects: Assessment of Effectiveness* (August 1975); Citizen Patrol Projects (January 1977); and *Citizen Crime Reporting Projects* (April 1977). Generally, the assessments are positive, but not without qualifications.

16. Chasen, *op.cit.*, 17.

17. This synthesis is from William C. Cunningham, John J. Strauchs, and Clifford W. Van Meter, *Private Security Trends 1970 to 2000* (Boston: Butterworth-Heinemann, 1990), 21.

18. C. Barnett, "The Measurement of White-Collar Crime Using Uniform Crime Reporting (UCR) Data" (www.fbi.gov/ucr/whitecollarforweb.pdf), 5.

19. *Ibid.,* 2.

20. FBI, "Financial Crimes Report to the Public" (www.fbi.gov/publications/financial/fcs_report052005/fcs_report052005.pdf), May 2005, C1.

21. University of Florida, "2002 National Retail Security Survey" (web.soc.ufl.edu/SRP/finalreport_2002.pdf), 4.

22. The Foundation for Taxpayer and Consumer Rights, Corporate Accountability-Factsheets (www.consumerwatchdog.org).

23. IRS, Criminal Investigations Division, "FY 1998 Annual Report," www.treas.gov/irs/ci/annual_report/progbk98.htm.

24. "Financial Crimes Report to the Public," *op. cit.,* E1.

25. "Fighting Fraud: Improving Information Security," FBI congressional statement, April 3, 2003, (www.fbi.gov/congress/congress03/farnan040303.htm).

26. The Economist, "Grokster and StreamCast face the music" (www.economist.com), March 30, 2005.

27. *Ibid.*

28. IFPI, "Internet Piracy: The Facts," (www.ifpi.org).

29. Michele Boldrin and David Levine, "The Economics of Ideas and Intellectual Property" (Minneapolis, MN: Federal Reserve Bank, Staff Report 357, February 2005).

30. Alex Viega, "Major Recording Artists Welcome Ruling on On-line File-Swapping" (www.detnews.com/2005/technology/0506/30/0tech-229916.htm).

31. Michael Sesnowitz, "The Returns to Burglary," *Western Economic Journal,* 10, no. 4 (December 1972), 477–481; William E. Cobb, "Theft and the Two Hypotheses"; Gregory Krohm, "The Pecuniary Incentives of Property Crime"; and J. Patrick Gunning, Jr., "How Profitable Is Burglary?" in Simon Rottenberg, ed., *The Economics of Crime and Punishment* (Washington, D.C.: American Enterprise Institute for Public Policy Research, 1973).

32. It should be noted that whether or not crimes against property yield net positive returns is not necessarily an indication of the validity of the economic model of behavior. If thieves have a preference for risk, crimes "will not pay" in the sense that net real returns after considering less risky (legal) alternatives will be negative. For a proof and discussion, see Gary S. Becker, "Crime and Punishment: An Economic Approach," *Journal of Political Economy,* 76, no. 2 (March–April 1968), 169–217, also represented in Neil O. Alper and Daryl A. Hellman, *op.cit.*; and Isaac Ehrlich, "Participation in Illegitimate Activities: A Theoretical and Empirical Investigation," *Journal of Political Economy,* 81, no. 3 (May–June 1973), 521–564.

33. Technically, each of these kinds of factors can be incorporated into the economic model if its impact on either gains or costs of committing crime is assessed.

34. Cf. Ehrlich, Isaac, "Participation in Illegitimate Activities," and David L. Sjoquist, "Property Crime and Economic Behavior: Some

Empirical Results," *American Economic Review,* 63, no. 3 (June 1973), 439–446. See also some estimated crime prevention production functions.

35. Studies using individual data to examine the economic model of criminal behavior include: Ann D. Witte, "Estimating the Economic Model of Crime with Individual Data," *Quarterly Journal of Economics* (February 1980), 57–84; Peter Schmidt and Ann Witte, *An Economic Analysis of Crime and Justice* (New York: Academic Press, 1984); and Llad Phillips and Harold L. Votey, Jr., "The Choice Between Legitimate and Illegitimate Work: Micro Study of Individual Behavior," *Contemporary Policy Issues,* vol. v, no. 4 (October 1987), 59–72.

36. Sharon Long and Ann Witte, "Current Economic Trends: Implications for Crime and Criminal Justice," in *Crime and Criminal Justice in a Declining Economy,* Kevin N. Wright, ed. (Cambridge, Mass.: Oelgeschlager, Gunn & Hain, 1981); and Richard Freeman, "Crime and Unemployment," in *Crime and Public Policy,* James Q. Wilson, ed. (San Francisco, Ca: ICS Press, 1983).

37. Philip Cook and Gary Zarkin, "Crime and the Business Cycle," *The Journal of Legal Studies,* vol. xiv (1) (January 1985), 115–128, also reprinted in Neil O. Alper and Daryl A. Hellman, *op.cit.*

38. Mocan and Bali, *op. cit.,* 16.

6

Crimes Against Persons

Crimes against persons include the FBI index crimes of **murder** and non-negligent manslaughter, **aggravated assault,** and forcible **rape.** While these crimes account for a much smaller percentage of reported index crime offenses than crimes against property, they are more serious in terms of harm done per offense. They also differ from crimes against property in the degree of passion or emotion that is often involved in the execution of the crime, and in the importance of psychological, or psychic, elements. For example, the "benefits" to be derived from committing a rape are psychic rather than monetary. Finally, these crimes differ from those against property in the relationship between criminal and victim. In 2003 more than half (53 percent) the time, crimes of violence took place within the family or among acquaintances. Rape, at least when it is reported and recorded as a rape, is the least likely of the crimes of violence to involve strangers (only 30 percent of the time in 2003).[1]

We begin our discussion of crimes against persons by reviewing the kinds of economic costs generated by these crimes. We then focus on the most harmful of these, murder, and we see whether an economic analysis of the "market for murder" makes any sense at all. We then examine aggravated assault and the links between murder and aggravated assault, using an empirical study of the two crimes. Next, we turn to a discussion of rape. We will end the chapter with a brief discussion of crimes of violence committed by youth since much of the crimes against persons involve juveniles. Throughout the chapter the emphasis is on developing effective public policy for dealing with these crimes.

ECONOMIC COSTS

How can we begin to assess the economic costs of a crime against a person, such as assault? First, if the victim is injured and requires medical attention, there is the cost of that medical care. Society as a whole expends scarce medical resources, including land, labor, and machinery and buildings, in caring for the victim. This use of resources would not be required if the crime had not been committed. Thus, society is worse off by the amount of medical resources used up.

Second, if the individual is incapacitated either temporarily or permanently, there is a loss of output. This can be evaluated by estimating what the person would have earned during the period that she or he is incapacitated. In the case of murder, the income loss would be calculated for the person's remaining working years had the crime not occurred.[2] In order to evaluate correctly what the loss in earnings is when the loss occurs over time, it is necessary to discount future dollars to their present value. This procedure is described in the appendix to Chapter 2.

Additional costs to society from crimes against persons are the psychic costs suffered by the victim and the victim's family, friends, and community. These may be severe, although they are difficult to assess. In cases of rape, for example, most physical injuries are minor, but the psychological aftereffects may be extreme and long-lasting. In some instances psychic losses may be demonstrated in measurable ways, such as when a family member is unable to work or seeks counseling because of mourning or grief.

There are additional impacts on society when one of its members is injured or killed. An economic evaluation of the loss focuses on the loss of a productive member of the economy—a unit of economic resources. But beyond being a productive member of the economy, the individual is also a member of social groups—family, community, and so forth. The lost contributions to these groups are not considered here, although admittedly these may be just as important as lost earnings.

A National Institute of Justice study of the cost of crime estimated the cost to society of someone's death associated with a number of crimes including murder, rape, arson and drunk driving. The total cost to society was estimated by accounting for productivity losses, medical costs, criminal justice system services and the impact on the quality of life. The reported cost of a murder was $2.94 million in 1993 ($3.90 million in 2005 dollars)[3]; the cost of a death associated with an arson was estimated to be slightly less, $2.74 million ($3.69 million in 2005 dollars); and the cost of a death associated with driving while intoxicated was estimated to be $3.18 million ($4.28 million in 2005 dollars).[4] The same study estimated that the cost of crime related deaths nationwide was over $93 billion ($125 billion in 2005 dollars).[5] This may be an over estimate in today's dollars since, as discussed in the first chapter, the amount of crime, including homicide, declined for much of the last decade.

Finally, the costs to society of crimes against persons include costs incurred by the public sector to enforce laws against these crimes and to punish those who break the law. These costs include those for police, courts, and prisons. Private expenditures by households and business firms to avoid being victimized by these crimes also constitute a cost to society.

THE MARKET FOR MURDER

In the preceding chapter we discussed the market for stolen property. In a similar way we will try to discuss crimes against persons within a market context. Initially, this may seem absurd, but we will find that a market approach yields useful insights with respect to public policy.

While a large percentage of murders are committed within family groups, between lovers, or as a result of arguments among acquaintances, not all of these crimes are **"murders of passion,"**[6] that is, emotion-charged crimes which occur in the heat of the moment. Some portion of these murders are rational in the sense that the crime is committed for monetary or psychic gain and the gains from the crime are compared with the costs in deciding whether or not to commit the crime.

Under such circumstances the economic model of criminal behavior fits very well.[7] While most people involved in this activity would consume (demand) and/or produce (supply) perhaps only one murder in a lifetime, if we combine all potential buyers and sellers of murder we have a market for murder. Notice that in many instances individuals are both consumers (they want the murder committed) and producers (they are willing to commit the murder) in this market. In other cases, buyers purchase services from sellers. The market for murder is described in Figure 6–1.

The demand simply indicates that some people value murder for either the monetary or the psychic gains to be derived from it. The demand curve has a typical negative slope, indicating that at relatively high prices few murders will be demanded. As price goes down, quantity demanded increases; less "lucrative" murders become feasible. The supply curve is another example of a supply-of-crime function, and it has a positive slope. At low prices, few murders will be supplied. As price increases, quantity supplied increases, either because existing producers increase output or because additional producers enter the industry. The equilibrium price and the equilibrium quantity of murders are indicated by the intersection of the supply

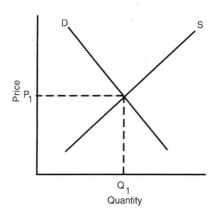

Figure 6–1 The Market for Murder

and demand curves. The equilibrium price in the murder market is P_1, and the quantity of murders produced is Q_1 per time period.

The Demand for Murder

The demand for murder will change if any of the determinants of demand change, i.e., consumers' tastes and income, and prices of related goods. Here our analysis of these determinants is very similar to that presented in the last chapter.

A change in the "taste" for murder would cause demand to change and the entire demand curve to shift. For example, a decrease in "tastes," perhaps because of an increased sense of horror or guilt associated with participating in violence, would cause demand to decrease and the demand curve to shift downward as shown in Figure 6–2. The market is willing and able to buy fewer murders at each price along demand curve D' than along demand curve D.

The effect of a change in income is less clear. Since the penalty for murder or accessory to murder is a prison term, the value of the penalty increases as income increases, demand for the product decreases, as in Figure 6–2. However, as income increases, it is likely that the monetary value of the crime increases, so that higher-income groups would be willing to pay higher prices for a murder directed at a particular target than lower-income groups would. Therefore, increases in income would increase demand—other things, including moral values, being equal.

The analysis of the effect of a change in the prices of related goods is more complicated. First, the effect depends on whether the related good is a

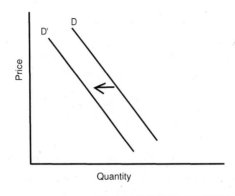

Figure 6–2 The Demand for Murder

substitute or a complement. If the good is a substitute, a drop in its price will cause the demand for murder to decrease. An increase in its price will have the opposite effect.

In some instances, murder may have no substitutes. In others, **blackmail** or **extortion** may be substituted as a means of financial gain, or aggravated assault may be substituted to inflict severe bodily injury. An increase in the price of one of these substitute "goods" could cause the demand for murder to increase. Notice again that we are talking about relative prices. As prices of substitute goods increase relative to the price of murder, murder will be used more often.

Changes in the prices of complementary goods can also cause demand to change and the demand curve to shift. An increase in the price of a complementary good will decrease demand, while a decrease in price will increase demand. What kinds of goods are complementary to murder? There are at least two kinds of complementary goods or services involved: information and transaction requirements.

In order to buy murder it is necessary to have information about what is available, where, and at what prices. If this kind of information becomes difficult to obtain (i.e., if the price of information increases), the demand for murder will drop. Similarly, if the transaction requirements of dealing in the murder market increase, demand will go down. (By transaction requirements we mean the time, trouble, and risk involved in buying.)

While the importance of information and transaction costs was emphasized in our discussion of the market for stolen property, the reverse is probably the case in the market for murder. In many instances individuals are both buyers and sellers, or rely on close associates to supply the crime. Thus, information costs and some portion of transaction costs (time and inconvenience) are minimized. Risk, however, or expected-punishment cost, remains an important consideration. Notice that both buyers and sellers are subject to risk.

Some portion of the market for murder is provided by firms that sometimes require murder in order to do business. These firms then buy murder from firms (or individuals) that produce it. In order to minimize information and transaction costs, the firms that demand murder often supply it themselves. Thus, the input is provided most cheaply by producing it "in house," an example of vertical integration.

The Supply of Murder

The supply of murder is simply another example of the supply of crime function discussed in Chapter 3. The function describes the relationship between price, or average gain from murder, and quantity of murder per time period. For the reasons discussed in Chapter 3, we would expect that relationship to be a positive one. When graphed, the supply curve has a positive slope, as shown in Figure 6–1.

The supply of murder will change and the curve will shift with a change in any of the costs of doing business. To review, for criminal activities such as murder, the costs of doing business are material costs, time costs, psychic costs, and expected-punishment costs. An increase in any one of these will cause the supply to decrease and the function to shift to the left; any quantity of murder will now require a higher price. On the other hand, a decrease in any of the cost categories will cause supply to increase, shifting the supply curve to the right.

PUBLIC POLICY TO REDUCE THE AMOUNT OF MURDER

If Figure 6–1 accurately describes the market for murder, any policy which will cause either demand or supply to decrease (a shift down to the left in the demand curve, a shift up to the left in the supply curve), or both, would reduce the amount of murder per time period. One possible direction for public policy would be to decrease the taste for violence. This would reduce the demand for murder, as well as for other violent crimes, and possibly reduce the supply by increasing the psychic costs of committing crimes involving violence.

A frequent criticism is that films and television are too violent, that they often glorify the cool, detached murderer, romanticize the use of guns, and show unrealistically attractive deaths. The head of a Chicago police homicide section stated that in several murders and robbery-murders investigated, "the killers, especially young men, copied the methods and exact language of recent films."[8] A study of the use of weapons on prime-time television shows concluded that the frequent appearance and use of weapons on TV, coupled with a large proportion of "misses" when shots are fired, and the negligible incidence of blood or other signs of suffering, give an unrealistic and potentially dangerous lack of severity to the consequences of weapon use.[9]

If **violence on film and television,** including the manner in which it is portrayed, has an impact on our taste for violence, then public policy to regulate the depiction of violence and weapon use on the screen might be appropriate. Effective regulation could reduce both the demand for and the supply of violent crimes, as well as possibly affect the choice of weapon in the commission of crimes, including crimes against property such as robbery. This kind of policy could therefore reduce the number of violent crimes, as well as possibly reduce the likelihood of injury or the severity of injuries involved in crimes such as robbery or aggravated assault. The costs of regulation, however, including reduced First Amendment rights, would have to be considered. We return to the question of choice of weapon later in the chapter.

Perhaps the most effective policy to reduce murder would be to increase expected-punishment costs. This would decrease both the demand for and the supply of murder. Expected-punishment costs can be increased by increasing either the probability of punishment or the value of the punishment.

The probability of punishment is the joint probability of being arrested, charged, convicted, and punished in a particular manner. This probability, therefore, depends on the amount of resources allocated to the various components of the criminal justice system, the efficiency with which these resources are used, and finally, the constraints placed on the use of these resources. For example, the probability of correctly identifying and punishing guilty persons is diminished to some extent by various protections guaranteed by our Constitution. We, therefore, trade a lower crime rate for personal freedoms. This is not to say that we should not do so; we must simply be aware of the choice involved.

The value of the punishment depends on several factors: the form of the punishment, the magnitude of the punishment, and (for these punishments, which are in the form of prison terms) the value of time to the prisoner. The value of punishment can therefore be increased by the use of longer sentences or by increasing the value of time to prisoners by increasing employment opportunities outside.

The form of the punishment is also a consideration. One debate surrounding the issue of appropriate punishment for murder is the question of **capital punishment** and its effectiveness as a deterrent. While we may object to capital punishment on various grounds—including unconstitutionality because it does not constitute due process of law or amounts to cruel and unusual punishment[10]—we should be able to predict its impact as a deterrent to murder by using our economic model of behavior. If, in considering the crime of murder, the potential offender weighs gains against costs, and if capital punishment is a more severe penalty than life imprisonment, then we should expect the introduction and use of capital punishment, other things equal, to increase expected-punishment costs, decrease the demand for murder and supply of murder (shift both curves to the left), and reduce the amount of murder.

This is what we would expect to see happen, yet various studies of capital punishment have concluded that it is not an effective deterrent to murder.[11] Only within the last 30 years has there been evidence supporting our *a priori* expectation.[12] However, many earlier studies suffered from methodological problems. First, no account was made for the probability of punishment. That is, while capital punishment was possible because it was "on the books" in particular states, it had not been used for many years, so that the probability of that particular form of punishment was zero. Expected-punishment costs for that form of punishment was, therefore, also equal to zero. Under such circumstances no marginal deterrent effect could be expected. Capital punishment could not be expected to deter murder any more effectively than life imprisonment.

A second major shortcoming of the earlier studies was the failure to correct for the influence of other factors which influence the murder rate. Therefore, when making comparisons from year to year, or from state to state, differences in murder rates could not be attributed to the form and expected value of the punishment used unless these other influences on murder were accounted for or held constant.

More recent studies of the deterrent effect of punishment, including capital punishment, have corrected for these deficiencies using sophisticated statistical techniques. One time-series study of the use of the death penalty in the United States since the 1930s concludes that it has had a measurable deterrent effect on murder. On the average, each additional execution imposed saved seven or eight murder victims.[13] A later cross-sectional study, using state data, concludes that "data from executing states indicate that, when enforced, the death penalty exerts a restraining effect on the frequency of murder and possibly robbery as well. . . . Indeed, because the effect of imprisonment is accounted for explicitly in the analysis, this investigation, more directly than the earlier time-series study, indicates that capital punishment has a differential deterrent effect over and above the actually enforced imprisonment terms."[14] Two recent studies using data for the period after the moratorium on the death penalty imposed by the U.S. Supreme Court in the early 1970s found that each execution leads to between three and 18 fewer murders.[15]

Other studies suggest that instead of capital punishment having a deterrent effect, in fact, it has a **brutalization effect** that leads to additional murders that would not have been committed had there not been an execution. Executions, it is argued, devalue life and demonstrate that it is correct and acceptable to kill someone who has seriously offended us. An empirical test of the brutalization hypothesis finds evidence of two additional homicides committed one month after an execution and one additional homicide two months later.[16] The third homicide may not be a net addition but simply a change in the timing of the crime since the researchers also find evidence of a reduction of one homicide three months after the execution.

Regardless of these results, a firm conclusion cannot be drawn. The more recent capital punishment studies have also been criticized on methodological grounds.[17] So the debate continues. While we argued that we would expect capital punishment to have a deterrent effect, our argument was based on two conditions: first, that the potential murderer weighs gains against costs before committing the crime, and second, that capital punishment is a more severe penalty than life imprisonment. While the evidence cited earlier supports the contention that capital punishment is the more severe penalty, many have argued that the reverse is the case for potential murderers. Under such circumstances capital punishment will not have an additional deterrent effect beyond the effect of life imprisonment.

Perhaps the more basic question, however, is whether or not potential murderers are rational and weigh gains against costs before committing murder. If they do not, expected-punishment costs, regardless of the form in which they are inflicted, will not deter crime. We then must ask ourselves whether or not public policy can be used at all to reduce murder rates.

As with any other public policy, the economist's view on the **death penalty** would be based on an assessment of its costs and benefits. While it may be relatively easy to measure many of the costs to society of imposing a capital sentence, measurement of the benefits are likely to be much more difficult. The investigative, legal (defense and prosecutorial), court (pretrial and appeals), incarceration and execution costs are all relatively easy to measure. Even the cost of possibly executing an innocent person can be estimated based on historical probabilities and estimates of the value of a person's life.

Studies have shown that death penalty cases are more expensive than similar cases where the death penalty is not in play because they generally involve: more experts; more attorneys for both the defense as well as the prosecution; a sequestered jury; and a longer trial. Since 1976 when the U.S. Supreme Court reinstated the death penalty, death penalty cases have actually involved two trials, one to determine guilt or innocence and the other to determine the penalty. Estimates place the costs to taxpayers of a death penalty case in Texas at approximately $2.3 million in 1992 ($3.2 million in 2005 dollars), which was three times more than the cost of spending 40 years in the highest security prison in the state, and the **cost of an execution** in Florida at $24 million in 2000 ($27 million in 2005 dollars).[18] A 2003 comparison in Kansas between the cost of a capital trial and the cost of a murder trial where the death penalty is not sought found capital trials to be seventy percent more expensive. The projected median cost to execution was $1.26 million while the for the non-death penalty case it was $740,000. The difference in trial costs was considerable. The death penalty cases were 16 times greater ($508,000 versus $32,000).[19] A study of federal trials over the 1990 to 1997 period found the cost of representing a defendant in a death penalty case that went to trial was five times more than in a case where the crime was punishable by death but the death penalty was not being sought ($270,000 versus $56,000 on average).[20] While the specific deterrent (incapacitation) benefit of the death penalty can be estimated relatively easily, based on the likelihood of the person killing again, it is the value of the retribution benefit that is very difficult, if not impossible, to determine. As we have seen, it is not clear whether there exists a general deterrent benefit so its inclusion in the benefit-cost analysis is questionable.

An additional debate that economists generally do not involve themselves in is whether the death penalty is being equitably administered. There is evidence to suggest that the **likelihood of receiving the death penalty** is related to factors that are not directly related to the circumstances of the crime. Researchers have found a strong relationship between the victim's and offender's race and the likelihood of being sentenced to death.[21] Since 1976 only 12 white defendants have been executed for killing a black while 193 black defendants have been executed for killing white victims.[22] What this says about the efficiency, or deterrent effect, of capital punishment is unclear, but what it says about equity, or fairness, in the application of this punishment is unmistakable. The question of fairness in the imposition of the death penalty has recently led to the declaration of **moratoriums on executions** in several states including Illinois where the 18th exoneration of a death row inmate recently took place. Nationally, there have been 119 exonerations since 1973.[23] These moratoriums and rising concerns regarding the death penalty are also being driven by religious leaders, from all aspects of the religious spectrum, and state and national legislators who are concerned about the ability of the poor and minority populations to afford competent lawyers, the quality and qualifications of public defenders assigned to their cases, and the funds for DNA testing that might exonerate those accused of a capital offense.

IRRATIONAL MURDER

By irrational murder we mean those instances in which the potential criminal does not, prior to the crime, consider the gains of committing the crime compared with the costs involved. These are the "murders of passion" in which the crime is committed almost impulsively, in the heat of intense anger or some other emotion. Under such circumstances our earlier analysis must be modified. Figure 6–1 does not accurately describe the market for this type of murder, since it describes a market based on the assumption of economic rationality on the part of buyers and sellers. How, then, can we describe the market for irrational murder?

Figure 6–3 describes the supply of and demand for irrational murder. The market depicted in the figure is a bit unusual and requires some explanation.

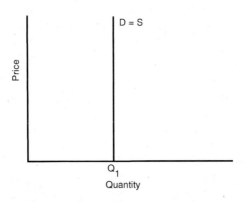

Figure 6–3 The Market for Irrational Murder

First let us consider the demand curve. It is drawn as a straight vertical line, indicating that the demand for irrational murder is, at the moment of passion, completely price inelastic. That is, regardless of the price to be paid for murder, buyers demand a constant amount per time period. Figure 6–3 indicates demand by the market as a whole, which is the summation of the amount that each buyer demands at every price. Consider the demand curve of one buyer. It, too, would be perfectly inelastic, indicating that at a particular moment, regardless of the price to be paid, the individual demands a specific number of murders, such as one, perhaps to avenge what is perceived to be an injustice.

The market demand curve is the summation of each of the individual demand curves. Obviously, at any point in time different individuals are "in the market." Under normal circumstances these individuals do not value murder and certainly would not be willing to pay a price for it. In the heat of the moment, however, a perfectly inelastic demand curve for murder exists—the person is "in the market," at least momentarily.

The supply curve is also perfectly price inelastic and is drawn as a straight vertical line. Regardless of price, the individuals (firms) "in the market" are each willing and able to commit a constant number of murders per time period. Again, the market supply is the summation of each individual's supply curve. For each person, or supplier, the supply curve is perfectly inelastic. The individual will commit a certain number of murders (e.g., one) regardless of price. And again, different individuals comprise the market at different moments, since normally each person would not supply murder at any price and enters the market only momentarily.

Finally, the demand and supply curves are drawn as the same line, indicating that at the moment of irrationality each person simultaneously demands and supplies a certain number of murders and the price to be paid and received is irrelevant. The person wants the crime and commits it herself or himself.

In the market for rational murder, even when the same person was both demander and supplier, the two functions were not identical and perfectly price inelastic. The demand curve had a negative slope, indicating that individuals compared the price to be paid with benefits received from murder and that marginal benefits typically decreased with increases in murder. The supply curve had a positive slope, indicating that suppliers compared the price to be received with the costs of committing the crime, and that marginal costs typically increased with increases in murder. The perfectly price inelastic demand/supply curve of Figure 6–3 indicates that no such rational comparisons are made by the demander/supplier in the market for irrational murder. The position of the demand/supply curve depends only on the number of murders required, not on the usual determinants of demand and supply.

If the market for irrational murder is described by Figure 6–3, it would appear that public policy directed at increasing expected-punishment costs, or toward any of the other determinants of demand or supply, would be a waste of resources. Perhaps efforts to reduce our tendency to have violent reactions to particular types of situations would help. We mentioned regulation of violence and weapon use in films and television earlier in the chapter. Or, more generally, maybe we can develop ways to control the appearance of moments of irrationality, whether they involve violence or not. Exploring this possibility would take us into disciplines other than economics. Is there anything an economist can offer as a possible solution?

When we consider the market for irrational murder described in Figure 6–3, we must realize that it consists of demand and supply which exist only momentarily for various individuals. After the heat of the moment passes, the individual is no longer willing to buy or sell murders but is quite possibly appalled at the thought. This being the case, if the production of murder could be made more difficult, the moment of passion or irrationality might pass before the murder has been completed. What we would like to do is to decrease the productivity of labor in the production of murder. This can be accomplished, given present levels of technology, by reducing the availability of inputs used in production; that is, by reducing the availability of capital, for example, handguns.

This is one argument for **handgun control.** Its advocates point out that the handgun is by far the most popular murder weapon. According to FBI figures, in 2003, handguns were used in 53 percent of all murders.[24] Where handguns are widely available, they make it possible for murder to be produced very efficiently. If an efficient weapon were not available during the moment of passion, it would take longer for a person to commit the crime and/or be more difficult to commit the crime in such an impersonal way— it would be necessary to have closer contact with the victim. Either effect would tend to cause the moment of irrationality to pass before the crime had been completed. Thus, while perhaps the moment of passion cannot be controlled, the outcome of that moment can be controlled by making efficient, impersonal weapons less available. Substitution of some other weapon, such as a knife, for the now more expensive handgun is very likely, and, in fact, has been found to occur when the cost of using a handgun has increased.[25] The cost of a handgun includes the difficulty of purchasing a handgun if they are entirely banned, or the increased punishment cost if there is a law requiring a mandatory sentence whenever a handgun is used to commit a felony.

It should be noted that, in addition to reducing the lethality of moments of passion, handgun control could also reduce the number of injuries and deaths resulting from other crimes, such as robbery, and the number of accidental injuries not associated with crime.

MURDER AND THE BUSINESS CYCLE

Whether murder is rational or irrational there is still the question of whether or not there is a statistical relationship between murder rates and the business cycle. Some researchers believe that recessions increase murder rates, while others believe the opposite.

Studies show that during a recession, the consumption of alcohol and other drugs tends to increase as people try to forget their economic problems. This increased consumption leads to an increase in alcohol and drug related murders. There are also fewer resources available for crime prevention because tax revenues are likely to decrease during a recession, although this may affect law enforcement productivity in a belated fashion and only impacts rational murder. Finally, a decrease in income associated with recession would tend to increase the supply of (rational) murder. All these factors would lead to a countercyclical pattern in murder rates. The decrease in income associated with recession, however, may also have the opposite effect by making it more difficult for a potential murderer to purchase a firearm, the most efficient way to produce a murder, leading to a decreased likelihood of successfully committing a murder.

A study by two economists found that there was no relationship between aggregate business cycles and murder rates in the United States.[26] For the post–World War II period they found a weak procyclical relationship, but when the data were extended to the pre-war period, no statistically significant relationship was found to exist. Therefore, they concluded that "[h]omicide is insensitive to the business cycle."[27] A study using more recent data reflecting the decline in the murder rate over much of the 1990s found some evidence of murder being a counter cyclical crime.[28]

AGGRAVATED ASSAULT

Aggravated assault can be analyzed in the same way as murder. As with murder, there are two markets for aggravated assault. In the first, the demand and supply look like those in Figure 6–1. Demand and supply will change, and the curves would shift, with a change in any of the determinants. The entire discussion of the market for murder, including public policy to reduce murder, with the exception of the discussion of capital punishment, could be repeated here and applied to aggravated assault.

The other market is the market for irrational aggravated assault; that is, assaults committed without a comparison of gains with costs. Here the demand and supply of aggravated assault would be as discussed above and the curves would look like those for murder depicted in Figure 6–3. In fact, we could argue that the two markets, the one for irrational murder and the one for irrational aggravated assault, are the same, for in the commission of an irrational violent act the outcome is not clear. The intent is to inflict severe bodily injury. If the violent act is extremely successful in inflicting injury (which in part depends on the choice of weapon), the victim dies and a murder is committed. If not, the crime is aggravated assault. Murder, the argument goes, is simply successful aggravated assault. For this reason there is no point in making a distinction between the two markets.

This is not to suggest that the two crimes are identical and therefore should have identical punishments. Murder is more harmful than aggravated assault and, therefore, must be punished more severely. (Recall our discussion of optimum punishments in Chapter 4.) However, punishments for aggravated assault should perhaps vary with type of weapon used, since the choice of weapon affects the probability that assault will become murder. Assault with a gun is five times as likely to kill the victim as assault with a knife.[29] But varying punishment by choice of weapon in order to deter lethal assaults assumes that we can affect the choice of weapon. This assumes that the criminal behaves in a rational way and considers the increased expected-punishment costs associated with using certain weapons. This would be true in the market for rational assaults but not in the market for irrational assaults.

Perhaps we have overemphasized the existence of a market for irrational murder/assault. While the price elasticity of demand and supply will vary for different individuals, perhaps there are few cases in which the functions are completely vertical. The problem is that we do not know enough about the characteristics of the markets for murder and aggravated assault, or their interrelationship. One study of the relationship between murder and aggravated assault presents some interesting evidence.[30] The purpose of the study was to see whether punishment deters crimes against persons; its focus was on homicide committed with firearms. The researcher argues that the rate of homicides committed with firearms depends on the rate of assaults committed with firearms. He then presents statistical evidence to support that argument. (The exact relationship includes the probability that death will occur, given that a victim has been assaulted with a firearm, as well as the rate of homicide with firearms occurring under other felonious circumstances.)

On the basis of this evidence a reduction in assaults by firearms would lead to a reduction in homicides. The question is, how can we reduce assaults using firearms? The researcher argues that while the rate of assault may not be subject to control, the choice of weapon used in the assault may be. Statistical evidence is presented which suggests that the use of guns in assaults can be deterred by increasing expected punishment costs, either by increasing conviction rates or by increasing the severity of punishment. There is weaker evidence which suggests that decreasing the availability of firearms would reduce the use of guns in assault.[31] The last result, of course, argues in favor of gun control.

FORCIBLE RAPE

The final crime considered in this chapter, forcible rape, is a different kind of problem, although a similar market analysis can be applied. The benefits from committing rape, as is often the case with many murders and assaults, are psychic rather than monetary. And again, the demanders of the crime are, in almost all cases, also the suppliers. Rapists most often, but not always, act alone.

One difference between assault and rape is in the kind of harm done. Most physical injuries from rape are minor, but the psychological harm is severe and long-lasting.[32] The characteristics of victims and offenders also differ. In 2003, over 90.1 percent of all rape victims were female,[33] with the highest victimization rates among persons 20-24 years old,[34] and offenders tend to be male and generally 25-44 years old.[35]

Another difference may be in the extent to which the crime is committed irrationally. Rape, contrary to some beliefs, is not solely or even primarily committed for sexual gratification; it is motivated by aggressive feelings toward women. Again we are straying from economics when we try to determine why individuals derive benefits from committing this crime, but an understanding of the type(s) of psychic benefits from rape may suggest the degree to which the crime is committed irrationally, during a moment of intense emotion, or rationally, after consideration of psychic gains versus the costs of committing the crime. A Boston police publication states that 90 percent of group rapes, 83 percent of pair rapes, and 58 percent of single rapes are planned.[36]

To the extent that rape is committed rationally, Figure 6–1 describes the market for it, and public policy to reduce rape should focus on ways to reduce the demand for and/or supply of rape. On the demand side, we could attempt to reduce the taste for rape. How this can be accomplished is material for research for psychologists, sociologists, and investigators in related disciplines. Improving the status of women, rather than reducing the taste for rape, may serve to increase it, at least in the short run. In the long run, one would hope that improving the status of women would reduce the need or "taste" for oppression of or aggression toward women, as well as the perception by potential rapists of women as receptacles for sexual gratification and oppression through sexual acts.[37]

On the supply side of the market the public policy options or programs are clearer. An increase in expected-punishment costs, other things equal, will decrease the supply of rape and shift the supply of rape function to the left, reducing the number of rapes committed. Again, expected-punishment costs can be increased in several ways—by increasing either the probability of punishment or the value of the punishment or both. Specific suggestions for increasing expected-punishment costs for rapists focus on increasing the penalties for rape and increasing the probability of conviction.

There are several ways in which conviction probabilities may be increased. A fundamental way is to increase the **percentage of rapes which are reported.** To encourage women to report the crime there have been a large number of efforts to improve police attitudes and sensitivity in handling rape cases, as well as to provide support services for victims.[38] Police rape squads headed by women, sensitivity training in law enforcement agencies, and establishment of rape crisis centers are examples of these efforts. The intention is to overcome the legitimate fear on the part of women that they, the victims, will be "victimized" again during the process of reporting, charging, and trying the case. Legislation to limit cross-examination of rape victims to what is relevant to the behavior of the defendant, and to repeal corroboration rules where they are still in effect, are additional ways to encourage reporting of the crime.

Finally, some programs to reduce the number of rapes focus on increasing the awareness level of potential victims and encouraging individuals to behave in self-protective ways. Information brochures, lectures, and media advertising are examples. These kinds of programs may be viewed as efforts to increase the probability of punishment for potential offenders (e.g., by advising potential victims to avoid dark, deserted streets or to carry a whistle) and/or to increase the time costs of committing the crime. An example of the latter is avoidance of **hitchhiking** by women. A reduction in the number of female hitchhikers reduces the number of potential targets for the crime for those who commit the crime via offering rides. This increases the time required to locate a "target." Either kind of approach, if it effectively increases the costs of committing rape, would reduce the number of offenses. The size of the decrease would depend on the extent of the change in supply. One serious concern here, however, is the impact that these kinds of programs have on the individual freedom of potential victims. This is one potential cost of such programs which would have to be weighed against the benefits of crime reduction.

JUVENILE CRIME

Crimes of violence are not limited to the adult segment of society. In fact, in 2002 almost 880,000 young people in the U.S. between the ages of 10 and 24 were injured by crimes of violence. Homicide is the second leading cause of death for young people in this age category, and for African-Americans of this age it is the leading cause of death. A firearm is, by far, the most frequently used weapon to commit these murders (almost 80 percent in 2001).[39]

Youth violent criminal activity has changed quite dramatically over the past 20 years. The period from 1983 through 1994 saw a dramatic rise in youths being arrested and therefore youth committed crime. Much of it apparently violence related to youth gangs being involved in illegal drug marketing activities. In 1994, according to the FBI, one in five arrests was of a juvenile under the age of 18.[40] The number of youths apparently involved in violent crime dropped dramatically over the next decade. In 2003 arrests of young offenders under the age of 18 for violent crimes were 20 percent below the 1994 level and accounted for 18 percent of arrests for violent crimes rather than almost 25 percent. The juvenile gangs are, apparently, less involved in drug-trafficking and are more involved in battling over "respect."[41] Additionally, the gangs are apparently comprised of younger members (14 to 17 versus 18 to 20) with a greater willingness to use force to deal with "trivial" disputes.

In the following chapter we will discuss crimes whose impact on individuals and society are quite different. In fact, although the validity of the term is debatable, these crimes are referred to as "victimless" crimes.

REVIEW TERMS AND CONCEPTS

Aggravated assault
Benefits
Brutalization effect
Business cycle
Capital punishment
Complementary goods
Consumers
Cost-benefit analysis
Costs
Countercyclical
Deterrent effect
Expected punishment costs
Forcible rape
General deterrence
Information
Irrational aggravated assault
Irrational murder
Juvenile crime
Market demand
Market supply

Material costs
Monetary gains
Murders of passion
Perfectly inelastic demand
Perfectly inelastic supply
Probability of punishment
Producers
Productivity of labor
Psychic costs
Psychic gains
Regulation
Specific deterrence
Substitute goods
Supply of murder
Taste for murder
Taste for violence
Time costs
Transaction requirements
Value of punishment

END OF CHAPTER QUESTIONS

1. How do economists distinguish between a rational murder and an irrational murder? Why is this distinction important in the analysis of the crime of murder?

2. If a beating (an assault) is a good substitute for a murder, what would be the impact of decreasing the punishment for an assault on the market for murder? Would this be a good public policy recommendation?

3. Educating women about the risks of becoming rape victims is good public policy because it decreases the supply in the market for rape. True or false and why?

4. What are some public policies that can ebe used to decrease the demand for rape?

NOTES

1. S. Catalano; *Criminal Victimization, 2003;* U.S. Dept. of Justice, Bureau of Justice Statistics, September 2004, Table 9, 9.

2. See Chapter 2 for a more detailed discussion of alternative approaches to valuation of loss of life.

3. Dollars here and throughout the chapter are adjusted for increases in the CPI through April 2005.

4. T.Miller, M. Cohen and B. Wiersema, "Victim Costs and Consequences: A New Look," *op.cit.*, Table 2, 9.

5. *Ibid.,* Table 5, 17.

6. According to FBI figures, in 2003 approximately 13 percent of murders were committed within family groups and 31 percent were between lovers or among acquaintances. In 45 percent of murders, the relationship between the victim and the murderer was not known to the police. U.S. Department of Justice, Federal Bureau of Investigation, *Uniform Crime Reports,* 2003 (www.fbi.gov/ucr/cius_031,Figure 2.4, 2).

7. Ehrlich applies his criminal choice model to crimes against persons as well as to crimes against property, and presents empirical evidence to support his argument that increases in the probability and severity of punishment can deter crimes against persons for the same reasons that they are expected to deter crimes against property. Isaac Ehrlich, "Participation in Illegitimate Activities: A Theoretical and Empirical Investigation," *Journal of Political Economy,* 8,1 no. 3 (May–June 1973), 521–564.

8. Bryce Nelson, "Handguns and Hooligans Boost Homicide Rates," *The Boston Sunday Globe,* January 26, 1975, A–2.

9. M. Wilson and P.B. Higgins, *Television's Action Arsenal—Weapon Use in Prime Time* (Washington, D.C.: U.S. Conference of Mayors, 1977).

10. Charles L. Black, Jr., *Capital Punishment: The Inevitability of Caprice and Mistake* (New York: W.W. Norton, 1974).

11. For a brief review, see Charles Tittle, "Punishment and Deterrence of Deviance," in Simon Rottenberg, ed., *The Economics of Crime and Punishment* (Washington, D.C.: American Enterprise Institute for Public Policy Research, 1973); Gordon Tullock, "Does Punishment

Deter Crime?" *The Public Interest,* no. 36 (Summer 1974), 103–111, also reprinted in Neil O. Alper and Daryl A. Hellman, *The Economics of Crime: A Reader* (Needham, Mass.: Simon & Schuster, 1997); Lawrence Katz, Steven Levitt and Ellen Shustorovich, "Prison Conditions, Capital Punishment, and Deterrence," *American Law and Economics Review* (2003); and Jeffrey Fagan, "Deterrence and the Death Penalty: A Critical Review of New Evidence," Testimony to the New York State Assembly (www.deathpenaltyinfo.org/Fagan Testimony.pdf), January 21, 2005.

12. Isaac Ehrlich, "The Deterrent Effect of Capital Punishment: A Question of Life and Death," *American Economic Review,* 65, no. 3 (June 1975), 397–417; "Capital Punishment and Deterrence: Some Further Thoughts and Additional Evidence," *Journal of Political Economy,* 85, no. 4 (August 1977), 741–788; Steven Stack, "Publicized Executions and Homicides, 1950–1980," *American Sociological Review,* 52 (1987), 532–540; Joanna Shepherd, "Murders of Passion, Execution Delays, and the Deterrence of Capital Punishment," *Journal of Legal Studies* (June 2004), 283-321; and Paul Zimmerman, "State Executions, Deterrence, and the Incidence of Murder," *Journal of Applied Economics* (May 2004), 163-193.

13. Ehrlich, "The Deterrent Effect of Capital Punishment," 414.

14. Ehrlich, "Capital Punishment and Deterrence," 778.

15. Shepherd, "Murders of Passion, Execution Delays, and the Deterrence of Capital Punishment," *op.cit.*; and Hashem Dezhbakhsh, et. al., "Does Capital Punishment Have a Deterrent Effect? New Evidence from Postmoratorium Panel Data," *American Law and Economics Review* (Fall 2003), 344-376.

16. W. Bowers and G. Pierce, "Deterrence or Brutalization: What Is the Effect of Executions?" *Crime and Delinquency,* vol. 26, no. 4 (October 1980), 453–484, also reprinted in Neil O. Alper and Daryl A. Hellman, *op. cit.*

17. William J. Bowers and Glenn L. Pierce, "Deterrence, Brutalization, or Nonsense: A Critique of Isaac Ehrlich's Research on Capital Punishment," *Yale Law Journal,* 85, no. 1 (1975–1976), 187–208; Peter Passall and John B. Taylor, "The Deterrent Effect of Capital Punishment: Another View," *American Economic Review,* 67, no. 3

(June 1977), 445–451; and Fagan, "Deterrence and the Death Penalty: A Criminal Review of New Evidence;" *op.cit.*

18. "Millions Misspent: What Politicians Don't Say About the High Cost of the Death Penalty," Death Penalty Information Center (www.essential.org/dpic/dpic.r08.html), 4.

19. Testimony of R. Dieter, "Costs of the Death Penalty and Related Issues" (www.deathpenalty.org/).

20. "Federal Death Penalty Cases: Recommendations Concerning the Cost and Quality of Defense Representation" (Washington, D.C.: Judicial Conference of the United States, Subcommittee on Federal Death Penalty Cases, May 1998), Executive Summary, 2.

21. William J. Bowers and Glenn L. Pierce, "Arbitrariness and Discrimination under Post-Furman Capital Statutes," *Crime and Delinquency*, vol. 26, no. 4 (October 1980), 563–635, also reprinted in Neil O. Alper and Daryl A. Hellman, *op.cit.*

22 These figures do not include cases of multiple victims of multiple races. "Race of Death Row Inmates Executed Since 1976," (www.deathpenalty.org/).

23. Steven Holmes, "Look Who's Questioning the Death Penalty," *The New York Times, News of the Week in Review,* April 16, 2000, 3. Death Penalty Information Center, "Facts About the Death Penalty" (www.deathpenalty.org/).

24. Other weapons and percentages of use (rounded) are as follows: knives (cutting or stabbing instruments), 13%; personal weapons (hands, fists, etc.), 7%; shotguns, rifles, and other or unidentified firearms, 3% each; blunt objects (clubs, hammers, etc.), 5%; and other weapons (poisons, fire, etc.), 13%. (Uniform Crime Reports, 2003, *op. cit.,* Tables 2.9, 19.)

25. William Bowers and Glenn Pierce, "The Bartley–Fox Gun Law's Short-Term Impact on Crime in Boston," *The Annals of the American Academy,* vol. 455 (May 1981), also reprinted in Neil O. Alper and Daryl A. Hellman, *op. cit.*

26. Philip J. Cook and Gary A. Zarkin, "Crime and the Business Cycle," *op. cit.*

27. *Ibid.,* 126.

28. S. Raphael and R. Winter-Ebmer, "Identifying the Effect of Unemployment on Crime," *Journal of Law and Economics* (April 2001) 259-83.

29. For a comprehensive look at firearm ownership, use, and violence, see G.D. Newton, Jr., and F.E. Zimring, Firearms and Violence in American Life (Washington, D.C.: National Commission on the Causes and Prevention of Violence, 1969). For a related discussion of robbery, choice of weapon, and robbery killings, see Frank E. Zimring, "Determinants of the Death Rate from Robbery: A Detroit Time Study," *Journal of Legal Studies,* 1, no. 2 (June 1977), 317–332.

30. Llad Phillips, "Crime Control: The Case for Deterrence," in Simon Rottenberg, ed., *op. cit.* The following discussion is based on this study.

31. One reason for the weaker results concerning availability of firearms is the difficulty of measuring the number of firearms available. The author was forced to use a proxy measure and recognizes its shortcomings.

32. A Boston Police Department publication indicates that in one-third of rape cases, roughness is employed by the rapist. In one-fourth, the victim is beaten nonbrutally during the rape. In one-fifth, the victim is choked and gagged by the assailant. Patricia Rehm, *Stop Rape* (Boston: Boston Police, Informational Services Section, n.d.).

33. Criminal Victimization in the U.S., 2003, *op.cit,* Table 9, 9.

34. Criminal Victimization in the U.S., 2003, *op. cit.,* Table 6, 7.

35. Uniform Crime Report 2003, *op. cit.,* Table 39. This age group accounts for 43.2% of total arrests for forcible rape.

36. Rehm, *op. cit.*

37. For a discussion and analysis of rape as the by-product of inequality between men and women in a system in which sexual relationships are power relationships, see Loreene M.G. Clark and Debra J. Lewis, *Rape: The Price of Coercive Sexuality* (Toronto: Women's Press, 1977). This study examines rape in Canada and concludes that to eliminate rape it is necessary to change social structures. For the classic argument on rape and male aggression, see Susan Griffin,

"Rape: The All-American Crime," *Ramparts,* 10, no. 3 (September 1971).

38. Robert Hendrickson, *Ripoffs—Complete Survival Guide* (New York: Viking Press, 1976).

39. Center for Disease Control, National Center for Injury Prevention and Control, "Youth Violence: Fact Sheet" (www.cdc.gov/ncipc/factsheets/yvfacts.htm).

40. U.S. Surgeon General, "Youth Violence: A Report of the Surgeon General" (www.surgeongeneral.gov/library/youthviolence/chapter2.sec1.html); and Uniform Crime Report 2003, *op.cit.,* Table 32, 274.

41. Brian Mac Quarrie and Suzanne Smalley, "Young, Armed and Dangerous," *Boston Globe,* October 17, 2004.

7

Crimes Without Victims

The so-called **victimless crimes** include a wide variety of offenses such as gambling, prostitution, homosexuality, and narcotics abuse. Whether or not such crimes are truly victimless is a debatable question,[1] and the extent of the harm done to participating individuals and society clearly varies from one such crime to another. In this chapter we start by examining the kinds of economic costs generated by victimless crimes. This will give us some sense of what it is worth to attempt to enforce laws prohibiting these activities. Next, we will establish a basic framework for economic analysis which is applicable to any of the victimless crimes. Finally, we apply the framework to a specific case—the market for prostitution.[2]

ECONOMIC COSTS

Negative Externalities

The kinds of economic costs imposed by these activities vary from one crime to another, but they fall into certain categories. The most important, although possibly not in terms of dollars, is the impact on the moral climate of society. Some would argue, for example, that prostitution encourages immoral behavior. It may also create sections within a city that are objectionable to look at, such as the Combat Zone in Boston.[3] These are examples of negative externalities; costs, even if only psychic, are imposed involuntarily on some people by the consumption and/or production decisions of others. **Negative externalities** are difficult to identify and measure. Some people may experience negative externalities only if an activity—say streetwalking by prostitutes, or drunks lying in gutters—is visible. For others, visibility does not matter; rather, they claim that the mere knowledge of the existence of the activity is harmful. Notice that if visibility were the only important characteristic, we might prescribe different public policies than we would if visibility did not matter.

Net Losses

Victimless crimes may also create net losses to society, measured by the amount of economic resources, including labor, machinery, land, and buildings, used up as an indirect result of the criminal activity. For the moment we ignore the resources used directly in the production of the illegal good or service. *Indirectly*, resources may have to be used as a result of consumption of the product. For example, purchasing the services of a prostitute may lead to venereal disease or AIDS, which may mean lost work time and hospital resources which would not otherwise be needed, and death, costing society the potential output and creativity of the victim. Some of these outcomes are possible, but not necessary, costs associated with **prostitution**. In fact, rates of venereal disease among prostitutes are lower than among other citizens, including college students. Prostitution may also generate medical, psychic, and other types of costs if prostitutes are assaulted by customers. Again, this outcome is possible but not necessary.

Drug abuse provides another example of potential costs in terms of net losses to society. The addict who is unable to work or dies prematurely represents potentially productive labor which is lost. Notice that welfare payments to an addict who is unable to work do not represent net social losses but are transfer payments; some individuals pay increased taxes (and therefore have less) so that others receive welfare payments (and therefore have more). From a social point of view the payments cancel each other out, and society as a whole is neither better off nor worse off (unless we could *prove* that a dollar is worth more to a poor person than to a rich one).

Opportunity Costs

Some would argue that the economic resources used *directly* in the production of illegal goods and services also represent a net loss to society in that they are being used to produce economic "bads" rather than "goods" and that, therefore, society sacrifices some output. This is the opportunity cost concept: by using scarce resources to produce "bads," we sacrifice the opportunity to produce "goods."

However, resources used directly in production are not net losses to society in the way that those used indirectly are (as in the case of the addict's lost labor). While it is true that we sacrifice output of some goods and services in order to produce illegal ones, the illegal output is obviously valued by at least some members of society. If no one valued the illegal output, there would be no demand for it and, therefore, no production of it and no use of resources for that purpose. Resources are simply being allocated in response to markets, albeit illegal ones. It is because certain goods and services are illegal that we consider their production a "waste of resources."[4] Production of legal products, such as cigarettes, is considered production of economic goods, and resources so used are not considered a net loss. Indirectly, however, as in some illegal markets, consumption of cigarettes leads to net losses to society.[5]

Transfers

In addition to the kinds of costs discussed so far, victimless crimes may also result in transfers of income or wealth from some individuals to others. From society's point of view there is no net change, but from the individual's viewpoint some individuals gain while others lose.

Several kinds of transfers can result from such activities. An obvious one is the lost income tax on illegally earned income. If some individuals avoid paying taxes, and if we assume that the government must raise a certain amount of money, then other individuals will have to make up for it by paying higher taxes.[6] To some extent, then, those who are employed in the production of legal goods and services pay higher taxes than would be necessary if illegal goods were made legal and incomes thereby derived were taxable.[7] While, in the aggregate, the gainers cancel the losers, at least in dollar terms, the size of the transfer is likely to be very large. For example, it has been estimated that in 1980 organized crimes' income from gambling alone was $22 billion,[8] or $52 billion in 2005 dollars.[9]

Another example of a transfer is property stolen by drug addicts in order to support their expensive habits. This time, real goods are transferred from some members of society to others. Robbery committed by prostitutes against their customers is another example.

This concludes our discussion of the kinds of costs generated by victimless crimes. Negative externalities are difficult to measure. The net losses may be quite costly, but not all of them are necessary results of illegal activities. From the point of view of society as a whole, transfers cancel out. These transfers, again, are not *necessary* results of the activities and may actually be due to the fact that the activities are illegal. For example, if prostitution were legalized, incomes derived from providing the service would be taxable. Robbery committed against customers would become more difficult because customers would be less hesitant to report the incident, and we would expect to see less of it as a result. The transfer costs associated with prostitution would therefore be reduced, if not eliminated, if the activity became legal.

Criminal Justice Costs

The final cost category also represents a cost that is imposed on us, not because of the activities per se, but because there are laws against the activities. This last kind of cost is the criminal justice expenditures that we make each year in an effort to police these activities and punish those who break the laws against them.

In 2003, six victimless crime categories (prostitution, drug abuse, gambling, liquor law violations, drunkenness, and driving under the influence) resulted in 4,373,179 arrests, which represented approximately 32 percent of total arrests in the country that year. Drug abuse violations accounted for more than 12 percent of all arrests, or slightly more than 76 percent of the combined total for the index crimes.[10] This may reflect the recent change in social attitudes towards viewing it as a very serious crime, leading to increased enforcement of drug abuse laws.

This arrest information suggests that a very substantial portion of our scarce criminal justice resources is being allocated toward policing the victimless crimes, and we might ask ourselves whether these resources are well spent. Before we rush to conclusions, however, we must realize that arrests for some of the victimless crimes (e.g., drunkenness) are easier to effect than arrests for such crimes as burglary; therefore, arrest figures are misleading indicators of the true amounts of effort or resources involved. In addition, some arrests for victimless crimes (as well as others) may be made in the course of other police activities.

Regardless of these qualifications, we do spend significant amounts of money each year, not only on police but also throughout the criminal justice system, in attempting to enforce the laws against victimless crimes. In 1994 approximately 350,000 Americans were incarcerated for victimless crimes. There were an additional approximately 1.5 million people who were on probation or parole for the same crimes. It was estimated that the cost of arresting and punishing these people for victimless crimes was $50 billion in 1994[11] ($66 billion in 2005 dollars).

Other, less easily measured costs are imposed on our criminal justice system by victimless crimes. It is argued that laws against these activities have led to **corruption of police and members of the judiciary.** The business of providing illegal goods and services is highly profitable. Sellers, therefore, find it desirable and affordable to make payoffs. The extent to which this affects our system is difficult to assess, but it does impose costs on all of us if the system is less efficient or less equitable as a result. Finally, partly because the public is aware of, or even overestimates corruption and partly because some people feel that at least some of the laws against victimless crimes are outdated and arbitrary, disrespect for the law in general is created. In 2002 approximately 40 percent of the U.S. population age 12 or older reported that they had experimented with or regularly used marijuana.[12] If individuals' opinions and behavior differ in part from those called for by the law, does it become more difficult to respect the authority of law in general? If so, additional social costs are generated.

AN ANALYTICAL FRAMEWORK

In recent years the laws against some victimless crimes have been eased. Public drunkenness is no longer criminal in well over half the states. Decreased penalties for marijuana use have been introduced, or a low priority has been given to arrests for this offense. "Anything goes" adult entertainment centers, which in effect legalize prostitution within their boundaries, have been proposed in some major cities. State-run "numbers" games have been introduced, and casino gambling was legalized in Atlantic City, New Jersey, on native-Americans' tribal lands as in Ledyard, Connecticut, and today legalized gambling exists in some form in all but two states and the District of Columbia. The trend is, therefore, in the direction of **legalizing,** or at least **decriminalizing,** these activities.[13] Whether or not this is appropriate depends on the estimated costs and benefits associated with the change. In this chapter we will develop a basic framework for analyzing the two extremes with respect to public policy: enforcement of stricter penalties versus legalization.

It is useful to view victimless criminal activities in a supply-and-demand framework. Thus, as shown in Figure 7–1, there is a market demand for an

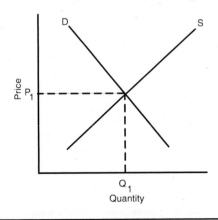

Figure 7–1 The Market for Prostitution

economic bad (e.g., prostitution). The curve describing it is labeled D. Few units of the service are demanded at relatively high prices. As the price decreases, the quantity demanded increases. There is also a supply of prostitution. The curve describing it is labeled S. As the price increases, the quantity supplied increases. The equilibrium price of prostitution and the quantity bought and sold are determined by the interaction of supply and demand and are illustrated by the intersection of the demand and supply curves. P_1 represents the equilibrium price established by the market, and Q_1 represents the equilibrium quantity.

Despite the fact that the activity is illegal, Q_1 units are bought and sold per time period. Associated with this is a certain level of employment of labor and other resources in the industry.[14] In addition, production and consumption of Q_1 units impose costs on society, as discussed at the beginning of the chapter. Included in these costs are criminal justice expenditures.

The demand for prostitution services is affected by the usual determinants of demand (i.e., consumers' tastes and income, prices of substitute goods, and prices of complements). A change in one or more of these determinants will cause demand to change and the entire demand curve to shift. This will, therefore, affect market price and quantity. If demand increases (i.e., the demand curve shifts upward), it means that people are willing to buy more services of prostitutes at every price. If demand decreases (i.e., the demand curve shifts downward), it means that people are willing to buy fewer services at every price.

Consider the impact of pornographic literature on the market for prostitution. Let us assume that prostitution and such literature are complementary goods, that is, that they tend to be consumed together. If this is so, and if the price of pornographic literature increases, it will cause the demand for prostitution to decrease and the demand curve to shift downward to the left. This shift from D to D' and its impact on the market for prostitution are illustrated in Figure 7–2.

Because demand has decreased and the curve has moved to D', P_1 and Q_1 no longer represent the market outcome. The price and quantity will be established through the interaction of the diminished demand and the existing supply of prostitutes' services, as illustrated by the intersection of the new demand and supply curves. This intersection has moved to P_2, Q_2. The equilibrium price for prostitution service has dropped to P_2, and the amount of services purchased by the market as a whole has decreased to Q_2.

We would get a very different result if the price of pornographic literature were to decrease. We would also get a different result if pornographic literature were not a complementary good but a substitute good. To see how

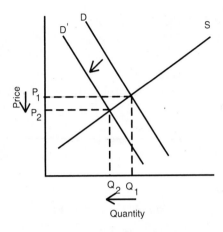

Figure 7–2 The Market for Prostitution

this changes the outcome, let us again assume that the price of pornographic literature increases, but this time we will assume that prostitution and pornographic literature are substitutes; that is, if you buy more of one you tend to buy less of the other. This time the price change will cause demand for prostitution to increase and the curve to increase to D′. In Figure 7–3 we can see how this shift results in an increase in price from P_1 to P_2 and an increase in the amount of prostitution bought and sold from Q_1 to Q_2.[15]

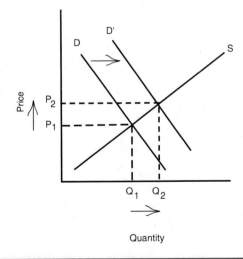

Figure 7–3 The Market for Prostitution

Whether or not pornographic literature and prostitution are complementary goods or substitutes is something that must be determined empiri-
cally. It is possible that there is a stronger relationship between pornography
and violent crimes, such as rape. At this stage in our investigation we are not
sure.[16] It is clear, however, that once the relationship between the goods has
been identified, it is possible to assess the impact of price changes on the
market via an economic model of supply and demand.

The supply for prostitution services is also subject to changes, leading to
shifts in the supply curve, if one or more of the determinants of supply
changes. These determinants consist of the costs of doing business, including
expected-punishment costs and time (opportunity) costs, and the number of
sellers in the industry.[17] An increase in any of the costs of doing business
(e.g., an increase in the price of hotel rooms) or a decrease in the number of
sellers will cause supply to decrease and the curve to shift to the left. An increase in the number of job opportunities for women would increase legal income alternatives and, therefore, would also cause supply to decrease and the
curve to shift in this direction. This is illustrated in Figure 7-4. Supply decreases as illustrated by the shift from S to S'; price increases from P_1 to P_2;
and quantity bought and sold drops from Q_1 to Q_2.

A decrease in any of the costs of doing business, or an increase in the
number of sellers, will cause supply to increase; the supply function will shift
to the right. In Figure 7–5 supply increases and the curve shifts from S to S'.
Equilibrium price drops from P_1 to P_2, and quantity bought and sold increases from Q_1 to Q_2.

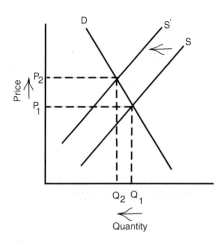

Figure 7–4 The Market for Prostitution

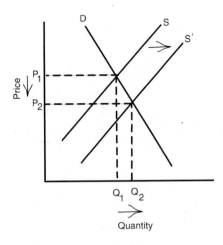

Figure 7–5 The Market for Prostitution

PUBLIC POLICY TOWARD CRIMES WITHOUT VICTIMS

With this understanding of how market price and quantity are established and how they can be affected by changes in either the demand for or the supply of prostitution services, we can analyze the likely impact of various public policies on the market for an economic "bad." While our analysis is limited to the market for prostitution, our methodology could be used to analyze other illegal markets.

We will assume that Figure 7–1 illustrates market equilibrium before a change in public policy. Using this as our starting point, we can demonstrate the market impact of two basic and opposite policy choices. These are not the only public policies possible, but they offer an interesting comparison. After demonstrating the impact, we can assess the possible costs and benefits of alternative actions.

First consider a "get tough" policy. Regardless of the particular tactics or procedures chosen, such a policy will be reflected in stricter enforcement of existing laws or the imposition of stiffer penalties, either of which increases expected-punishment costs. The impact on the market for the economic "bad" depends on (1) the extent to which expected-punishment costs are increased (this will determine how much supply and/or demand changes and the functions shift) and (2) whether we "get tough" on sellers, buyers, or both parties. Typically, law enforcement efforts have concentrated on the sellers of economic "bads" rather than on their buyers, although it is clear that if there were no buyers there would not be sellers. It was estimated that nationwide, in the late 1980s, 70 percent of those arrested for prostitution were female prostitutes, 20 percent were male prostitutes and the remaining 10 percent were their customers.[18]

We will initially assume, then, that "getting tough" means increasing the expected-punishment costs to sellers of prostitution, primarily females. Since this represents one of the costs of doing business, supply will decrease and the curve will shift to the left, to S′, reflecting the increased cost of doing business. Figure 7–6 illustrates the impact on market price and output. The price increases from P_1 to P_2, and the quantity bought and sold decreases from Q_1 to Q_2. The employment of resources in prostitution would decrease along with the reduction in output. Female unemployment rates might increase, not because unemployed prostitutes are counted in the official unemployment statistics, but because the unemployed prostitutes might enter the legal market in an attempt to find jobs and not initially be very successful.[19] The extent to which the supply functions and, therefore, the extent to which price increases and output decreases depends on the extent to which the expected value of the punishment is increased.

If we were also to increase the expected punishment costs to buyers, or consumers, of prostitution, which has been the direction of some more recent policy,[20] the reduction in output would be even greater. The expected-punishment costs for buying illegal services may be looked at as part of the transaction costs associated with buying the product. Analytically, we can consider transaction costs as a complementary good (i.e., the two things go

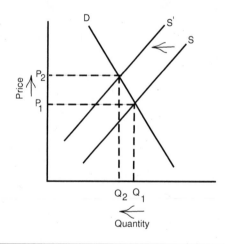

Figure 7–6 The Market for Prostitution

together). If transaction costs increase, the impact on demand is the impact which results from an increase in the price of a complementary good. When the price of a complement goes up, the demand decreases and the curve shifts downward. Getting tough on buyers, therefore, results in a downward shift in the demand curve for prostitution, from D to D'.

In Figure 7–7 we see the impact of the decrease in demand added to that of the decrease in supply. The result is to further decrease output, from Q_2 to Q_3. This results, of course, in further reductions in employment in the industry. The impact on price is complicated. While the decrease in demand will put downward pressure on prices, it is not clear whether the resulting price, P_3, will be equal to, less than, or greater than the initial price, P_1. In Figure 7–7 we show P_3 as slightly greater than P_1. This is because the demand decrease is less than the supply decrease. If the opposite were the case, P_3 would be less than P_1. The point is that the impact on price depends on how much tougher we get, and on whom. Regardless of these factors, however, it is clear that such a policy can reduce the consumption of prostitution services. The question is, does this kind of policy make good economic sense?

To answer this question we need an accounting of the costs and benefits of the policy change. Clearly, getting tough will mean devoting more resources to law enforcement unless existing resources have been used inefficiently and, therefore, could be reorganized to produce more, or we reduce or eliminate some of the constraints which currently affect the use of law

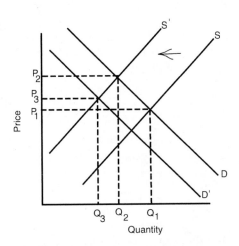

Figure 7–7 The Market for Prostitution

enforcement resources, such as rights to privacy. If neither of these is possible or desirable, we will simply have to spend more on law enforcement to reduce the consumption and production of prostitution.

The benefits associated with the increased spending would be reductions in all the costs associated with prostitution described earlier, with the exception of criminal justice costs. How large and how real some of these costs are—and, therefore, how large and how real the benefits would be—is open to some question. If the benefits of reduced prostitution exceed the costs of increased law enforcement, the policy change is economically rational. If the reverse is the case, society would be better off not making the change. A San Francisco study commission estimated that in 1994 it cost that city $7.6 million ($9.97 million in 2005 dollars) to arrest, prosecute and incarcerate the approximately 5,300 prostitutes it arrested. This is an average cost of $1,442 per arrest (or $1,892 in 2005 dollars).[21] Really getting tough would therefore cost even more. The question is, would it be worth it?

If "get tough" policies are economically inefficient, what about going to the opposite extreme and **legalizing prostitution**? First we must ask what impact this would have on the market for prostitution. On the basis of this analysis we can begin to discuss the likely costs and benefits of the policy change.[22]

Legalization of an economic "bad" will have impacts on both the demand and supply sides of the market; that is, we would expect both to change. The impact on price and quantity will depend on the magnitudes and directions of the changes. Let us begin analyzing this more complicated series of impacts by considering the impact on the demand function.

The demand will change if there is a change in consumers' tastes, in the prices of substitute or complementary goods, or in income. The question is, would legalization affect any of these? The answer is "yes." First consider consumers' tastes. Tastes for prostitution can be affected by legalization in a number of ways. First, for those whose taste for prostitution was diminished simply because of its illegal status, taste will increase. On the other hand, there may be some individuals for whom taste was enhanced by the illegal status and whose taste for prostitution will decrease after legalization. On balance, the likely impact is a net increase and, therefore, for the demand to increase resulting in a shift upward and to the right in the demand curve. At every price people will be willing to buy more services.

There is another way in which tastes may be affected, namely through advertising. Currently, there is informal advertising among some classes of prostitutes in the form of streetwalking. Whether this continues or is substituted for by some other type of advertising (e.g., in newspapers) depends on the details of the legalization scheme. If advertising were permitted and tastes for prostitution were increased by additional advertising expenditures, the consumers' demand would increase again and the curve would experience an additional upward shift. Depending on the type of advertising used, the negative externalities visibly generated by prostitution may increase or decrease per unit of prostitution services marketed. For example, if advertising in the *Yellow Pages* were substituted for streetwalking, the visible negative externalities associated with any amount of prostitution would be decreased.

Legalization can have another impact on the consumers' demand. To the extent that there are expected-punishment costs associated with buying prostitution services, these would be eliminated with legalization. As mentioned earlier, the expected-punishment costs for buying illegal services may be looked at as part of the transaction costs of buying those services. Transaction costs and the illegal services are complementary goods. Thus, as expected-punishment costs (or transaction costs) decrease, the demand for the service increases. A decrease in the price of a complementary good causes demand to increase. The extent of the change in demand depends on the size of the price reduction. Since in the past our law enforcement efforts have focused on the sellers of illegal goods and services, this impact would probably be relatively small.

Altogether, we would expect legalization to increase demand and shift the demand curve for prostitution upward and to the right. In addition, there will be an impact on the supply side of the market. The impact on the supply side is caused by the reduction in expected-punishment costs to sellers. This represents a decrease in the costs of doing business; any amount of prostitution can now be produced at a lower price. The supply increases and the function shifts outward, to the right. While each existing firm, or seller, can now produce at lower costs, it is also true that there is likely to be an increase in the number of sellers. Legalization will remove one barrier to entry into the industry, since sellers who were previously kept out by psychic costs may now enter. For both of these reasons, the supply function shifts to the right.

The final impact of the changes in demand and supply is illustrated in Figure 7–8. In our illustration the change in supply exceeds the change in demand. As a result the price drops from P_1 to P_2. If the opposite were the case, the new price would be higher. Given the reasons for the changes in the functions, it is reasonable to conclude that the supply change would dominate.

In addition to the price change, there is an increase in the quantity bought and sold from Q_1 to Q_2.

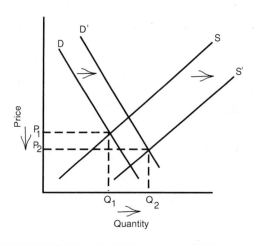

Figure 7–8 The Market for Prostitution

Regardless of whether demand or supply increases more, it is clear that the production and consumption of prostitution will increase. Employment in the industry will also increase.

Competition in the industry may increase as well. Whether or not this happens will depend on whether production is increased primarily by existing firms producing more or by new firms entering the industry. Which of these outcomes occurs will depend on whether or not there are economies of scale in the production of the product; that is, on whether larger producers have lower average costs of production than smaller producers. To answer this question we would need detailed information concerning how the product is produced and what inputs, including advertising, are used. In other words, we need information concerning the production function. In the absence of this information we can only "guesstimate" the outcome. If we can conclude that competition would increase, then we know that monopoly profits in the industry will be removed and product quality will likely improve.[23]

The final question to answer is whether legalization makes economic sense. What are the costs and benefits to society by making this change in public policy?[24] The costs to society will come in the form of increases in some, but not all, of the costs associated with prostitution discussed earlier in the chapter. Negative externalities are likely to increase. Since it is possible that with legalization the visible externalities *per unit of service* decrease, the total amount of negative externalities generated as more of the service is bought and sold need not increase. If legalization does not decrease the negative externalities per unit, then it is clear that the total amount generated will increase. The dollar price tag associated with this effect is hard to estimate.

Net losses resulting indirectly from consumption of the product are likely to drop even though more of the product is consumed. This is because increased competition would improve the product (or **licensing** may be required to maintain sanitary standards) and reduce medical costs to buyers. In addition, assaults on sellers would be reduced with legalization because of the increased likelihood that the incident would be reported to the police. Since these cost categories are reduced, they actually represent benefits associated with legalization.

Opportunity costs are eliminated by legalization. Opportunity costs are the legal economic goods we sacrifice by using our resources to produce illegal economic "bads." By changing the status of a product from illegal to legal we erase this cost category.

Transfer costs are also reduced by legalization and, therefore, represent benefits of the policy change.[25] Incomes derived from prostitution now would be taxable. Robbery committed against customers would become more difficult because customers would be less hesitant to report incidents, and we would expect to see less robbery as a result.

Finally, criminal justice costs, both those which are easily measured and those which are not, such as disrespect for the law, would be reduced significantly. We would no longer have to spend scarce resources policing the activity, and society would feel that, at least in this instance, our law enforcement efforts and expenditures were no longer wasted or allocated arbitrarily.

On balance, it appears that legalization would result in a net increase in social welfare; that is, the benefits to society as a whole would exceed the costs.[26] However, before going this route we should compare legalization with alternatives which may yield still larger increases in social welfare. In addition, there are some qualifications which must be recognized.[27] First, although negative externalities are hard to measure, they should not be underrated. We have suggested that visible externalities may be affected by legalization and could be decreased. Nonvisible externalities, however, will continue to exist, at least in the immediate future until attitudes change, if they do. If these are the primary negative externalities generated by prostitution, then we may be underestimating the costs of legalization.

Another important qualification revolves around the issue of **regulation.** Some of the benefits of legalization may be eliminated or reduced, depending on the extent of regulation introduced. Extensive regulation of firms may result in the same kind of corruption of law enforcement officials, or others responsible for regulation, that exists today. Severe constraints on sellers may impose unnecessary costs, monetary and psychic, on those employed in the industry. For example, in Nevada, where prostitution is legal, some counties have established regulations which impose apparently excessive restrictions on the lives of the prostitutes, including the hours when the women can be in town and the buildings and residential areas in which they are permitted. One town, for example, does not allow prostitutes to have friends within the town.[28] If they are used only to reduce negative externalities, such restrictions can be justified. If they are used to restrict the civil liberties of those who are legally employed in an industry which some people disapprove of, they cannot. If prostitution is legalized, we must be careful not to substitute excessive regulation and licensing requirements as a punishment for selling prostitution. Doing so may be as expensive to society as enforcing existing laws against prostitution.

In the next chapter we turn to a detailed discussion of one "victimless" crime market: the market for illicit drugs—cocaine and heroin. Much of what we have learned in this chapter, with some refinement and elaboration, can be applied to the study of the illicit drug problem.

REVIEW TERMS AND CONCEPTS

Advertising
Barriers to entry
Competition
Corruption
Decriminalization
Economic resources
Economic "bads"
Economies of scale
Equilibrium
Expected punishment costs
Legalization
Legalizing
Licensing
Monopoly
Moral climate
Negative externalities

Net losses
Nonvisible externalities
Opportunity cost
Production function
Profits
Public policies
Regulation
Social welfare
Streetwalking
Time costs
Transaction costs
Transfer costs
Transfers of income
Unemployment rate
Victimless crimes
Visible externalities

END OF CHAPTER QUESTIONS

1. Because there are no victims in a victimless crime they do not impose costs on society. Is this a true statement? Why?

2. What are some public policies that can be used to decrease the demand for victimless crimes, such as gambling and prostitution?

3. What are some examples of behavior that at one time were victimless crimes that are no longer criminal? What are some examples of behavior that were not victimless crimes that now are crimes?

4. If the legalization of prostitution required government regulation would this decrease or increase the expected benefits of legalization? Explain.

NOTES

1. For a discussion of the argument against classifying prostitution as a victimless crime, see Nancy Erbe, "Prostitutes: Victims of Men's Exploitation and Abuse," *Law and Inequality,* vol. 2:609 (1984).

2. For a public-policy-oriented textbook which discusses some other examples of crimes without victims, see Edwin M. Schur, *Crimes Without Victims—Deviant Behavior and Public Policy: Abortion, Homosexuality, Drug Addiction* (Englewood Cliffs, N.J.: Prentice-Hall, 1965). See also Edwin Schur and Hugo Bedau, *Victimless Crimes: Two Sides of a Controversy* (Englewood Cliffs, N.J.: Prentice-Hall, 1974).

3. The Combat Zone is an area of a few blocks in downtown Boston zoned for adult entertainment activities. It is the only area so zoned in the city.

4. Consistent with this thinking, output of illegal goods and services is not counted in the Gross Domestic Product (GDP) of the U.S.

5. For a detailed cost-benefit analysis of quitting smoking for both the individual and society, see Gerry Oster, Graham A. Colditz, and Nancy L. Kelly, *The Economic Costs of Smoking and Benefits of Quitting* (Lexington, Mass.: Lexington Books, 1984).

6. If public-sector expenditures are reduced by the amount of revenue lost, it is still a transfer; however, the distribution of gainers and losers is different.

7. There is also the possibility that increased tax rates reduce work incentives, at least in the legal sector of the economy.

8. Reported in the Report to the President and the Attorney General, *The Impact: Organized Crime Today* (Washington, D.C.: U.S. Government Printing Office, April 1986), 444, from James Cook, "The Invisible Enterprise," *Forbes* (September 29, 1980), 60–71.

9. Dollars here and throughout the chapter are adjusted for increases in the CPI through April 2005, *op.cit.*

10. U.S. Department of Justice, Bureau of Justice Statistics, *Uniform Crime Reports, 2003* (*op.cit*), Table 29, 270.

11. "Operation Safe Streets presents: Talking Points on Crime," LP News Archive (www.lp.org/lpn/9409-oss-talking.html).

12. Office of National Drug Control Policy, "Fact Sheet: Marijuana" (www.whitehousedrugpolicy.gov/February 2004), 1.

13. Decriminalization means that the activity remains illegal but is no longer punishable as a criminal offense. For a discussion and analysis of the impact of decriminalization of public drunkenness, see David E. Aaronson, C. Thomas Dienes, and Michael C. Musheno, "Changing the Public Drunkenness Laws: The Impact of Decriminalization," *Law and Society Review,* 12, no. 3 (Spring 1978), 405–436. The question of and references relevant to the decriminalization of drugs are in the next chapter.

14. This is determined by the production function for the product.

15. Notice that if we wanted to decrease the consumption of prostitution services, it would be to our advantage to encourage increases in the prices of complements and/or decreases in the prices of substitutes.

16. For empirical studies and discussions of the relationship between pornography and sex crimes and other antisocial behavior, see President's Commission on Obscenity and Pornography, *Technical Report of the Commission on Obscenity and Pornography,* vol. 7, *Erotica and Antisocial Behavior* (Washington, D.C.: U.S. Government Printing Office, 1971), and 8, *Erotica and Social Behavior.* Also see Attorney General's Commission on Pornography, *Final Report,* Vols. I and II (Washington, D.C.: U.S. Government Printing Office, July 1986). For an alternative perspective suggesting that the availability of pornography decreases sex crimes see Milton Diamond and Ayako Uchiyama, "Pornography, Rape and Sex Crimes in Japan," *International Journal of Law and Psychiatry* (1999), 1-22.

17. The organization of the industry (i.e., competitive or monopolized) will also affect the supply curve if there are economies of scale.

18. Prostitutes Education Network (PEN), "Prostitution in the United States—The Statistics" (www.bayswan.org/stats.html), 1.

19. To be officially considered unemployed, a person must be not working at a legal sector job, must be willing to work, and must be actively seeking a job. Since prostitution is legal only in Nevada, prostitutes who were formerly employed in a legal Nevada brothel would be the only ones who could be officially counted as unemployed.

20. In 2004, Paterson, NJ, passed an ordinance permitting police to seize the cars of anyone arrested for driving into the city to purchase the services of a prostitute. (www.phillyburbs.com/pb-dyn/news/278-05032005-484602.html) Minneapolis posts the photos of people convicted for soliciting on the city's web site for a period of six months after being convicted. (www.ci.minneapolis.mn.us/police/prostitutionconvictions/convictions.asp#TopOfPage) In June 2005 Chicago started posting photos of prostitutes and their customers who have been arrested, not convicted, for selling or soliciting. (E. Ferkenhoff, "A Tangled Web of Sex, Technology, and Civil Liberties," *Boston Globe,* June 27, 2005)

21. San Francisco Task Force on Prostitution, Fuel Report 1996 (www.bayswan.org/5cost.html).

22. For a discussion applied to gambling, see Lillian Deitch and David Weinstein, *The Impact of Legalized Gambling* (New York: Praeger, 1974).

23. Profits from victimless crimes may be a source of capital for organized crime. If industry competition increases from legalization, this will reduce monopoly profits to organized crime. If not, as the industry expands, monopoly profits will increase. The degree of competition and involvement of organized crime most likely varies among types of victimless crimes. See the discussion in Chapter 9.

24. An extensive review of the costs and benefits of legalizing prostitution can be found in Barbara Milman, *op. cit.*

25. Technically, of course, a reduction in transfers does not represent a *net* benefit to society, although indirectly net benefits may result.

26. For some members of society the opposite may be the case (e.g., for an individual with a strong moral distaste for the product regardless of who consumes it).

27. For two discussions that favor decriminalization of prostitution, see Therese M. Wandling, "Decriminalization of Prostitution: The

Limits of the Criminal Law," *Oregon Law Review,* 55, no. 4 (1976), 553–566, and Pennsylvania Program for Women and Girl Offenders, *The Decriminalization of Prostitution—the Movement Towards Decriminalization* (Philadelphia, 1975).

28. Elizabeth and James Vorenberg, "The Biggest Pimp of All: Prostitution and Some Facts of Life"; *Atlantic Monthly,* 239, no 1. (January 1977), 30.

8

The Markets for Heroin and Cocaine

With the preceding chapter as background, we will discuss in detail two additional examples of "victimless crime" markets—the markets for **heroin** and **cocaine.** They are a large part of a global market that, the United Nations Office on Drugs and Crimes, estimates generated $320 billion in retail business in 2004 and involved approximately five percent of the world's population 15-64 years old, or approximately 200 million people, as consumers, with approximately $60 billion per year from the U.S. market alone.[1] It is an industry that affects the economic, social, and political wellbeing of many countries throughout the world. It is also an industry that is affected by changes in the economic, social, and political circumstances of countries throughout the world.

The heroin market deserves special attention because heroin abuse is perhaps the least victimless of the victimless crimes and therefore represents a more serious challenge to policy makers. Analysis of the heroin market is also interesting because it is somewhat complicated. The cocaine market, which has many similarities to the heroin market, is also singled out because it comprises a significant part of the U.S. market for illicit drugs.

THE HISTORY OF HEROIN AND COCAINE IN THE U.S.

Prior to examining contemporary heroin and cocaine markets, we will provide a brief historical review of the markets.[2] **Opium** was brought to this country by the early European settlers to be used straight or mixed with alcohol as a pain reliever. Its addictive nature was noted in the medical literature of the early 1800s, but the first major problem of addiction emerged from the use of morphine to relieve pain during the Civil War. Heroin was not synthesized until the early 1870s and became known by that name when the Bayer Company introduced it in cough syrup. Restricting the distribution of opium and its derivatives to doctors' prescriptions started late in the 19th century in some states, but without a federal restriction on the interstate transportation of these drugs all users had to do to obtain it was travel to a state where the desired drug was not restricted.

Cocaine's history in the U.S. is not as long. It was not until the 1880s that purified cocaine became readily available. It was often incorporated into a drink. In fact, Coca-Cola was introduced in 1886 as a drink containing the benefits of coca (the name of the plant from which cocaine is refined) without the risks of alcohol, the most common base up to that time.[3] It, along with opium and its derivatives, was widely advertised and sold all over the country by the pharmaceutical companies of the time. In 1894, Parke-Davis marketed an emergency kit that included cocaine, morphine, atropine and strychnine along with a syringe. It was the passage at the federal level of the **Harrison Act in 1914,** which required a strict accounting of these drugs from their importation into the U.S. to their distribution to the final consumer and the imposition of a tax at each stage, that created the incentives for the illegal markets of today.

THE HEROIN MARKET

Illegal trade in the heroin market grew steadily during the 1960s and into the early 1970s. Nationally, narcotic drug law arrests of persons age 18 and older increased over 600 percent between 1960 and 1970. **Addiction rates** and drug-related crime and deaths also increased substantially. In Boston, the total heroin user population increased ten times over the decade. Federal spending to solve the problem also grew rapidly over the period. From 1968 to 1973 federal expenditures for drug-related programs increased twelvefold, from $66.4 to $791.3 million.[4]

Several factors have been cited as reasons for the rapid growth of the problem during that period. Rising incomes increased the demand for new forms of recreation or leisure goods; social pressures, unrest, and dissatisfaction increased tastes and, therefore, demand for products which represented escape or rebellion; finally, the availability of the drug in Southeast Asia led to the introduction of heroin to a significant number of troops stationed there during the **Vietnam War.**

Sometime between 1971 and 1973 the problem peaked, owing at least partly to the expenditure of hundreds of millions of dollars by the federal government on efforts to sever the European heroin connection. In Massachusetts, drug arrests and deaths from overdose began decreasing in 1971. Nationally, drug-related deaths began to level off or drop in 1973, and the quality of street-level heroin was down to as little as two or three percent in 1973.

While these figures appeared encouraging at the time, we still have not turned the corner on drug abuse, including heroin. In the late 1970s the problem appeared to be increasing in severity. Overall the **number of arrests for drug abuse violations** began increasing around 1977 with the total number of arrests peaking in 1989 at a level that was up more than 105 percent from what they were in 1979. Drug arrests decreased in both 1990 and 1991 and ended the period approximately 25 percent below what they were in 1989, but since then they have increased to the point where drug arrests in 2000 were almost 60 percent higher than in 1991. As a percentage of total arrests for all crimes, drug arrests went from approximately seven percent in 1991 to almost 11 percent in 2000.[5] At the same time the federal government's expenditures to combat drug abuse (including funds for drug law enforcement, international narcotics control and health-related drug abuse activities) increased from almost $1.2 billion in fiscal year (FY) 1982 ($2.6 billion in 2005 dollars) to more than $17.9 billion in FY 1999 ($20.9 billion in 2005 dollars), a nominal increase of more than fourteen times over the seventeen year period.[6] The federal FY 2005 budget is $12.2 billion and the proposed budget for FY 2006 is $12.4 billion.[7]

While the Turkish-French flow of heroin may have been slowed in the early and mid-1970s, major new sources were developed in Mexico and Southwest Asia. From the early 1990s to today South America, especially Colombia, has played an increasingly important role in opium cultivation. Also, with the demise of the Soviet Union new sources of opium were developed in the former republics and eastern block nations including Poland, the Ukraine, Moldava, and Kazakhstan where the cultivation of opium poppies is legal. With the overthrow of the Taliban in 2001, Afghanistan has once again become the world's premier provider of opium. Current estimates are that it is providing 90 percent of the world's supply.[8] New transit routes for the Turkish and Southwest Asian opium have also developed through Poland, Hungary, and the Czech Republic (the former Czechoslovakia).[9] Today it is believed that the primary source of heroin in the U.S. is South America, primarily from Colombia. The next largest source is heroin from Mexico, followed by Southwest Asia and Southeast Asia.

Indicators of the supply of heroin, since it cannot be directly measured, are its quality and the amount seized by law enforcement agencies. It is believed that the higher the heroin's quality and the more heroin seized, the greater the supply. The quality (purity) of the heroin bought in the U.S. changes over time. It is believed that the **purity of heroin** in the U.S. increased in the late 1980s and early 1990s, remained relatively stable for the next six years and increased even more through 2000.. This, in part, reflects the changes in the **sources of the heroin coming into the country.**[10] In 2000 it was believed that the South American heroin was the purest while the Mexican heroin was the poorest quality. While the quality of heroin in the U.S. has been increasing, the amount of heroin seized by various federal agencies has increased. In fiscal year 1995 almost 2,600 pounds were seized and in fiscal year 2001 almost 5,500 pounds were seized[11] representing an increase of more than 100 percent and a likely increase in the supply of heroin in the U.S. All of this has led some experts to conclude that as long as there are drugs there will be drug abuse, and that we might as well save money and legalize all drugs.

This conclusion is premature before we have carefully analyzed the heroin market and its ramifications. As noted above, opium and its derivatives became illegal in the United States in 1914 with the passage of the Harrison Act. Prior to that time a legal opium habit could be maintained for a minimal expenditure. In the early 1900s addiction to opium and its derivatives was relatively prevalent, partly because the product was cheap and partly because of ignorance about its addiction potential. The incidence of addiction was 0.57 percent of the population in 1914, compared with 0.025 percent in 1967. The price of heroin, corrected for changes in the cost of living, rose by about 3,000 percent over the same period.[12] It has been estimated that by 1984 the incidence of heroin addiction had increased to 0.21 percent.[13] This possibly reflected the effect of a period of relatively stable nominal retail prices for heroin which occurred over the period from 1978 to 1982,[14] and, therefore, a decreasing real price during this period of relatively high inflation. From the early 1980s to the late 1990s it has been estimated that the **price of heroin** purchased at the retail level dropped considerably, from $3,115 for one-tenth of a gram or less in 1981 to $1,799 in 1998. At the same time its purity at the retail level has increased from 4.7 percent to 24.3 percent.[15] Recent estimates of **drug addiction rates** in the U.S. today range from .26 percent to .34 percent for heroin (2003) and .95 percent for cocaine (2001).[16] In 2001 the estimate for the retail price of heroin was $10 for a dose (50 to 100 mg of heroin) and for purity the estimate was 36.8 percent nationwide.[17] This is likely to reflect an increase in the supply of heroin to the domestic market.

THE COCAINE MARKET

The roots of the cocaine epidemic in the United States were in its use as a fashionable drug of the wealthy. Today it is a drug that is used by individuals at all levels of the socioeconomic scale. A rapid increase in **cocaine consumption** occurred in the early 1980s and continued through the mid-1980s. The number of people who used cocaine (including crack) in 2003 was estimated to be approximately 5.9 million people, or approximately 2.5% of the U.S. population 12 and older, which was considerably less than the 9.8 million people, or approximately 5.1% of the population, who used cocaine in 1985.[18] Cocaine consumption grew 133% over the period of 1982 to 1985, from 31.0 metric tons to 72.3 metric tons and continued to grow to more than 352 tons in 2002.[19] It was estimated that by 2003 almost 15 percent of the people in this country had tried cocaine, and three percent had tried crack. The 2003 **National Survey on Drug Abuse** found only one percent of the population 12 and older, or approximately 2.28 million people, used cocaine during the month prior to the survey. In comparison the survey found that 6.2 percent of the population were current users of marijuana and 50 percent consumed alcohol.[20] While cocaine is not physiologically addictive like heroin, experts believe it is psychologically addictive and that "[t]he differences between so-called physical dependence and so-called psychological dependence may be more a matter of semantics and sensitivity of measures than of neurochemistry."[21] Thus, in the analysis that follows we will consider addiction to both heroin and cocaine.

The growth in cocaine consumption can be attributed to several factors. One factor that certainly contributed to the increase was the dramatic drop in its retail price. From 1976 to 1979 cocaine's retail price rose approximately 47 percent, from $530 to $780 per gram. From its peak, the price of cocaine decreased dramatically. By 1993 the retail price was estimated to range between $120 to $151 per gram, with most of the decrease occurring since 1982. The **price of cocaine** has fluctuated somewhat since its 1993 low. The per gram retail price ranged from $25 to $110 in late 2004 and early 2005.[22]

Another, not unrelated factor, was the introduction of "crack" during 1981. **Crack** is a form of cocaine that is processed for smoking, generally prior to retail sale, by mixing cocaine with water and either baking soda or ammonia. It is a less risky process than the alternative method of refining cocaine because it does not utilize ether, which is very volatile when heated. This decreases the danger in production and, therefore, decreases the cost to the producer. It also reduces the cost to the consumer who purchases raw cocaine and processes it himself/herself. Finally, crack is shorter lasting than other forms of cocaine and highly addictive. Studies have found that addiction to crack can occur within several months as opposed to taking three to four years with cocaine "snorting."[23]

Law enforcement efforts to deal with cocaine have also grown over recent years. This is especially true of the U.S. Customs Service's effort to prevent the importation of cocaine. In FY 1975 approximately one-thousand shipments of cocaine were seized with a total weight of almost 730 pounds and an estimated value of $155,400,000 ($561,520,000 in 2005 dollars). In FY 2003 the number of shipments seized was more than two and a one-half times the number seized in 1975, while the weight increased to more than 257,804 pounds with an estimated value of approximately $3.5 billion ($3.7 billion in 2005 dollars).[24] Efforts within the country have also increased with more than a doubling in the number of cocaine processing laboratories seized from 1983 to 1988. Since then there has been a significant decrease with only six laboratories seized in the 1993 to 2003 period.[25] There was an increase of 120 times in the amount of cocaine removed by the Drug Enforcement Administration over the period from 1978 to 1989. The amount removed each subsequent year through 1998 decreased so by 1998 the amount removed was 63 percent less. From 1999 through 2003 the amount removed has grown annually.[26] While it would seem that the war was being won, the purity of the cocaine being seized at the retail level increased for some time. The average purity of a kilogram of cocaine ranged between 80% and 83% over the 1990 to 1997 period and has decreased recently to 69% in 2001.[27] Along with the price decline discussed above, this indicates significant amounts of cocaine are still entering the country.

ECONOMIC COSTS

Following the outline of the preceding chapter, we can classify the economic impacts of victimless crimes into one or more of the following categories: negative externalities, net losses, opportunity costs, transfers, and criminal justice system costs. Heroin and cocaine production and consumption generates each of these types of costs.

Negative externalities are imposed on those members of society who are not directly involved in the consumption of heroin or cocaine. Some members of society are offended, distressed, or outraged by *seeing* addicts on the streets. For other members of society, simply *knowing* that people are consuming heroin and cocaine imposes costs. Estimating the value of these negative externalities is very difficult.

Negative externalities are also imposed on the unborn children of pregnant women who continue to use drugs during their pregnancies. **Crack babies and heroin babies** require significant medical care at birth, and in many cases, throughout their entire lives. A 1991 study in the U.S. estimated the cost of prenatal exposure to cocaine to be $32.3 billion in 2005 dollars and for prenatal exposure to heroin the costs were estimated to be $1.9 billion in 2005 dollars.[28]

Net losses in the form of lost labor are imposed on society when **a heroin or cocaine user dies prematurely from an overdose or unsanitary conditions.** Potential productive labor is also lost to the extent that persons who are addicted are unable to work and lead normal lives.[29] If heroin or cocaine users require medical attention that would not otherwise be necessary, this represents additional net costs or losses to society. Property destroyed during a criminal act by a drug user is another example.

The problem of unsanitary conditions among intravenous heroin users is an even greater public health concern with considerable evidence identifying dirty needles used by heroin addicts as an important conduit for the spread of AIDS. In 2001 exposure to drugs accounted for about 31.5% of men living with AIDS and about 38.0% of women living with AIDS.[30] The provision of sterile needles to addicts, so called **needle exchange programs,** as a method to address this problem is controversial, even though it is an alternative being used in parts of the United States, Canada, and Europe.[31] There is some evidence that heroin users are adjusting by smoking and snorting heroin rather than by injecting it.[32]

There are opportunity costs associated with the heroin and cocaine markets, too. Those scarce economic resources, including land, labor, and capital, which are used up in the production and distribution of heroin and cocaine could be devoted to the production of goods and services which are socially desirable. Again, however, we must recognize that while some members of society would rather see those resources used to produce, for example, books or food or televisions, other members of society clearly prefer the production of illegal drugs. We know this because consumers of heroin and cocaine are willing to pay prices which are sufficient to compensate resources for their production.

This brings us to the next category of costs. In some, even many, cases we might wonder how heroin and cocaine consumers are *able* to pay prices which are sufficient to call forth a supply of these drugs. A study of arrested heroin users in 1993 estimated that a weekly "hardcore" heroin user's habit cost $328 per week in 2005 dollars. This amounts to about $17,080 a year.[33] From a study of arrested "hardcore" cocaine users in 1993, it was found that the median weekly expenditure per user on cocaine was $289 in 2005 dollars.[34]

In order to support this expensive habit, for many addicts it is necessary to turn to crime, most often property crime. It has been estimated that one-third to two-thirds of all property offenses in big cities are committed by addicts.[35] In a Detroit study, almost 90 percent of the crack users indicated that they had relied on crime for the money needed to support their habits.[36] This represents a tremendous involuntary transfer of wealth and property.

Critics point out, however, that many of the people involved are not addicts first and criminals second; rather, they are criminals first and addicts second. This suggests that even if heroin and cocaine were free or all addicts could be cured, we would not see a significant decrease in the amount of crime against property.[37] Others question whether the causal relationship between **drugs and property crime** is as strong as is suggested by law enforcement agencies. In part, they point out that increasing the resources allocated by police towards dealing with drug crimes decreases the resources available to combat other types of crime, like property crime. Therefore, the increased property crime may in part be caused by this reallocation, not by the addicts.

Another form of transfer cost is imposed when individuals who earn money in the production and consumption of heroin or cocaine do not pay taxes on their illegally earned income. Those of us who do pay taxes make up for this loss by paying more.

The final cost category is criminal justice system costs. Clearly, we spend billions of dollars a year attempting to enforce laws against heroin and cocaine importation, sale and use. In 2002, 15.5 percent of arrests at the state and local levels were for drug crimes and 34 percent of inmates in prisons and jails are there due to drug abuse. This is an increase since 1987 of more than 55 percent in the proportion of drug arrests.[38] On the federal level, drug offences represented 28 percent of arrests in 2001.[39] The number of drug dealers incarcerated increased twelve fold from 1980 (24,000) to 2004 (325,000) with most of the increase among cocaine dealers.[40] Indirectly, costs are imposed on the criminal justice system and on the entire government to the extent that participants in the markets for illegal drugs bribe and corrupt the police and public officials. This erodes public trust in the criminal justice system and the public sector and may create general disrespect for the law.

Some of the costs we have mentioned are rather easily measured and estimated. A study of drug abuse in 1992 and updated to 2002, originally undertaken by the National Institute on Drug Abuse, estimated the **total cost of drug abuse** to be almost $181 billion for 2002, more than $25 billion less than the cost of alcohol abuse. The largest cost of drug abuse was due to lost productivity associated with premature death, illness and the lost earnings of the incarcerated drug users and the victims of drug-related crimes. The estimated lost productivity cost was $129 billion. Health care expenditures associated with rehabilitation, drug treatment and health problems from the use of the drugs, such as HIV, was estimated to be almost $16 billion, slightly more than half the health care costs of dealing with alcohol abuse. Additional costs associated with drug abuse, primarily associated with the criminal justice system, were estimated to be approximately $36 billion. For drug abusers most of this cost comes from the income generating crimes they commit to be able to purchase their drugs and for the alcohol abusers most of this cost is associated with the violent crimes they commit while under the influence.[41] (See Table 8-1.)

In the study that surveyed the behavior of addicts in New York City discussed earlier, it was found that the daily users of heroin (used heroin six to seven days per week) imposed $55,000 per year of costs on society

TABLE 8–1
ESTIMATED COSTS OF DRUG AND ALCOHOL ABUSE—2002
(MILLIONS OF DOLLARS)

	Drugs	*Alcohol*
Health Expenditures		
Specialty services	$9,076	$ 8,240
Medical Consequences	6,768	20,900
Lost Productivity		
Premature death	24,646	40,280
Illness	35,448	96,700
Crime and victims	68,471	11,140
Other costs		
Criminal justice, etc.	36,413	26,590
Total	$180,822	$203,780

Source: ONDCP, *The Economic Costs of Alcohol and Drug Abuse in the United States—1992-2002* (Washington, DC: Executive Office of the President, December 2004), various tables, and "Estimated Economic Costs of Alcohol Abuse in the United States, 1992 and 1998," (www.niaaa.nih.gov/databases/costs.htm) with adjustment for inflation.

($263,180 in 2005 dollars). Regular users (used heroin three to five days per week) imposed about $32,000 in costs per year ($153,120 in 2005 dollars). Irregular users (used heroin two days per week or less), or dabblers, imposed about $15,000 in costs per year ($71,776 in 2005 dollars). These were costs "in addition" to foregone legal sector employment opportunities, criminal justice system costs, private prevention costs, and psychic costs. Another study estimates "the annual cost of illegal drugs, both monetary and human casualty costs, is comparable to the total ten-year cost of the Vietnam War" which was estimated to cost $342 billion in 2005 dollars.[42]

THE STRUCTURE OF THE HEROIN AND COCAINE INDUSTRIES

While later in this chapter we will be analyzing the heroin and cocaine markets within a supply-and-demand framework, it makes sense to first describe some of the details of the industry and the distribution chain for both heroin and cocaine.

Heroin

Heroin is derived from the opium poppy, which is grown in various parts of the world. Turkey and Southeast Asia used to be the primary sources of heroin for the U.S. market; in the mid-1980s they were replaced by the countries of Southwest Asia and Mexico. With the overthrow of the Taliban in Afghanistan there has been a resurgence of Southeast Asian heroin, but today South American heroin, primarily from Colombia, is estimated to be the source of most of the heroin for the U.S. market.[43] It is also believed that the U.S. market can be separated into three relatively distinct markets based on the source of the heroin. One market encompasses the east coast of the U.S.; one encompasses the U.S. west of the Mississippi River; and the third the mid-west. The east coast market is dominated by heroin from South America, the western market is dominated by Mexican heroin and the mid-west market by Southeast Asia heroin.[44] The basic structure of the heroin industry appears to be very much like the structure of any industry that produces a legal good, though there are a few more steps in the production and distribution processes and it is certainly more hidden from public view.[45] There is the farmer, the provider of the raw material, who grows the opium poppies. Brokers then purchase the opium from the farmers and deliver it to the manufacturers where the raw opium gum is refined into heroin. The refiners use brokers to minimize their exposure in dealing with the large number of farmers who grow the opium. This is important because the refining process is quite capital intensive requiring a great deal of financial resources and therefore they have a great deal to lose.

There is a complex distribution process between the manufacturer of the heroin and the consumer. This process includes those who would be known as importers, wholesalers and retailers in legal markets. The manufacturers either sell their product to or use the services of smuggling syndicates. These are firms that have an expertise in importing the heroin into the U.S. From Southeast Asia it appears that there are two primary groups who dominate this level, the Nigerian syndicate and the Chinese syndicate. From South America, where most of the U.S. heroin comes from, there are the Dominicans who front for the Colombian heroin producers and the Mexicans who bring in their own heroin. At the import level these few large firms appear to have a great deal of monopoly power.

It is felt that organized crime has the tightest grip on the market at this point. **Organized crime** could, of course, be characterized as a large-scale firm which attempts to monopolize particular markets.[46] The question is, why is there **monopoly** at the top? Why are there not a large number of small firms importing heroin? One reason may be the tremendous amount of capital required. This would tend to restrict entry to those with large amounts of capital available for investment in illegal markets. Traditional sources of capital funds would, of course, be unavailable. It may also be that monopoly is necessary at the top in order to make effective "payoffs" to appropriate officials and therefore to decrease risk. Once established, monopoly could be maintained and enforced by means of an effective system of bribery.

It appears that the importers generally become the wholesalers or domestic distributors of the heroin in the U.S. The Mexicans apparently bring their drugs over land through the long border between the U.S. and Mexico with Los Angeles being the headquarters for their domestic distribution throughout the U.S. west of the Mississippi. The Nigerians appear to be headquartered in Chicago and cover the upper Midwest. They, too, use Mexico as an entry port but also use couriers who enter the U.S. via non traditional countries such as Britain and France. The Dominicans bring their heroin in through Florida and New York City where their distribution center covering the east coast is located. The Chinese, who are relatively small participants in the heroin market, operate through the large Chinese communities in San Francisco and New York City. These wholesalers sell their heroin to large quantity dealers/retailers who redistribute the heroin to the smaller cities and towns throughout the U.S.

At the bottom of the distribution chain, the street dealer and "juggler" level, there are many small firms. There are fewer barriers to entry at this level.

First, the capital requirements are smaller. Second, many dealers at his level are also addicts, so their opportunity costs in the legal sector are relatively low. This means a larger supply of retailers. Finally, the stigma of dealing in heroin may be lower at the lower levels, where dealers are also users. This means lower psychic costs of doing business. While there are a larger number of smaller firms at the bottom, it is argued that monopoly power still exists here since sellers have strict territorial rights. Thus, there may be geographic monopolies.

The price of heroin at any level is determined by the interaction of supply and demand. As the heroin moves along the chain of production/distribution, it undergoes a series of price markups. The magnitude of the markup at each successive stage depends on two things: the costs of doing business at that stage, which consist primarily of expected punishment costs; and the ability to pass higher prices on to the next stage (i.e., market power).

As we move down the heroin distribution chain, market power diminishes, so we would expect to see price markups get smaller. On the other hand, the risk of arrest increases because the number and frequency of transactions increases. This does not necessarily mean that expected punishment costs are higher. If they are, however, we would expect to see price markups increase as heroin moves down the chain. Some evidence on pricing and profits is provided in Table 8–2. From the figures we can see the value added at several stages of distribution. Value added represents the difference between costs of materials (price paid at the previous stage) and sale price. The figures suggest either that expected-punishment costs decrease at lower levels or, more likely, that market power diminishes (or both).[47]

The total markup on a given quantity of heroin was recently estimated to be 5,000 times the price received by the farmer in Southeast Asia.[48] This incredible figure is due partly to the fact that the original kilo is diluted by each distributor, usually by 50 percent. In Baltimore it was recently estimated that one-kilo of heroin brought to the city by its large quantity retailers becomes seven-kilos by

TABLE 8–2

ESTIMATED VALUE ADDED AT VARIOUS STAGES OF HEROIN DISTRIBUTION

Importer	200%
Kilo connection	167%
Street dealer	61%
Juggler	35%

the time it reaches the street.[49] This kilo has probably traveled through at least six different countries and changed hands at least 100 times as well.

It is interesting to note that the amount of law enforcement expenditures affects not only the overall price of heroin but also, through its allocation along the distribution chain, the price structure and markups, and ultimately the price on the street. Thus, a given increase in risk, hence in the costs of doing business, at the importer level will cause a larger price increase than the same cost increase at the street level if the importer has greater market power and, therefore, greater ability to pass along a price rise.

Cocaine[50]

Cocaine is derived from the leaves of coca plants which are harvested four times a year. They are primarily found in South America, especially Colombia, Bolivia and Peru. The coca base from the leaves is refined in laboratories which are primarily located in the jungles near where the coca is grown. It is further refined, often in Colombia, into cocaine hydrochloride. The refined cocaine is then imported to the United States leaving via ship from Venezuela, Ecuador and Brazil. There are apparently three main routes for the cocaine to enter the United States. The one that accounts for the majority of the cocaine entering the country goes through Central America and Mexico often entering the U.S. along the 2,000 mile border with Mexico. This route has grown in importance in part due to NAFTA (North American Free Trade Agreement) and the increased trade between Mexico and the U.S. that it generated. The second most important route is through various Caribbean countries and islands including the Dominican Republic, Haiti and Puerto Rico to the major ports along the Gulf and the Atlantic coasts, especially Miami and New York City. The third route is directly to the U.S. without transshipment but this is estimated to account for less than five per cent of the cocaine entering the country. The wholesale and retail distribution in this country is much like that for heroin.

Up until recently the structure of the cocaine industry was characterized as a vertically integrated industry. This meant that the firms in the industry own or control more than one level in the production and distribution process. The major firms in the cocaine industry were involved in the wholesale marketing of the coca base; they owned the refineries; they transported the cocaine to this country; they imported the cocaine into the country and sold it to the major distributors throughout the country, but were not involved in retail sales at the street level; and they were heavily involved in laundering the money that derives from these activities. Some independent domestic refining of the cocaine occured in laboratories principally located in south Florida, with others in New York, California, and several other states.[51]

Another characteristic of the industry during the period of rapid growth was its **oligopolistic structure.** It was an industry dominated by a relatively small number of large firms. Since there was apparently **collusion** among the firms with respect to market share, price, confronting law enforcement efforts, and dealing with the political environment, the cocaine oligopoly was believed to have operated as a **cartel** or several cartels. The major cartels were centered in Colombia, and were the source of between 75 and 80% of the cocaine imported to this country,[52] with the headquarters of the major cartels in Medellin, Cali, and Bogota. There were apparently a total of 20 "families" in the Medellin cartel, with four dominant families. The development of the cartels, and their ability to grow, was due in part to the willingness of the cartels to use violence,[53] political pressure, and to take advantage of the economic conditions in the countries in which they operate. The growing U.S. demand for cocaine was also an important factor.

During the early 1990s law enforcement efforts in Latin America led to a change in the industry. Direct competition to the Colombian based firms, e.g., the Medellin and Cali cartels, in the production and importing of cocaine developed in Bolivia. Mexican based crime groups also began to dominate the wholesale distribution of cocaine throughout the western and midwestern U.S. Peru remained the largest producer of coca leaf, coca paste and cocaine base, but Colombia increased its production of leaf and base, thus increased the degree of vertical integration in the cocaine industry there.[54]

The mid to late 1990s saw a more dramatic change in the industry in part due to additional law enforcement efforts, including the incarceration of two leaders of Colombia's cartels. The big change was not in the production of cocaine since the firms in Colombia still dominate this aspect of the industry, but it was in the importation of cocaine to the U.S. and the distribution of it in the U.S. A number of firms entered this aspect of the industry from those who were already involved in other aspects, such as ones in Peru and Bolivia who had previously been primarily involved in the production of cocaine base. In addition firms from Italy, Nigeria, Russia and the Ukraine have entered and are involved in the cocaine market in the U.S. and other parts of the world. Perhaps the biggest gainers associated with the decline of the Colombian cartels were the Mexican cartels, one located in Juarez and the other in Tijuana, who apparently controlled more than three-quarters of the importation of cocaine into the U.S. and one-third of the cocaine market in the country in the early part of the 21st century.[55]

TABLE 8–3

COCAINE PRICES THROUGH THE DISTRIBUTION CHAIN, (2004 DOLLARS)

At the farm (Colombia, per kg)[1]	$1.80
Refined base (Colombia, per kg)[1]	807
Wholesale (100 pure grams or more, per kg)[2]	27,260
Mid level distributor (10 to 100 pure grams)[2]	56,140
Retail (1-gram units)[2]	247,950

Source: [1]United Nations, Office on Drugs and Crime, "World Drug Report 2005" (www.unodc.org/unodc/en/world_drug_report.html), 63.
[2]Office of National Drug Control Policy, "The Price of Illicit Drugs: 1981 through the Second Quarter of 2001," October 2001, Table 1, 30, adjusted to 2004 dollars.

As we discussed above in the market for heroin, the price of cocaine at any level in the chain of production/distribution is a function of the interaction between supply and demand. Again, the magnitude of the price markups is due to the costs of doing business at each stage, and the market power of the firms, i.e., their ability to pass along higher prices. The information in Table 8–3 suggests that considerable markups exist at various levels.

The estimated $8 billion in annual earnings for the Colombian cartels in 1986 ($14.2 billion in 2005 dollars), which was more than the gross national product of one-third of the world's countries, was very important to the maintenance of the cartels.[56] In Medellin, where the average police officer earned $160 per month[57] at that time and the earnings of others were equally low, it was not difficult to understand the cartel's ability to operate with little pressure from local law enforcement officials or to hire people to work for them. It is also not difficult to understand the importance to the entire country's economy of that much U.S. currency entering the country. This provided the cartels and the current drug firms with a good deal of political leverage at the national level as well. A 1999 estimate of the illegal drug trade in Colombia places its annual value at between 25 percent and 33 percent of the country's total exports.[58]

In this country the domestic distribution of cocaine[59] at the wholesale level is dominated by Mexican and Colombian criminal groups with Dominican groups playing a significant, but smaller, role, especially in the northeast. The retail level is dominated by various ethnic gangs who have expanded beyond their traditional urban neighborhoods to establish national distribution networks. Powder cocaine is distributed at the retail level by African American and Hispanic gangs along with local independent dealers who tend to be Caucasian, Cuban, Haitian or Puerto Rican. The retail distribution of crack cocaine which is primarily found in metropolitan areas, especially the inner city and lower income neighborhoods, is also dominated by African American and Hispanic gangs. There is also evidence that Haitian, Jamaican, Puerto Rican, Cuban, Mexican, Middle Eastern, Dominican and Pacific Islander groups are involved in the retail distribution of crack cocaine in U.S. cities. Many of these gangs are comprised of recent immigrants (legal and otherwise) who are apparently more willing to use violence to obtain control of the market than their predecessors. They, too, are apparently willing to "buy" protection from U.S. law enforcement officials and a virtually unlimited supply of employees with the money they earn from their business.

A study of the economics of a drug selling inner-city neighborhood gang in a large industrial U.S. city provides some interesting insights into the operation of the cocaine market, primarily for crack cocaine.[60] The study was based on a local or neighborhood gang that existed for four years but which no longer exists. It was part of a city-wide structure led by approximately 16 people whose responsibilities included long-term strategies for the organization; maintaining relationships with suppliers; recruitment of new members; and punishment. There were approximately 100 similar local gangs covering the city's neighborhoods. In many ways the structure of this market is similar to that of a legal franchised company, like McDonalds. Here, the local gang leaders make payments to the central leadership, the franchisers, which provides the local gang with: protection both for its market (i.e., turf) and in prison; stable relationships with neighboring gangs, other franchisees; access to wholesale drug dealers; and the opportunity for advancement in the organization.

The local gang in the study had a leader, three officers below him and the street dealers or 'foot soldiers.' The officers had the responsibilities for providing: safety for the gang, the 'enforcer;' management of the gang's liquid assets, the 'treasurer;' and transportation of large quantities of both drugs and money, the 'runner.' The street dealers reported to the enforcer and numbered between 25 and 75 over the four year period.

Over the years there has been evidence that in Los Angeles, "pee-wees" (children nine to eleven years old) earned $400 per week ($657 in 2005 dollars) as look-outs and sales people, other evidence suggests that the get-rich-quick image for low-level operatives in the cocaine industry is not entirely accurate.[61] The evidence suggests that most of the people work long hours, in some cases dealers have customers coming 24 hours a day, for six or seven days a week, in a climate dominated by physical threat. The long hours of work often lead to low hourly wages. A study of lookouts in East Harlem (New York City) identified some who made only $30 ($49 in 2005 dollars) for a 12 hour work day, which was considerably less than the minimum wage. Another study in Washington, D.C., estimated the median hourly earnings of street-level dealers to be $30 ($49 in 2005 dollars), which was significantly higher than the $7 ($11.16 in 2005 dollars) per hour median found for their legal sector jobs, but "few of the street-level dealers . . . reported the kinds of incomes from which Mercedes and great fortunes spring."[62]

The study of the inner-city cocaine dealing local gang found that the only one who earned significantly more than the minimum wage on an hourly basis and considerably more than what he could have earned in the legal sector, given his education and experience, was the leader of the local gang. During the study period he earned between $4,200 and $10,900 per month (in 1995 dollars, or $5,360 and $13,910 in 2005 dollars). The three officers each earned approximately $1,000 per month[63] ($1,276 in 2005 dollars) or only slightly more than the minimum wage. The street dealers in this study only worked approximately 20 hours per week selling drugs and earned about $200 per month ($255 in 2005 dollars) which was well below the federal minimum wage at that time.[64] They survived by living at home and working in low level service sector legal jobs.

MARKET CHARACTERISTICS

Analytically we can describe the markets for heroin and cocaine in similar terms, focusing first on the demand side of the market, and then on the supply side.

Demand

The market demand for heroin or cocaine by consumers as a group can be derived from each individual's demand for the drug.[65] While tastes for the product differ from one individual to another, for purposes of analysis, heroin and cocaine users can be broadly grouped into two distinct markets: addicts and "dabblers." Users in the addict market are physiologically or psychologically dependent on the drug. In the extreme, this means that a certain amount of the product must be consumed per time period, regardless of price. Translating this into a demand curve yields a perfectly price inelastic curve as illustrated in Figure 8–1.

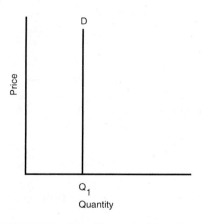

Figure 8-1 The Demand for Heroin (Cocaine) by Addicts

Regardless of price, addicts as a group demanded Q_1 units of heroin (cocaine) per time period.

For the addicted users, tolerance for the drug increases with usage. This means that with the passage of time demand increases and the inelastic demand curve shifts outward to the right as taste (tolerance) for the drug increases as illustrated in Figure 8–2.

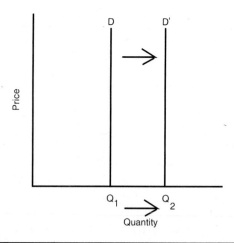

Figure 8-2 The Demand for Heroin (Cocaine) by Addicts

After the increase in demand, the addict market requires and demands Q_2 units of heroin (cocaine) per time period, regardless of price.

The high degree of inelasticity of the addict demand suggests that there are no good substitutes for the product. An interesting empirical question is, what is the real value of the price elasticity of demand by addicts? Is it different for individuals addicted to heroin as compared to those addicted to cocaine? Is it truly zero? As we will see, design of an optimum public policy depends, in part, on this value. It is the addicted user who generates most of the economic costs to society associated with heroin or cocaine consumption-costs in the form of negative externalities, lost labor, medical resource costs, involuntary transfers of property, and criminal justice system costs.

The other segment of the heroin and cocaine markets is the "dabbler" market. Dabblers are experimental, infrequent, or potential users. For this group, the demand for the drug can be represented by a standard, negatively sloped demand curve as illustrated in Figure 8–3.

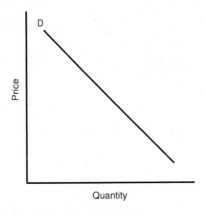

Figure 8–3 The Demand for Heroin (Cocaine) by Dabblers

At relatively high prices, dabblers demand relatively few units of heroin (cocaine) per time period. As price decreases, quantity demanded increases. The position of the demand curve is affected by the usual determinants of demand (i.e., consumers' tastes and incomes, prices of substitute goods, and prices of complements). For dabblers, there *are* substitutes for heroin (cocaine), including alcohol and other drugs. A change in the price of any of these goods will change consumers' demand and shift the demand curve. When marijuana prices rose in the mid-1970s as a result of "Operation Intercept," some consumers shifted to heroin, thereby increasing the demand for heroin. For dabblers, as compared to addicts, the economic costs to society of heroin (cocaine) consumption are relatively small. The typical dabbler is inconspicuous, leads an otherwise normal and productive life, and does not have to steal property to buy the product. Why, then, should we concern ourselves with their consumption of heroin (cocaine)? The obvious answer is that some, but not all, dabblers become addicts.

Supply

On the supply side of the market, there are also some interesting complications. Within the heroin and cocaine industries there is monopoly power, at least at the upper stages of distribution and perhaps all the way down to the street level.[66] Monopoly in the sellers' market means restricted output in order to maintain high prices and maximize profits. Oddly enough, since heroin and cocaine are social "bads," restricted output via monopoly power is beneficial to society. From a public-policy point of view, we may want to encourage monopoly in the heroin and cocaine markets. Perhaps we are better off if organized crime distributes heroin and cocaine than if the industry is competitive.[67] Before we come to this conclusion, however, we must note some qualifications. To understand these, we will first compare market outcomes when the industry is competitive with market outcomes when the industry is monopolized. Initially we assume that supply conditions are the same regardless of market structure; that is, the market supply curve is the same whether there is one large supplier or a thousand small ones.[68]

The market demand curve in Figure 8.4 is represented by D, which measures the average revenue (AR) to the monopolist. The marginal revenue (MR) to the monopolist lies below the average revenue and is indicated by the curve labeled MR_m. Under competitive conditions, Q_c units will be produced and will be sold at a price of P_c per unit. On the other hand, if the industry is monopolized, only Q_m units will be produced and will be sold at the higher price, P_m. Thus, monopoly restricts output and thereby reduces the consumption of heroin (cocaine). However, this assumes that supply, or cost conditions, are the same under the two market structures.

What if there are **economies of scale** in the production and/or distribution of heroin (cocaine)? This means that average and marginal costs of doing business decrease with increased size of the producers in the industry. As a result, a large monopolist's costs will be lower than those for a collection of smaller firms.[69] Therefore, the comparison made in Figure 8–4 is no longer valid. A different supply characterizes the monopolist's behavior so that a separate supply curve must be indicated for the monopolist.

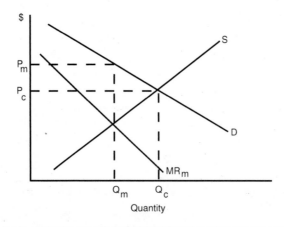

Figure 8–4 The Heroin (Cocaine) Market: Competition versus Monopoly (1)

In Figure 8–5, S_c represents the supply curve for the **competitive industry** while S_m represents the supply curve of the monopolist. Notice that we have drawn S_m considerably below S_c, indicating substantial economies of scale. Notice that now, because we have indicated such substantial economies, the output under competition, Q_c, is less than the output under monopoly, Q_m. Relative prices are also reversed. The competitive price, P_c, exceeds the monopoly price, P_m. Thus, whether or not we want to encourage monopoly in the heroin and cocaine markets depends very much on the existence and extent of economies of scale.

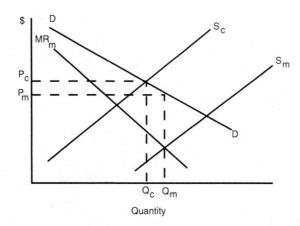

Figure 8–5 The Heroin (Cocaine) Market: Competition versus Monopoly (2)

There is one further consideration. We suggested earlier in the chapter that street dealers, while large in number, may have geographic monopolies. If there are strict territorial rights and if dealers know the needs (tastes) of the consumers within their territories, then the dealers may operate as perfectly discriminating monopolists.[70] That is, they charge each consumer a different price, depending on how badly each buyer needs the heroin (cocaine). The seller charges each customer the maximum amount that each will pay. Under these circumstances the market outcome is again different. Assuming no economies of scale, we can compare competition with a perfectly discriminating monopolist in Figure 8–6.

Now the market demand curve, D, represents marginal revenue to the monopolist, MR_m. Because of this, under either market structure we get the same output and consumption of heroin (cocaine): Q_c equals Q_m. Which, then, would we prefer? This time we would prefer competition because, while the output is the same, the price, P_c, is lower than that which would be charged under monopoly. Remember, the price charged by the monopolist is different to different customers and therefore is not labeled in Figure 8–6. We know, however, that the average price charged is higher than P_c, since P_c is the lowest price the monopolist charges to the last, least needy, customer. Lower prices under competition would mean cheaper habits and less property crime by addicts.

The worst of all possible worlds would be a perfectly discriminating monopolist with economies of scale. We leave it to the reader to illustrate this possibility. The outcome, however should be clear: the monopoly output would exceed the competitive one and would exceed Q_m in Figure 8–6.

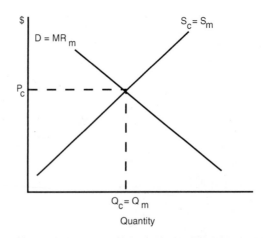

Figure 8–6 The Heroin (Cocaine) Market: Competition versus Monopoly (3)

PUBLIC POLICY OPTIONS

The optimum public policy toward the market for illegal drugs is difficult to formulate. The choice depends on a comparison of the costs and benefits of alternative approaches. It may be that the best policy is a combination of approaches blended in a complementary way. In the following sections we review the policy options available for dealing with the heroin and cocaine markets and analyze the impact of each. It may be that what is appropriate for one market may not be appropriate for the other.

Restricting Supply

Both federal and local law enforcement efforts have attempted to restrict the supply of heroin and cocaine. Approximately 60 percent of the $12.2 billion budgeted by the federal government in FY 2005 on drug control was for **supply reduction**.[71] Past attempts with heroin include efforts to break the kilo connection links in international efforts, federal purchase of foreign crops or subsidies to farmers not to produce, and local efforts to increase risk and, therefore, the costs of doing business to weight dealers, street dealers, and jugglers. Recent efforts to stem the flow of cocaine have also included financial and U.S. military support for other countries' efforts to eliminate the cultivation of coca and the laboratories where it is processed to make cocaine. An example of the role of the U.S. military was its invasion of Panama in December 1989 to "arrest" the country's president, Manuel Noriega, on trafficking charges. In 2001 there were hundreds of U.S. troops and military contractors in South America, especially Colombia, fighting a guerrilla war and spending $1.3 billion as part of the U.S.'s counter drug policy.[72]

The primary focus of current federal efforts to restrict the supply of heroin, and especially cocaine, have been aimed at blocking its importation into the country by using a great deal of resources to close our borders. In April 1986, President Reagan signed the National Security Decision Directive on Narcotics and National Security directing all federal agencies, including the Department of Defense, to more actively counter narcotics smuggling into the United States. Early congressional support for this effort amounted to providing $700 million in an attempt to seal the country's borders.[73] The federal budget request for fiscal year 2005 included more than $2.7 billion to be spent in attempting to seal the borders.[74] Heightened border security since the events of 9/11 has had the additional affect of strengthening drug supply restriction efforts at the borders, though it is still a difficult task. U.S. Customs estimates that almost 11.3 million trucks, 121.4 million vehicles and 468 million passengers and pedestrians entered the country in FY 2004.[75]

Additionally, a reduction in the supply of drugs can be obtained by increasing the costs of production. Seizing the money and property (e.g., boats, airplanes, and land) belonging to drug traffickers and others is a way to increase the costs to the offender that is gaining in popularity. There is an additional incentive for law enforcement agencies to seize property since they are allowed to retain some of the financial gain from the sale of the seized property or retain the property for their own use. From 1985 through 1991, approximately $2.6 billion in cash and property had been obtained in more than 35,000 federal seizures. The amount had increased in value 18 times over those six years. From FY 1992 through 1995, the Drug Enforcement Administration, alone, seized almost $2.9 billion in assets. In 2003 the DEA made almost sixteen thousand seizures valued at almost $458 million.[76] State and local law enforcement agencies have their own forfeiture programs based on state laws. Considerable criticism of the use of **civil forfeiture** has come from judges, legislators, and citizens groups. Two reasons for it are that civil forfeiture is a sanction that does not require the individual to be convicted or even charged with a crime. Also, it may create a financial incentive for law enforcement agencies that may distort their efforts to fairly enforce all the laws, not just the drug laws.[77] These factors have lead to reforms in the federal statute on civil asset forefeiture.

While initially any reduction in supply may be reflected in decreased access to the drug (i.e., it will take longer to make a buy), ultimately the supply shift will be reflected in increased prices and/or decreased quality. Presumably, the intention of restricting supply is to decrease consumption of the product. However, the effectiveness of this approach depends on what the demand for the drug looks like; more specifically, it depends on the price elasticity of demand for the drug.[78] Figure 8–7 illustrates the impact of a supply reduction in each of the two submarkets—addicts and dabblers.

In the dabbler market, a reduction in supply is illustrated by a shift in the supply curve from S to S′. Before the reduction, the price of heroin (cocaine) was P_1 and consumption by dabblers was Q_1. Because of the reduction in supply, price increases to P_2 and consumption decreases to Q_2. Thus, our law enforcement efforts are successful to the extent that consumption has been reduced. However, in the addict market something very different happens. There, the same supply reduction leads to increased price, from P_1 to P_3.[79] Because the demand curve is perfectly price inelastic, consumption, or quantity demanded, does not respond to the price change. Addicts continue to consume Q_1 units of heroin (cocaine) per time period. The only thing that has changed is the cost of the addicts' habits, which has become more

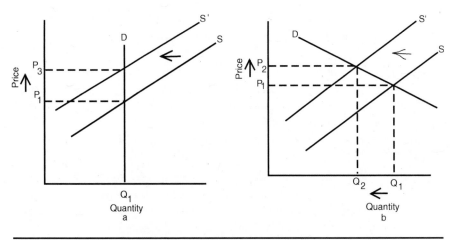

Figure 8–7 The Addict Market (a) and the Dabbler Market (b)

expensive. It is likely, therefore, that our law enforcement approach has indirectly led to increased crime by addicts. This hardly seems a desirable result; unfortunately, however, any program which reduces supply in general is going to have such an impact.

Additionally, a policy of interdiction at the borders, which reduces the supply at the wholesale level by increasing the risks and therefore the costs of importing drugs, apparently has little impact on retail prices. The cost of importing cocaine has been estimated to be less than one-tenth its retail price, so a 50 percent increase in the wholesale cost will increase retail prices by less than five percent.[80] Perhaps what we need is an approach which leads to increased prices, and, therefore, decreased consumption, in the dabbler market and at the same time leads to reduced price, and therefore, less crime, in the addict market. That is, price discrimination appears desirable.

Price Discrimination

For **price discrimination** to be practiced in any market, certain conditions must exist. First, the seller(s) must have some degree of monopoly power. If the market is competitive and a seller attempts to charge certain customers more than others, those buyers who are being discriminated against will simply shop elsewhere. Earlier we argued that sellers of heroin (cocaine) do have monopoly power, perhaps even at the street level. If so, price discrimination can be practiced.

The second condition for price discrimination is that there must be separate markets with different price elasticities of demand. If the submarkets have essentially similar demand functions, with the same price elasticity at various prices, there is no point in charging different prices. In the heroin (cocaine) market as we have described it, there clearly exist different submarkets with different price elasticities, so price discrimination would be desirable from the seller's point of view.

Finally, for price discrimination to work it is necessary that the submarkets be kept apart or that the cost of keeping the markets separate be relatively low. If not, those buyers who are receiving the same product at a lower price will turn around and resell excess product to those customers who are being charged a higher price. How truly separate the addict and dabbler markets are is unclear. As we will see, the problem of keeping these markets apart is a major obstacle to designing effective public policy.

Assuming for the moment that the markets can be kept separate, at least to some extent, it is interesting to note how price discrimination in the market would work. With all the necessary conditions to make price discrimination practical and profitable, heroin (cocaine) dealers would charge different prices to different customers. Generally, higher prices would be charged to addicts and lower prices to dabblers.[81] Notice that this is just the opposite of what we might like to see: lower prices to dabblers would encourage consumption, while higher prices to addicts would lead to more crime!

In the absence of some sort of intervention by the public sector, this kind of undesirable price discrimination is likely. The question is, is it possible to turn the price discrimination around? Is there some law enforcement approach which we could use to encourage price discrimination in the other direction? One suggestion is to have more undercover police agents on the street making buys. The idea is that by doing this we would increase the risk of selling to unknown buyers. Therefore, dealers would attempt to decrease their risk by selling in larger volume, with fewer transactions, to regular buyers. The effect is to reduce the supply to dabblers and to increase it to addicts, thereby raising prices to dabblers[82] and reducing them to addicts. Dabbler consumption would be reduced as a result. The effectiveness of this approach would depend on the extent to which the dabblers are kept separate from the addicts. Increasing the risk to sellers would mean higher costs for law enforcement. This expense must be weighed against the advantage of reduced consumption by dabblers and lower prices to addicts.

Law Enforcement on the Demand Side

An alternative law enforcement approach would focus on the demand side of the market in an effort to reduce the demand for heroin or cocaine. Approximately forty percent of the federal government's FY 2005 budget of $12.2 billion for drug control was targeted toward demand reduction programs.[83] The advantage of this approach, if it is effective, is that prices are reduced while consumption by dabblers is decreased. Figure 8–8 illustrates how this happens. The demand curve, D, represents the total demand for heroin (cocaine) by both addicts and dabblers.[84] We now assume that we focus law enforcement efforts on the demand size of the market. That is, we increase the expected-punishment costs to buyers of heroin (cocaine). As we argued in the previous chapter, increasing the expected-punishment costs of buying illegal goods may be looked at as an increase in transaction costs, a complementary good. As the price of the complementary good is increased, demand decreases and the demand curve shifts downward. Thus, increased law enforcement efforts on the demand side of the market would lead to a decrease in demand and a shift from D to D'.

The impact on the market is interesting. The quantity bought and sold is reduced from Q_1 to Q_2, while price drops from P_1 to P_2. The reduction in consumption is, of course, desirable. Since the addicts' demand is insensitive to price (i.e., perfectly price inelastic), it is also insensitive to changes in the

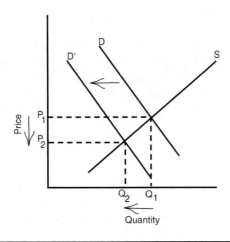

Figure 8–8 The Heroin (Cocaine) Market: A Demand Shift

price of a complementary good.[85] Therefore, the change in demand must be a result of decreased demand by dabblers. The reduction in consumption is due to reduced consumption by dabblers; addicts are still buying the same amount. Because of this, the reduction in price is desirable. Addicts can now support their habit at a lower cost.

How likely is it that this policy would be effective? Remember that it is the dabbler demand which is subject to change and that therefore this is the portion of the market which must be approached. How easy is it to increase expected-punishment costs to dabblers? These are the infrequent or experimental users, who are harder to identify and therefore harder to arrest. We could increase penalties to dabblers, and this would serve to increase expected-punishment costs; but how popular would this be with the public? The public may resist a program which involves increased penalties to dabblers but not to addicts! After all, the addicts' consumption is more harmful to society.

A variation on this approach is incarceration of addicts—sometimes called "street sweep" programs. While increased expected-punishment costs may not deter addicts, incapacitation through incarceration will reduce the demand for heroin (cocaine) during the incarceration period. Whether or not this is an efficient way to fight drug problems depends on the costs of such programs compared with the benefits.

The Medical Approach

There is another approach that would also attempt to change the addicts' demand. The argument is that the addicts' demand may be insensitive to price and income but will respond to a change in tastes. That is, medical approaches are used to reduce the physiological dependence of heroin addicts and the psychological dependence of cocaine addicts. If it is effective, addicts' taste for heroin or cocaine is reduced and the addicts' demand decreases shifting the curve to the left. Ideally, the entire market disappears and consumption by addicts is reduced from Q_1 to Q_2, where Q_2 is equal to zero as illustrated in Figure 8–9.

This approach would seem to solve our problems, but it has some drawbacks. First, it is extremely expensive.[86] This expense must be weighed against the value of reducing the consumption of heroin (cocaine). Second, and of more immediate concern, there is the problem of low success rates. Various studies indicate relapse rates of 90 to 95 percent for heroin addicts. This means that the reduction in demand is only temporary. Once the

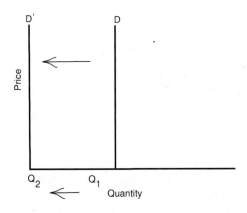

Figure 8–9 The Heroin (Cocaine) Market: Addict Demand Shift

treated addict has been separated from the treatment facility or program, the taste for heroin increases again. Perhaps the medical approach must be expanded to include or treat other aspects of dependence on the drug besides physiological ones. That is, to reduce tastes permanently it may be necessary to alter the addict's social or economic environment. A twelve year follow-up of approximately 400 male heroin addicts admitted between 1969 and 1972 to 18 multimodality treatment centers throughout the country found that only 25 percent never relapsed to daily use during the follow-up period.[87]

Beyond that, it may be necessary to combine the medical approach with a law enforcement effort to reduce availability of the drug. Higher prices and reduced supply to a newly treated addict may be effective. Finally, even if the medical approach works, there remains the problem of the dabbler market. Clearly, the medical approach must be coupled with other efforts to reduce consumption by dabblers. However, with addicts eliminated from the market it would be much easier to deal with dabblers.

The federal government has allocated considerable resources to the treatment of people who use illegal drugs. In fiscal year 1981 it spent $514 million ($1.1 billion in 2005 dollars). This was approximately one-third the **total spent by the federal government on drug control** at that time. The fiscal year 2005 budget included a request for $3.1 billion to be spent on treatment. This is a significant increase over 1981, but represents approximately 25 percent of the drug control budget request for 2005.[88]

Methadone Maintenance

If traditional medical approaches are ineffective, it may be possible to reduce the addicts' demand for heroin artificially; that is, through a maintenance program using methadone or one of four other drugs. (For the cocaine addict there is no methadone equivalent substitute.) If a legal, low-cost substitute for heroin is provided, perhaps the demand for heroin can be reduced. If this approach is completely effective, the impact will be the same as that illustrated in Figure 8–9: addicts' consumption of heroin will be reduced to zero. In its place, addicts are consuming methadone, an artificial substance which blocks the craving for, and the "high" from, heroin.

Methadone has been in use in the U.S. for more than 30 years and has been found to have significant benefits to both the addict and to society. Properly medicated addicts under a doctor's supervision are able to live a relatively normal life since it is not sedating or intoxicating. Studies have found it to be a cost-effective substitute for incarceration with an overall benefit-cost ratio of 4:1. Its use has led to significant reductions in various diseases associated with heroin use including HIV/AIDS, hepatitis and sexually transmitted diseases. It has been found to decrease the criminal activity of its users by half since they no longer need to commit crimes to support their habits. It has also been found to increase the users full-time employment by almost 25 percent.[89]

As with any program, there are some problems with methadone maintenance. First, some would argue that it is just as bad to consume methadone as it is to consume heroin, and therefore this program has no advantages. That is, for some individuals the negative externalities generated by methadone consumption are as great as those generated by heroin consumption. Nevertheless, the costs to society are lower with methadone maintenance to the extent that individuals can consume methadone and otherwise lead healthy, productive lives. Providing methadone free or at a low price would mean cheaper maintenance for addicts and a reduction in the number of crimes committed by addicts.

A second problem centers on the question of how effective a substitute methadone really is. If it is not a close substitute for heroin, making the product available at very low prices or even giving it away will not reduce the addicts' demand for heroin. There is some evidence that only the older, "burnt-out" addicts find methadone an attractive alternative. Admissions data from 1983 for methadone maintenance programs in 23 states and the District of Columbia found that almost 62 percent were 30 years old or older, while only 52 percent of clients entering alternative programs were in the same age cohort. Additionally it was found that more than 22 percent between 30 and

44, and more than 35 percent over the age of 44 reported having used heroin for more than 25 years.[90] Therefore, it is likely that methadone maintenance will be effective for only a portion of the addict market and additional ways of dealing with the problem will have to be implemented.

How effective a substitute methadone is may depend on the circumstances under which it is consumed. If the addict is forced to take the methadone orally in a very controlled, clinical situation, it may not be attractive. If however, its consumption is not regulated, methadone may become a better substitute for heroin. But as it becomes a better substitute it may also become more of a problem to society. If methadone is misused, it too can lead to reduced productivity or death.

Additionally, if methadone can be readily substituted for heroin, then it will be attractive not only to addicts but also to dabblers. Then we must go back to the problem of how to keep the two markets separate, unless we argue that methadone consumption is costless to society and that increased consumption by dabblers is therefore of no concern. If we want to keep dabblers from consuming methadone, then what we are really condoning, again, is price discrimination: make methadone available to addicts but not to dabblers. With a public monopoly over the product, this can be accomplished if the two markets can be kept separate. However, accounts of abuses in the black market for methadone suggest that such separation is difficult to maintain.[91]

A final problem with a methadone maintenance program is its impact on the heroin market. If the program is successful, demand for heroin by addicts will be reduced and heroin prices will drop. This means that consumption by dabblers will increase unless methadone maintenance is coupled with a law enforcement effort to reduce the supply of heroin and increase heroin prices to dabblers. As heroin prices rise, the quantity demanded by dabblers will decrease.

Drug Maintenance

If methadone is not an attractive enough substitute for heroin, and since there is no similar substitute for cocaine, then why not use heroin (cocaine) in a maintenance program, as is done in Britain?[92] Here the intent is not necessarily to reduce addicts' demand for the drug but to satisfy that demand legally by providing the drug under somewhat controlled circumstances, either free or at a low price.[93]

The possible advantages are several: to the extent that consumption circumstances are controlled, premature death from overdose or unsanitary conditions can be avoided; when the heroin is regularly available, a large problem of uncertainty is removed from the addict's daily life, perhaps allowing the addict to lead a more normal existence; since the drug would be free or relatively inexpensive, the need to commit crimes in order to support an expensive habit is removed; and "strings" can be tied to the continued receipt of the drugs which could include counseling, regular medical examinations, and proof that the addict is living a lifestyle that is not harmful to either himself/herself or society.

On the other hand, there are some problems with this approach. First, we again have the problem of negative externalities. Since the addicts would continue to consume drugs, the negative externalities generated by that consumption would continue, although they would be reduced to the extent that monitored consumption is more acceptable. Somewhat offsetting this reduction might be public concern over a government-sponsored program which hands out drugs. A second problem is whether or not a maintenance program can be a close substitute for heroin or cocaine purchased and consumed illegally and clandestinely. Can equally "attractive" conditions for consumption be provided in a sterile clinic? If, to make the maintenance program attractive, injection at the clinic is not required, how is resale to other users avoided? This gets us back to the problem of keeping dabblers and addicts separate. Again, the intent is to practice price discrimination by providing drugs to addicts at low or zero price while maintaining or even increasing the price paid by dabblers. As with methadone maintenance, it would be necessary to increase law enforcement efforts in the illegal (dabbler) market for drugs in order to reduce supply and raise prices there.

Legalization

A final, perhaps extreme, alternative is to **legalize the heroin (cocaine) market,** or at least **decriminalize** it. Legalization can take a variety of forms. It can be a market that is essentially free of government intervention, similar to the market for most U.S. consumer goods. It can be a market in which the government has a significant role guaranteeing product quality, restricting who can sell or buy the product, or marketing the product on its own. Decriminalization, which can also take many forms is generally when possession of a drug for use by an individual is legal or mildly punished with its sale remaining illegal.[94]

For a period of almost 50 years, starting in 1924, the United Kingdom decriminalized drug use, but this policy[95] was abandoned in 1968 to deal with a growing number of addicts. The British experience suggests that legalization or decriminalization could lead to an increase in demand.[96] Today, the British have two policies in place. One focuses on supply reduction with criminal sanctions. The other is a program of decriminalization for users incorporating a social services approach to the addicts' problems.[97] Drug policies in the Netherlands are very similar to the British.[98] Drug use is viewed as a public health problem and drug laws are used to reduce the supply of drugs. Demand reduction is integrated into all the country's social programs with an emphasis on creating more market separation among drug users, in order to prevent 'soft' drug users from switching over to 'hard' drugs. For example, soft drug users are able to purchase soft drugs in a setting apart from the criminal underworld, where they would otherwise be exposed to hard drugs.

It has only been since the late 1980s that serious consideration of legalization or decriminalization has taken place in this country. This was brought about, at least in part, by the increased costs to society of the crime, especially violent crime, associated with the cocaine industry. Today economists, like Nobel Laureates Milton Friedman and Gary Becker, political commentators, like William F. Buckley, Jr., politicians, like former Baltimore Mayor Kurt Schmoke, and others are voicing their support for repealing the drug-prohibition laws.[99]

As we saw in the preceding chapter, legalization or decriminalization of heroin (cocaine) would lead to changes in both demand and supply. Both would increase, shifting the curves to the right. Consumption increases from Q_1 to Q_2, and price may drop from P_1 to P_2. Since consumption of the product increases, the costs to society generated by that consumption increase. On the one hand, expenditures by the criminal justice system to enforce laws against heroin (cocaine) would be reduced. Since the price drops in Figure 8–10, there may be less crime by addicts. On the other hand, there will be more consumers. It is not necessary for the price to drop. If the change in demand exceeds the change in supply, the new price will be higher.

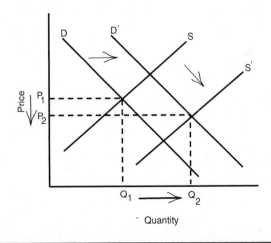

Figure 8–10 The Heroin (Cocaine) Market: Legalization

How much the demand and supply change is an empirical question that can only be answered after legalization or decriminalization takes place.[100] We do know, however, that regardless of which change is larger, the quantity bought and sold will increase. While we save criminal justice costs, the increased consumption is undesirable. It should be noted that in Britain and the Netherlands, where drug use is decriminalized, addiction rates were estimated to be .062 percent and .15 percent, respectively, while in the U.S. the addiction rate was estimated to be .21 percent of the population.[101] Also, it should be noted that in the ten years immediately following the repeal of Prohibition in the U.S. homicide decreased by more than one-third, and assaults with firearms decreased by more than 40 percent.[102]

One way to avoid the possibility of increased consumption is to legalize or decriminalize heroin (cocaine) and then subject it to taxation.[103] The tax could be imposed on buyers or sellers or both. A tax on buyers will decrease demand and shift the demand curve downward, while a tax on suppliers will decrease supply and shift the supply curve to the left. Both changes are in the direction of reduced consumption. By designing an appropriate tax scheme, we could decrease supply and demand until the amount consumed and the price would be the same as it was prior to legalization (what was originally shown in Figure 8–10).

If we think about it, imposing a tax on buyer and seller is very similar to what we do now, except that the tax (penalty) is paid with uncertainty and, rather than generating revenue, costs us money for criminal justice system expenditures. Legalization or decriminalization with taxes, then, may leave heroin (cocaine) market prices and consumption unchanged but may save us law enforcement expenditures and provide us with tax revenues. The law enforcement savings depend on the enforcement costs of dealing with the black market that is likely to develop.

There is one final consideration with regard to legalization or decriminalization. As discussed in the preceding chapter, legalization may change the market structure; that is, it may lead to increased competition in the industry. Whether or not this will happen depends on whether there are effective barriers to entry into the industry. If there are substantial economies of scale which are not removed with legalization or decriminalization, then competition will not increase. As pointed out earlier in this chapter, competition in this market may or may not be desirable.

In the next chapter we turn to a discussion of a crime problem which is often associated with "victimless" crimes: organized crime. As we will see, however, to get an accurate assessment of the impact of organized crime and develop rational policies for dealing with the problem, it is necessary to separate organized crime per se from the products in which it deals.

REVIEW TERMS AND CONCEPTS

Addicts
Average revenue
Barriers to entry
Black market
Capital
Cartel
Civil asset forfeiture
Coca
Collusion
Costs and benefits
Criminal justice system costs
Dabbler market
Dabblers
Decriminalization
Distribution stages
Drug maintenance
Economies of scale
Expected punishment costs
Exports
Fiscal year
Franchise
Geographic monopoly
Gross national product (GNP)
Importer
Juggler
Kilo connection
Legalization
Liquid assets
Marginal revenue
Market power
Medical approach
Methadone maintenance
Minimum wage

Monopoly
Monopoly power
Morphine
NAFTA
Needle exchange programs
Negative externalities
Net losses
Oligopoly
Opium
Opportunity costs
Optimum public policy
Organized crime
Perfectly discriminating monopolists
Perfectly price inelastic
Physiologically addictive
Price discrimination
Price elasticity of demand
Price markups
Prohibition
Productivity cost
Psychologically addictive
Public trust
Retailers
Risk of arrest
Street dealer
Street sweep programs
Transfers
Transnational industry
Value added
Vertical integration
Vertically integrated industry
Weight dealer
Wholesalers

END OF CHAPTER QUESTIONS

1. As related to the market for illegal drugs, what is the economic justification for making it illegal to possess hypodermic needles (unless you are diabetic)?

2. Why does restricting the supply of heroin have a different impact on the market for addicts than it does on the market for dabblers?

3. What is the largest cost to society caused by illegal drug use? How does this differ from the largest cost to society caused by alcohol use?

4. How would an economist evaluate the legalization of drugs?

5. Why is the importation of illegal drugs often undertaken by large firms rather than small ones?

NOTES

1. United Nations, Office on Drugs and Crime, "World Drug Report 2005," www.undoc.org/undoc/en/world_drug_report.html, 2 and 5; 31; and Jonathan Caulkins, Peter Reuter, Martin Iguchi, James Chiesa, "How Goes the 'War on Drugs?'" Santa Monica, CA: Rand, 2005,1; re-spectively.

2. The historical material draws on David F. Musto, "Opium, Cocaine and Marijuana in American History," (*Scientific American,* July 1991, 40–47); Thomas Hobbler and Dorothy Hobbler, *Drugs & Crime* (New York: Chelsea House Publishers, 1988); and Edwin M. Schur, *Crimes Without Victims—Deviant Behavior and Public Policy: Abortion, Homosexuality, Drug Addiction* (Englewood Cliffs, N.J.: Prentice-Hall, 1965), 130–134.

3. Cocaine was removed from Coca-Cola around 1900. Musto (*op.cit.,* 44) indicates it was 1900 while Hobbler and Hobbler (*op. cit.,* 27) suggests it was 1903.

4. A description for the 1960s and 1970s of the U.S. drug problem, its impact, and policy recommendations, see National Commission on Marijuana and Drug Abuse, *Drug Abuse in America: Problem in Perspective* (Washington, D.C., 1973). Additionally, see the President's Commission on Organized Crime, Report to the President and the Attorney General, *America's Habit: Drug Abuse, Drug Trafficking and Organized Crime* (Washington, D.C., March 1986).

5. U.S. Department of Justice, Federal Bureau of Investigation, *Uniform Crime Reports, 1988* (Washington, D.C., 1989), Table 27, 172; ONDCP, "Drug Use Consequences" www.whitehousedrug-policy.gov/publicaitons/policy/13neds/table27.html, Table 27.

6. *America's Habit,* Appendix D, 1; *Drug Control: Status Report on DOD Support to Counternarcotics Activities* (Washington, D.C.:

U.S.G.A.O., June 1991), 8; and ONDCP, *Drug Data Summary* (Washington, D.C., April 1999), 5.

7. National Drug Control Strategy, FY 2006 Budget Summary, February 2005 (www.whitehousedrugpolicy.gov/publications/policy/06budget/), 1.

8. Scott Baldauf and Kay Bowers, "Afghanistan Riddled with Drug Ties," **Christian Science Monitor,** May 13, 2005 (www.csmonitor.com/2005/0513/p01s04-wosc.html).

9. Stephen Flynn, *op.cit.,* 6–8, and Joseph B. Treaster, "U.S. Links Trail of Heroin to a 'Soviet Connection,'" *The New York Times,* April 15, 1992, 1. *The NNICC Report 1997: The Supply of Illicit Drugs to the United States* (Washington, D.C., U.S. Drug Enforcement Administration, November 1998).

10. National Narcotics Intelligence Consumers Committee (NNICC), *The NNICC Report 1997: The Supply of Illicit Drugs to the United States* (Washington, D.C.: U.S. Drug Enforcement Administration, November 1998), 39–40, and U.S. Drug Enforcement Administration; "Drug Trafficking in the United States" (www.usdoj.gov/dea/drug_trafficking.html).

11. ONDCP, *Drug Data Summary* (Washington, D.C., April 1999), 2, and ONDCP, Fact Sheet, "Heroin, June 2003," (www.whitehousedrug policy.gov/publications/factsht/heroin/index.html).

12. Arthur D. Little, Inc., *Drug Abuse and Law Enforcement* (Cambridge, Mass.: President's Commission on Law Enforcement and the Administration of Justice, 1967), D9–D12, cited in Edwin T. Fujii, "Heroin Addiction and Public Policy," *Journal of Urban Economics,* 2, no. 2 (April 1975), 181–198.

13. President's Commission on Organized Crime, *op.cit.,* Figure 9, 46.

14. *Sourcebook,* Table 3.107, 277.

15. ONDCP, *Drug Data Summary* (Washington, D.C., April 1999), 4.

16. Data on the number of addicts is from: ONDCP, Fact Sheet, "Heroin, June 2003," *op.cit.,* and ONDCP, Fact Sheet, "Cocaine, November 2003" (www.whitehousedrugpolicy.gov/publications/facts/cocaine/index.html). Authors' calculated addiction rates using the U.S. Census Bureau's population estimate for July 1, 2003, U.S. Statistical Abstract, Table 2, 7.

17. ONDCP, Fact Sheet, "Heroin, June 2003," *op.cit.*

18. Office of Applied Studies, *1998 National Household Survey on Drug Abuse* (Washington, D.C., Department of Health and Human Services, August 1999), Tables 4A and 4B, and SAMHSA, "Results from the 2003 National Survey on Drug Use and Health: National Fundings," (www.oas.samhsa.gov/nhsda/2k3nsdah/2k3results.htm #lot), Table G.1.

19. ONDCP, Fact Sheet, "Cocaine," *op.cit.* A metric ton is 2204.6 pounds.

20. SAMHSA, *op.cit.*, Tables G.1 and G.16.

21. National Institute on Drug Abuse, "Cocaine, Pharmacology, Effects, and Treatment of Abuse," (Rockville, MD: NIDA, Research Monograph 50), 48.

22. *Sourcebook (1988),* Table 3.87, 372; *Drug & Crime Data: Fact Sheet, op.cit.,* 4; *What America's Users Spend on Illegal Drugs, 1988–1993* (Washington, D.C.: Office of National Drug Control Policy, Spring 1995), Table 4, 18; and ONDCP, *Drug Data Summary* (Washington, D.C., April 1999), 4; and National Drug Intelligence Center, "National Drug Threat Assessment 2005: Threat Matrix" (www.usdoj.gov/ndic/pubs11/13817/13817t.htm).

23. NNICC, *op.cit.,* and *The Border War on Drugs* (Washington, D.C.: Office of Technology Assessment, March 1987); and Mary G. Graham, "Controlling Drug Abuse and Crime: A Research Update," *Reports* (March/April 1987), 2.

24. *Sourcebook (1988),* Table 4.28, 520–521; and U.S. Statistical Abstract, *op.cit,* Table 316, 199. Estimated value for 2003 calculated by author using a price of $30,000 per kilo (*National Drug Threat Assessment 2005, op.cit*).

25. *Sourcebook Online,* www.albany.edu/sourcebook/, Table 4.39.

26. *Sourcebook Online, ibid.,* Table 4.37.

27. See NNICC, *op.cit.,* Figure 12, 18; *The National Drug Control Strategy: 1997, op.cit.,* 21; NNICC, 1998, *op. cit.,* 1; and Fact Sheet, "Cocaine," *op.cit.*

28. Joel W. Hay, "The Harm They Do to Others: A Primer on the External Costs of Drug Abuse," in Melvyn B. Krauss and Edward P. Lazear, *Searching for Alternatives: Drug-Control Policy in the United States* (Stanford, Ca., Hoover Institution Press, 1991), Table 12.4,

215. In comparison, Hay estimates the costs of prenatal exposure to tobacco and alcohol at $110.5 (approximately $160 billion in 2005 dollars) and $14.9 billion (approximately $22 billion in 2005 dollars), respectively (Table 12.4, 215).

29. The U.S. Chamber of Commerce reported that industry lost $60 billion in 1986, or approximately $107 billion in 2005 dollars, to lost output due to workers' drug problems. (Reported on ABC's "Drugs: A Plague Upon the Land," April 10, 1988.)

30. Office of National Drug Control Policy, "National Drug Control Strategy Update 2003," (www.whitehousedrugpolicy.gov/ publications/policy/ndcs03/tables.html), Table 27.

31. In 2000 there were 126 programs in 34 states and Washington, D.C. (2000 National Syringe Exchange Survey, www.opiateaddictionrx. info/survey/2000/statetables.html).

32. Joseph B. Treaster, "The Nation: A More Potent Heroin Makes a Comeback in a New, Needleless Form," *The New York Times*, April 28, 1991, E4.

33. The 2005 dollars are obtained by inflating the relevant estimate for consumer price index (CPI) increases through May 2005. This method is used throughout the chapter (www.bls.gov).

34. *What America's Users Spend on Illegal Drugs, 1988–1993, op.cit.*, Table 2, 14.

35. During the second quarter of 1991, 79% of male arrestees in Manhattan (New York City) and 77% in Philadelphia (Pa.) tested positive for the presence of at least one illegal drug. The comparable numbers for female arrestees in the same cities were 74% and 75%, respectively. Cocaine was by far the most likely drug to be found in their systems. ("Drug Use Forecasting, Second Quarter 1991," U.S. Department of Justice, National Institute of Justice, *Research in Brief,* February 1992, 3–4.)

36. Mieczkowski, T., "Some Observations on the Scope of Crack Use and Distribution," in Mieczkowski, ed., *Drugs, Crime, and Social Policy* (Boston: Allyn & Bacon, 1992), Table 2.3, 43.

37. Peter Reuter, Robert MacCoun, and Patrick Murphy, *Money from Crime: A Study of the Economics of Drug Dealing in Washington, D.C.* (Santa Monica, Ca.: The Rand Corporation, June 1990). Bruce L. Benson, "Do We Want the Production of Prison Services

to Be More 'Efficient'?" (Tallahassee, Fl.: Florida State University, Department of Economics Working Paper Series, no. 91–06–6).

38. ONDCP, "The Economic Costs of Drug Abuse in the United States, 1992–2002," Washington, DC, December 2004, xi.

39. Drug Data Summary, March 2003 (www.whitehousedrugpolicy .gov/publications/factsht/drugdata/).

40. Mark A.R. Kleiman, "Drug Enforcement, Drug Prices, and Drug Abuse" (www.markarkleiman.com/archives/drug_policy_/2004/09/ drug_enforcement_drug_prices_and_drug_abuse.php).

41. Drug abuse accounted for between 25–30% of all income generating crime, while alcohol abuse accounted for between 25–30% of all violent crime. H. Harwood, D. Fountain, and G. Livermore, *The Economic Costs of Alcohol and Drug Abuse in the United States—1992, Executive Summary* (Rockville, MD: National Institute on Drug Abuse, September 1998), Sect. 1.6; and ONDCP, "The Economic Costs of Drug Abuse in the United States, 1992–2002," *op.cit.*

42. Bruce D. Johnson, et al., *op. cit.,* Figure 11-1, 106 (New York City heroin users); and Joseph D. Douglass, Jr., *op. cit.,* 30 (costs in comparison to the costs of the Vietnam War).

43. It was estimated that in 1985 the countries of Southwest Asia (Iran, Afghanistan, and Pakistan) were the source of 47 percent of the U.S. heroin, Mexico was the source of 39 percent, and Southeast Asia (Burma, Thailand, and Laos) the source of 14 percent. (Source: NNICC, *op.cit.,* Figure 23, 70). The distribution for 1991 was 58 percent Southeast Asia, 21 percent for both Southwest Asia and Mexico (*The NNICC Report 1991, op.cit.,* 23); and *The National Drug Control Strategy: 1997, op.cit.,* 21. In 2001, the distribution was estimated to be 75 percent South America, 14 percent Mexico, 8 percent Southwest Asia and 3 percent Southeast Asia. (Drug Availablility Steering Committee, "Drug Availability Estimates in the United States," December 2002, Table 2-7, 61).

44. Mathew Brzezenski, "Re-engineering the Drug Business," *The New York Times,* June 23, 2002.

45. The source for much of the material describing the heroin industry is Matthew Brzezinski, "Re-engineering the Drug Business," *op.cit.*

46. We will discuss this in more detail in the next chapter. For additional material, see Thomas Schelling, "Economic Analysis and Organized

Crime," in President's Commission on Law Enforcement and Administration of Justice, *Task Force Report: Organized Crime* (Washington, D.C., 1967), 119–126.

47. Mark H. Moore, *The Economics of Heroin Distribution* (Croton-on-Hudson, N.Y.: Hudson Institute, 1970), 69–70.

48. Brzezenski, *op.cit.* Similar estimates for cocaine (115 times) and marijuana (134 times) suggest that a significantly greater degree of market power exists in the distribution of heroin than in either of the other two drug markets. (Mark H. Moore, "Supply Reduction and Drug Law Enforcement," mimeo, March 1, 1989, Table 4.)

49. Brzezinski, *op. cit.*

50. A four-part series in *The Miami Herald*, "The World's Deadliest Criminals: The Medellin Cartel" (February 8 through February 11, 1987); an article in *Newsweek*, "Cocaine's 'Dirty 300'" (November 13, 1989); *The NNICC Report 1991*, *op.cit.*; and ONDCP, "Measuring the Deterant Effect of Enforcement Operations on Drug Smuggling, 1991–1999," (August 2001) are the basis for much of the material on the cocaine industry.

51. NNICC, *op.cit.*, 31.

52. It was reported in NNICC, *op.cit.*, Figure 14, 36, that in 1985 and 1986 Colombia was the probable source of 75% of the cocaine available in the U.S. with Bolivia the source of 15%, Peru 5%, and Ecuador, Argentina and Brazil the source of the remaining 5%. *The Miami Herald* (February 6, 1987) indicated that Colombia was the source of 80% of the cocaine in the U.S.

53. In Colombia the murder of at least 30 judges, several cabinet ministers, and numerous law enforcement officials and others have been attributed to the Medellin cartel. In southern Florida the "cocaine wars" of 1979–1982, which involved the killing of approximately 250 people, can be attributed to the cartel's interest in controlling the importation and wholesaling of cocaine in this country. *(The Miami Herald, op.cit.)* From August 1989 to mid-January 1990, 209 people were killed by bombings in Colombia attributed to the cartel's activities (*The Boston Globe*, April 5, 1990).

54. NNICC, *op. cit.*, 1–37.

55. National Drug Intelligence Center, "National Drug Threat Assessment 2005," February 2005, Figure 14, 12; and "Measuring the

Deterrent Effect of Enforcement Operations on Drug Smuggling, 1991-1999," *op. cit.* 72.

56. *The Miami Herald,* February 8, 1987, 1A.

57. *The Miami Herald,* February 6, 1987, 12A.

58. Larry Rohter, "Colombia Adjusts Economic Figures to Include Its Drug Crops," *The New York Times,* June 27, 1999, A3.

59. The material about the domestic distribution of cocaine is from NNICC, 1998, *op. cit.,* 12, and "National Drug Threat Assessment 2005," *op.cit.*

60. Steven Levitt and Sudhir Venkatesh, "An Economic Analysis of a Drug-Selling Gang's Finances," *The Quarterly Journal of Economics,* August 2000.

61. This material draws upon G. Kolata, "Despite Its Promise of Riches, The Crack Trade Seldom Pays" in *The New York Times,* November 26, 1989.

62. Peter Reuter, et al., *op.cit.,* viii.

63. Levitt and Venkatesh, *op.cit.,* 770.

64. *Ibid.,* 771. The federal minimum wage in 1995 was $4.25 per hour.

65. If utility functions are independent and additive, the market demand is simply the horizontal summation of the individual functions.

66. As discussed earlier in the chapter, the market structure is probably best described as oligopolistic rather than monopolistic. However, both market structures involve some degree of market power.

67. This question will be examined in detail in the next chapter.

68. Strictly speaking, there is no supply curve under monopoly conditions. Rather, we are arguing that the marginal cost curve is the same.

69. We assume that economies of scale have not been exhausted.

70. This is also referred to as first degree discrimination. The monopolist extracts from each consumer the full value of her or his consumer surplus.

71. ONDCP, "National Drug Control Strategy, FY 2006 Budget Summary," (www.whitehousedrugpolicy.gov/publications/policy/06budget/), Table 1.7.

72. "U.S. Military Aid to Latin America Linked to Human Rights Abuses," The Center for Public Integrity (www.publici.org/report .aspx?aid=252&sid=100), July 12, 2001.

73. *The New York Times,* March 9, 1988, D2.

74. ONDCP, "National Drug Control Strategy, FY 2006 Budget Summary," *op.cit.,* Table 1.7.

75. U.S. Customs and Border Protection, "Performance & Annual Report, FY 2004" (www.customs.gov/linkhandler/cgov/toolbox/ publications/admin/cbp_annual.ctt/cbp_annual.pdf), pp. 6 and 54.

76. "Where the Innocent Lose," *Newsweek,* January 4, 1993, 42; and *Sourcebook Online, op.cit.,* Table 4.42.

77. *Ibid.,* 43.

78. A study done by the U.S. Coast Guard estimated that a doubling of the retail price for cocaine would only decrease consumption by six percent (Peter Passell, "Economic Scene: A Demand Side Cocaine Policy," *The New York Times,* March 16, 1988, D2). The demand for cocaine is highly inelastic (–.06).

79. Prices may or may not be equalized in the two markets, depending on the extent of price discrimination practiced. Comparison of quantities consumed in the two submarkets is difficult without knowing the number of addicts and dabblers.

80. Based on the research of Mark Kleiman at Harvard's Kennedy School of Government (Peter Passell, "Economic Scene: Faulty U.S. Logic in Cocaine Policy," *The New York Times,* March 9, 1988, D2).

81. To maximize profits, the seller charges the lower price in the market with the high price elasticity of demand.

82. Raising prices to dabblers in the heroin market may have a smaller-than-expected impact on the consumption of heroin since most first time users of heroin are given it rather than purchase it. (Mark A.R. Kleitman and Jonathan P. Caulkins, "Heroin Policy for the Next Decade," *The Annals of the American Academy of Political and Social Science,* May 1992, 165.)

83. ONDCP, "National Drug Control Strategy, FY 2006 Budget Summary," *op.cit.,* Table 1.7.

84. If the demand functions are independent of one another, the total market demand is the horizontal summation of the two submarket functions.

85. With a change in the price of a complementary good the demand curve does shift. In the special case of a perfectly inelastic demand curve, the upward (downward) shift due to a decrease (increase) in the price of the complement is a vertical movement of the demand curve which visually is no different than the original curve.

86. A national survey from 1996 to 1999 of facilities to rehabilitate addicts estimated the cost of non-hospital residential therapy and counseling was $62.10 in 1997 dollars per resident or almost $23,000 per year. (Substance Abuse and Mental Health Services Administration, "The ADSS Cost Study: Costs of Substance Abuse Treatment in the Specialty Sector," DHHS: Rockville, MD, Table 4.2, 21.)

87. D. Dwayne Simpson, "Relapse," *NIDA (National Institute on Drug Abuse) Notes,* vol. 4 (December 1986), 10–11.

88. ONDCP, "National Drug Control Strategy, FY 2006 Budget Summary," *op.cit.,* Table 1.7.

89. ONDCP, "Fact Sheet: Methadone" (www.whitehousedrugpolicy .gov/publications/factsht/methadone/), April 2000.

90. B. Brown, "Methadone Maintenance," *National Institute on Drug Abuse, Notes,* vol. 4 (December 1986), 12–13.

91. Gary Hoenig, "The Infinite Resilience of Drug Abuse," *The New York Times,* February 9, 1975.

92. For a description of the British system for dealing with drug addicts, see David Turner, "Pragmatic Incoherence: The Changing Face of British Drug Policy," in M. Krauss and E. Lazear, *op.cit.,* 175–190.

93. Municipal drug clinics, which dispensed low-cost narcotics to addicts, operated between 1912 and 1925 in over 40 U.S. cities, with varying success. (Schur, *op.cit.,* 159–160.) In Britain it is prescribed by doctors and obtained in local pharmacies. This is all paid for by the country's national health system. (David Turner, *ibid.*)

94. Mark A.R. Kleiman, *Against Excess* (New York: Basic Books, 1992) provides an excellent discussion of alternative models for drug use decriminalization.

95. The policy was known as the British Treatment System and was based on the belief that addiction was an illness to be dealt with in the medical arena. Addicts were to be weaned from their addiction if possible; if not they were to be maintained on a nonincreasing dose of the drug. (D. Turner, *op.cit.*).

96. Some Boston data, while not based on legalization or decriminalization, are also informative. From 1960 to 1970 expected-punishment costs to a heroin user in Boston decreased substantially. The chances of an arrested user going to prison decreased from 0.5 in 1960 to 0.1 in 1970. The average sentence fell from 23 months in 1961 to less than 15 months in 1969. Over the same period the estimated number of addicts increased tenfold. James Q. Wilson, Mark H. Moore, and I. David Wheat, Jr., "The Problem of Heroin," *The Public Interest,* no. 29 (Fall 1972), 19. While this does not prove cause and effect, the figures are suggestive.

97. The social services approach is locally oriented and includes a variety of services such as medical care (drug maintenance, etc.), housing services, education counseling, employment services (training, placement, etc.), counseling, etc. (D. Turner, *op.cit.*, 181–186, and Robert Meier, *Crime + Society,* Boston: Allyn and Bacon, 1989, 245–249.

98. Eddy Engelsman, "Drug Policy in The Netherlands From a Public Health Perspective," in Krauss and Lazear, *op.cit.,* for a description of the Dutch policies and programs.

99. The literature for and against legalization or decriminalization has grown dramatically since the public debate started in earnest. Some examples are: E. Nadelmann, "The Case for Legalization," *The Public Interest,* no. 92 (Summer 1988); Mark A.R. Kleiman, *op.cit.;* and M. Krauss and E. Lazear, *op.cit.,* is a collection of papers by economists and noneconomists on both sides of the issue from a conference held at Stanford University in 1990. The recent testimony before Congress by David Boaz, Executive Vice President, Cato Institute ("Drug Legalization, Criminalization, and Harm Reduction," June 16, 1999, www.cato.org/testimony/ct-dbz061699.htm) provides an excellent summary of the arguments in favor of legalization.

100. John P. Morgan, "Prohibition is Perverse Policy: What was True in 1933 is True Now," in Krauss and Lazear, *op.cit.*, is an attempt to use information from the prohibition of alcohol in the U.S. as a method of predicting what would happen with legalization or decriminalization.

101. The British and U.S. rates are for the mid-1980s (R. Dennis, *op.cit.*, 130) and the rate for the Netherlands is for 1990 (E. Engelsman, *op.cit.*, 172).

102. James Ostrowski, "Thinking About Drug Legalization," *Policy Analysis,* May 25, 1989.

103. A fine example of a detailed plan for the use of taxation in conjunction with decriminalization can be found in M. Kleiman, *op.cit.*

9

Organized Crime

In the last chapter we referred to something called **organized crime.** While most of us have read or heard or seen descriptions of the activities and tactics of organized crime, we are probably not sure exactly what is meant by organized crime. In fact, it may interest you to know that some people doubt that a thing called organized crime even exists.[1] In 1967 the President's Commission on Law Enforcement and Administration of Justice issued a report which describes a criminal organization which has been organized at the national level since 1931.[2] Essentially, this organization is a national cartel, that is, a group of oligopolists, or "families," joined together in a "confederation" in order to reduce uncertainty and competition among themselves and thereby maximize profits for the group as a whole. Territories and markets are divided up among the various oligopolists.

Economic analysis should be useful in defining the structure of organized crime. Thomas Schelling, an economist who served on the Crime Commission's Task Force on Organized Crime, equates organized crime with "large-scale continuing firms with the internal organization of a large enterprise" which make a conscious effort to control or monopolize the market.[3] Whether or not organized crime exists, then, depends on whether or not economic conditions support business firms which operate on a continuing basis, are large scale, and monopolize. These questions will be examined later in the chapter. Assuming, for the moment, that these large-scale firms do exist and that they do attempt to control the market, it is logical to conclude that "trade associations" or cartels would develop. Even in legal markets characterized by a few large-scale producers, or oligopolists, there are strong incentives to collude, or join together, in order to reduce risk and uncertainty, discourage competition and entry into the industry, and thereby increase profits to the group. **Cartels,** however, are illegal in the United States, so ideally they do not exist in legal markets. But if the market or industry is illegal to begin with, there is no reason to believe that an illegal form of business organization would not be used to advantage.

BACKGROUND

The basic organization which the Crime Commission describes as characteristic of organized crime today emerged in 1931. It was during the 1920s that the organization made its "take-off into self-sustained growth."[4] This period was conducive to growth for several reasons.[5]

First, and most important, was the adoption of **Prohibition** by constitutional amendment in 1920. This created an economic opportunity for firms to produce, import, and retail illegal alcohol, since the public's demand for alcohol was not seriously reduced by the introduction of Prohibition. The large capital requirements for production facilities and the need to corrupt public officials were incentives to such firms to organize on a large scale. The decade of the 1920s was characterized by considerable competition for territories and control of particular operations, and violence was common. In order to control this bloody rivalry which might threaten public apathy toward enforcement of Prohibition, it was necessary to reduce interorganizational competition; that is, to join together in a cartel.[6]

Public apathy played an important role during this period. Because of it, law enforcement efforts were hampered and, therefore, expected punishment costs to those participating in the illegal industry were reduced. Public apathy also meant that working in the illegal sector did not carry a stigma; this reduced the psychic costs associated with breaking the law.

Thus, economic opportunities in the illegal sector existed. At the same time, there were individuals who had very few economic opportunities in the legal sector. The United States had unrestricted immigration until the 1920s. Large numbers of primarily rural people immigrated to this country and became concentrated in urban centers. They had only their labor as a resource and were not readily assimilated into the industrialized economic system. The existing governmental system and programs offered very little to improve the situation. Distrust and alienation developed and compounded the problem of lack of economic opportunity. Secret ethnic societies were established, and alternative ways of providing economic opportunities and upward mobility were sought. In addition, various criminal leaders from southern Italy immigrated to the United States when Mussolini adopted and enforced an anti-**Mafia** policy.

The 1920s, then, provided the economic as well as social conditions for the growth of large criminal enterprises. The huge profits earned meant that capital was available for reinvestment—to expand or to diversify into other markets and activities.

Additional evidence suggests another explanation for the growth of organized crime.[7] During organized crime's formative years the FBI, the law enforcement agency that should have been involved in combating the development of a national crime cartel, took a hands off approach. In fact it was not until the President's Commission's report in the late 1960s that the FBI admitted that organized crime existed. This has been attributed, by some, to the fact that organized crime had information regarding the personal lifestyle of **J. Edgar Hoover,** FBI director from 1924 to 1972, that was apparently used to influence him and his management of the Bureau.

DIVERSIFICATION AND CHANGE

Until recently it was felt that most of organized crime's revenue came from gambling. **Gambling** and **loansharking** together were the two most profitable and important illegal services produced by organized crime, but other goods and services were and still are produced including bootlegging, fencing, narcotics, prostitution, protection, and racketeering. In recent years narcotics have become an increasingly important activity of organized crime. In 1986 the President's Commission on Organized Crime concluded that "[d]rug trafficking is the most serious organized crime problem in the world today."[8] In the same year it was estimated that organized crime's net income from narcotics (heroin, cocaine, and marijuana) accounted for between 30 percent and 65 percent of the net income from criminal activities.[9] A recent report from the United Nations ranks trafficking in narcotics, trafficking in arms and trafficking in humans as the three most important sources of revenue for organized crime, in decreasing order of importance.[10]

Organized crime has become increasingly active in legitimate businesses as well. It has been involved in legitimate businesses from the beginning, but diversification into such businesses has increased recently. There are good reasons for this. First, such investments decrease risk; it makes sense to balance a portfolio of investments with profitability and risk. Legitimate business investment also provides an outlet for idle funds. Profits from illegal markets cannot be continuously reinvested in illegal markets. At some point reinvestment and expansion cannot be profitable. Investment funds are therefore available for alternative ventures. A final reason for diversification into legal markets and legitimate businesses is to provide a respectable source of income to report to the Internal Revenue Service.

The diversification of organized crime and its increased involvement in complex financial arrangements has led to greater need for technical expertise (e.g., legal, financial, and accounting expertise) within the organization. Acquiring such expertise may require structural changes which could create problems in the maintenance of efficiency and loyalty within the organization.[11] For example, "outsiders" may have to be placed in traditional positions of authority and respect within the organization, creating interpersonal, intraorganizational rivalries. This would be an interesting question for management theorists to investigate.

Recent evidence suggests that organized crime is undergoing a transition similar to some legal sector industries. The larger, stalwart firms in the industry, those that comprise the American Mafia or Costa Nostra, are "fading out of existence" according to some law enforcement officials,[12] and are being replaced by new firms. The new firms include Asians, Colombians, and other ethnically based crime groups who are "wild groups"[13] that tend to be more violent. In fact the FBI now has separate investigative units to deal with Eurasian, Asian and African organized crime firms. The members of the Eurasian crime firms come from Eastern Europe and Western Asia, i.e., the former Soviet republics. The Asian firms have roots in many of the countries in East and Southeast Asia including China, Korea, Japan and Thailand. The African firms are primarily from Nigeria, Ghana and Liberia.

A number of reasons have been suggested for the Mafia's decline including: increased law enforcement efforts, especially through the use of the **Racketeer Influenced and Corrupt Organization Act (RICO)**; an aging leadership who were not quick enough to think globally; a breakdown of traditional loyalties among members of the crime organization; offspring who have become very successful in the legal sector making it difficult to recruit a new generation of leaders; and a dispersal of their traditional markets, the urban ethnic communities, to the suburbs and beyond.

ECONOMIC COSTS

Provision of Economic "Bads"

Many of the economic costs associated with organized crime are those which result from the provision of economic "bads," such as heroin and cocaine. The costs to society of these criminal activities were described in the preceding chapter. It is important to note that these costs are not necessarily a result of organized crime. If there were no such thing as organized crime, but these illegal markets remained in existence, all of the costs associated with the illegal markets or economic "bads" would persist. Thus, the important question is whether or not production of these illegal products requires an ongoing, large-scale monopoly. If not, the costs associated with the illegal markets are not costs inherent in organized crime. It is true, of course, that some of the costs resulting from these markets, and therefore from organized crime, are very large. Take tax avoidance, for example. While this represents a transfer from honest taxpayers to those who do not pay taxes, it is a very large transfer in the case of organized crime, whose net profit is in the billions of dollars. A recent estimate of the net income of organized crime ranges from $8.1 billion to $80.6 billion in 1986 dollars[14] or $14.4 billion to $216.8 billion in 2005 dollars. Recent estimates are that the **"criminal underworld"** receives over $40 billion in 1999 or $46.7 billion in 2005 dollars from illegal drugs and $100 billion a year from illegal gambling in 1994 or $131.2 billion in 2005 dollars.[15]

The Costs of Organized Crime Per Se

What costs are due to organized crime per se? One category of costs is negative externalities. The existence and tactics of a large-scale criminal enterprise and its infiltration of legitimate business causes concern on the part of some law-abiding citizens. This concern is a psychic cost. How large this impact is, is hard to estimate. On the other hand, it is true that some people seem to derive psychic benefits from the knowledge that organized crime exists. For some, organized crime holds the same romantic attraction and adventure that the heroes of the Wild West did. Other people are concerned by the tremendous power that organized crime has over our economy, owing not so much to its tactics as to its tremendous wealth. Concern is also growing that organized crime's wealth has given them significant power over the economies and governments of other countries, especially in areas where the political stability is already tenuous, such as the Latin American countries involved in the cocaine trade.[16] Here the problem of organized crime is no different from that of legal monopolies or **conglomerates,** except that we attempt to control the latter domestically with antitrust regulations.

The tactics used by organized crime can also generate real losses to society in the form of injury or property damage (e.g., from murder or physical intimidation) or involuntary transfers (e.g., from extortion). Again, however, these practices may not be unique to organized crime and might be used in these markets even if they operated without organized crime. Since illegal markets do not enjoy the protection in business dealings that legal ones do (e.g., contracts and the courts), other methods of enforcing agreements and discipline must be used. It is even possible that not only would the same tactics be used in the absence of organized crime, but they would be resorted to more often.

Organized crime, since it represents monopoly power, has an impact on the price and/or quality of the products it sells as well as on the output it produces. In the preceding chapter we saw how a monopolist tends to restrict output and sell the same product that a competitive firm would sell, but at a higher price (or a product of lower quality at the same price). We also showed that this is not necessarily the case but depends on whether or not economies of scale are important in production or distribution. If economies of scale are not significant, organized crime sells its products at higher prices than would be the case if the markets were competitive, and it produces and sells less of the product. The effect on output is actually desirable if we are talking about the production of illegal goods and services. By restricting output we have less of the problem. But remember that organized crime is also involved in legitimate enterprises, and here the reduced output is undesirable.

Organized crime can have another impact on prices, and that is when harassment of legitimate businesses or other questionable business tactics increase the costs of doing business for these firms and thereby force their prices up. Prices are increased, and output and employment of resources in these firms or industries are reduced. Profits are transferred from legal enterprises to illegal ones.

If we look back and summarize what we have said about the impacts of organized crime per se, the impacts stem from two characteristics of organized crime: monopoly power and unethical or illegal business practices. The first problem is common to all industries in which there is an element of monopoly, whether the product is legal or illegal. The second problem is more complicated. Some of it stems from the fact that the products are illegal, so that production is forced "underground," and therefore alternative ways of enforcing business agreements and discipline must be sought. Monopoly power may actually reduce the amount of such activity. But some of the undesirable tactics (e.g., harassment of legitimate businesses and selling of protection services) are due to monopoly power. Without control of the market and of harassment activities, adequate protection cannot be guaranteed.

Criminal Justice System Costs

The last category of impacts is criminal justice system costs—money spent each year on police, courts, and prisons in order to deter and punish participation in organized crime. These include evidence gathering, arrest, post arrest processing, trial, and sentencing costs. In the case of organized crime, these costs are particularly high relative to the number of defendants handled. One reason for this is that organized crime can afford highly trained lawyers. Another reason is that organized crime systematically corrupts law enforcement officers and public officials. The Crime Commission's Task Force on Organized Crime concludes that organized crime can flourish only in areas where it corrupts local officials. It has been estimated that about one-third of the annual net income from gambling alone goes to **corruption.** This corruption then makes arrest, prosecution, and conviction of offenders particularly difficult. It also depreciates the value and functioning of our entire criminal justice system, as well as other systems in the public sector. Efficiency and equity are diminished, and public trust and cooperation suffer as a result.[17]

AN ECONOMIC ANALYSIS OF ORGANIZED CRIME[18]

The most useful way to view the problem of organized crime is in the context of illegal markets and illegal enterprises. Organized crime is a group of large-scale enterprises operating within illegal markets to maximize profits. A distinction should be drawn between organized crime and the "underworld" economy of which it is a part. Many unorganized criminal business (e.g., robbery) operate within a highly organized economic framework. That economy has a labor market and recruitment system, a marketing and distribution system, a communications system, a financial network, and a diplomatic system. (By the latter we mean a system responsible for the maintenance of relations with law enforcement officials.) One question that is interesting to ask at this point is, "To what extent is the organized underworld economy affected by organized crime (i.e., by a large-scale monopoly organization)"? For the underworld economy to be organized, is it necessary for a large firm or cartel to assume a leadership role? Perhaps for the underworld economy to run smoothly, it is necessary to have certain activities centralized in a large firm—say, the diplomatic activities, or financial relations with the "upper world." Paul Rubin argues that organized crime is "a criminal firm whose function is the selling of goods and services to other criminal firms."[19] The kinds of goods and services which organized crime might provide to other firms in the underworld economy include capital, violence, and police nonenforcement, which is accomplished through bribery. Organized crime may also provide specialized services, depending on the market.[20]

If the links between the large-scale firm, or cartel, and the underworld economy can be defined, the next question is, "What conditions determine the existence of the large-scale firm? What economic conditions provide the incentives or make it necessary for certain criminal enterprises to organize?" Perhaps there is one key activity or market in which organized crime is involved, which is the reason that organized crime has to be large and organized.

Of course, there is an incentive to be large and to monopolize illegal markets: it can increase profits. This is particularly true in markets where demand curves are relatively inelastic and/or price discrimination is feasible. But this is true in other markets as well, and monopoly is not necessarily the result. For monopoly to persist, there must be barriers to entry—something which keeps competing firms out of the industry.

To some extent we set up barriers to entry into any illegal market by making the production of certain goods and services illegal. This restricts entry to those who are willing to break the law. But again, this does not necessarily mean that monopoly will result. It simply means that the costs of doing business are higher than they would be if the markets were legal. What, then, are the real barriers to entry?

One possibility is the existence of technical economies of scale; that is, to utilize certain equipment or personnel fully it is necessary to be a large-scale operation.[21] A wire service for illegal horse race betting is an example. If this service can be provided only by a firm which is large relative to the size of the market, then this part of the gambling industry will be monopolized. Note that the rest of the industry, even bookmaking, need not be monopolized. Organized crime would simply sell the specialized service to bookmakers. The need to utilize certain personnel (e.g., a disciplinarian or enforcer) completely may be another source of technical economics of scale. Thus, violence may be provided more efficiently by a large-scale organization, and may therefore be monopolized.

Financial economies of scale are another barrier to entry and another source of monopoly power. Some illegal markets require substantial capital outlays, at least in certain activities. As mentioned in the last chapter, heroin requires large amounts of capital at the import stage. Thus, this stage of distribution is monopolized by organized crime, or at least financed by it. The spreading of risks in gambling is another example.

An additional advantage of being large is the ability to control factors that would otherwise be out of the firm's control. This is referred to as internalizing externalities. It is for this reason that effective provision of violence may have to be centralized, or monopolized, by organized crime. Excessive violence arouses public attention and ultimately imposes costs on all criminals. If violence, or enforcement of agreements among criminals, is done individually by each small firm or criminal, the total amount of violence will be larger than would be the case if violence were centrally provided. This is because each small firm thinks a little violence will go unnoticed. Since each small firm thinks the same thing, each provides a little violence and the end result is an excessive amount. A monopolist realizes the consequences of violence, controls it, and avoids this kind of problem.

Which of these advantages of large-scale operation is the reason some criminal activities are organized is not known for certain. Rubin feels that financial economies of scale are the key.[22] Regardless of which factor it is, however, the point is that if the economic condition or conditions which require a large-scale criminal organization can be identified, it may be possible to restructure the economic environment so that a large-scale organization is no longer required. This would permit entry into the markets and would result in less organized crime, although not necessarily in less crime.

It is possible that if organized crime became disorganized, there would be an adverse impact on the entire underworld economy so that criminal activity as a whole would become more difficult and would therefore diminish. But it is also possible that the underworld economy would be unaffected.[23] The question then is, "Which is to be preferred, organized crime or disorganized crime?" The answer may be organized crime. This is because of the advantages to society of reducing violence in industries in which organized crime is involved. Organized crime may also fill a leadership role in the underworld economy and therefore enforce a kind of discipline on other criminal activities; for example, it may enforce avoidance of certain classes of crime or prevent random destruction of property. In reaction to the recent increases in criminal activity associated with the cocaine trade, a criminologist suggests that he's "beginning to long for the 'good' old days when the Mafia ran the drug trade. For when the Mafia ran the drug trade there was a lot less crime and violence."[24]

A final advantage of organized crime is the possibility of restricted output of economic "bads." We described in the last chapter how monopolists tend to restrict output and produce less than competitive firms as a group would produce. (We also discussed some qualifying conditions.) This is an advantage to society when monopolists operate in illegal markets. Because we are talking about illegal markets, there is an additional reason for a monopolist to hold back production. This is to reduce risk if law enforcement efforts tend to increase when output gets too large. Small sellers would tend to ignore this effect, and therefore as a group would produce and sell more than a monopolist.

All of this discussion does not lead us to any firm conclusions. It suggests that if we cannot eliminate certain criminal activities we may be better off with organized crime than without it. But we would still have the problem of crime. Perhaps the most rational response to the problem of organized crime is to attempt to reduce the profits to be earned by operating in illegal markets and to fight the abuse of monopoly power via anti-trust regulations. This requires that the problem of organized crime be viewed as a problem of illegal firms operating in illegal markets—which is what we have been arguing throughout this chapter. Before deciding on the most appropriate public policy, it is useful to review the various strategies that have been or could be used against organized crime.

Strategies for Fighting Organized Crime[25]

Law Enforcement Strategies

One way to fight organized crime is to attempt to enforce existing laws more vigorously. While some of the techniques may be similar, there are several law enforcement strategies which are possible, depending on the focus of the activity.[26]

The Violation Strategy The first of these is a violation strategy. Here the focus is on events, or violations. The strategy is a reactive one: offenders are arrested and prosecuted whenever they break the law. Simple as it sounds, it is a difficult strategy to implement because the events are unknown. Because the violations of the law represent "victimless" crimes, there is no complaint or victim to report the violation. Beyond this, if it is true that organized crime sells goods and services, primarily capital, to other criminals, then a violation strategy, even if it is successful, does not focus on organized crime. Organized crime may be financing the operation, but it is not doing the selling to the public.

The Attrition Strategy A second law enforcement approach focuses on individuals rather than events. Efforts are concentrated on identifying, arresting, and prosecuting key individuals within the organization in an attempt to disrupt the organization.

There are two problems with this approach. First, it is very difficult to carry out. Successful bribery by organized crime leads to selective nonenforcement of the law. Coupled with expert legal advice, it makes it very hard to convict and punish individuals associated with organized crime.

The second problem is the likely impact of such a strategy if it is successful. While it may disrupt the organization temporarily, it is unlikely to do so permanently. As long as there are profitable business opportunities in illegal markets, individuals will rise to the occasion. Those individuals who have been removed from the organization will simply be replaced.

The Market Strategy The last law enforcement strategy focuses on market structure and the supply and demand for illegal or controlled goods and services. While each of the other law enforcement strategies has an impact on illegal, as well as legal, markets, this last approach focuses on that impact. Thus, to the extent possible, complementary market strategies can be devised which have the desired outcomes in terms of prices, output, and consumption of products. Since one objective of law enforcement is to reduce the consumption of illegal goods and services, this approach would focus on attempts to decrease the demand for and/or the supply of the illegal products.

One possibility would be to identify the supporting structure required for the smooth working of the various markets and attempt to undermine that structure. This gets us back to the question of the links between organized crime and the underworld economy in which it functions. It may be possible not only that organized crime is essential to the underworld economy, but also that the reverse is true. This means that efforts to diminish the efficiency of the underworld economy will have an adverse impact on organized crime's operations, leading to a decrease in supply of their activities.

The question still remains as to how to undermine a supporting structure and decrease demand or supply via law enforcement, and whether or not this is the most effective public policy. It is possible that via such a policy the consumption of economic "bads" will be decreased and society will gain, but this must be compared with the costs of effectively increasing law enforcement efforts.

Preventive Strategies

A second set of strategies is preventive in nature. Rather than relying on increased enforcement of existing laws against certain activities, these strategies rely on altering the economy and social environment.

The Public-Education Approach The first of these is a program of public education. By informing the public about the dangers of organized crime and the goods and services in which it deals, it may be possible to reduce the demand for illegal goods as well as decreasing the supply by increasing risk and, hence, the costs of doing business. Ideally, risk is increased because the public at large is aware and watching.[27]

Whether or not this type of strategy would be effective is questionable. First, public information may have no impact on the demand for goods and services or the willingness of the public to watch for violations of the law. And even if the public were watching more carefully, this may not significantly increase the probability of punishment for those who participate in organized crime.

Eliminating Business Opportunities Since we have defined organized crime as large-scale firms operating in illegal markets, perhaps the most logical approach to dealing with organized crime is to eliminate profitable illegal business opportunities. While one obvious way to do this is to legalize certain markets, there are some other possibilities. Eliminating interstate tax differentials on alcohol and cigarettes is one. This would eliminate the illegal and profitable business of running contraband. Making gambling debts legal contracts would lead to a decrease in loansharking.

There are doubtless other such possibilities, but the greatest potential for eliminating opportunities for illegal profit making is to provide legal substitutes via either the public sector or the private sector. State lotteries, reintroduced in 1964, are an example. Here, in an increasing number of states, the public sector attempts to compete with the illegal numbers game.[28] The idea is that if the state can provide a very similar game at competitive prices, demand for the illegal game will be reduced and illegal activity and profits will decline.

For this strategy to work, the publicly provided legal games must be competitive with equally high payoffs, daily winners, easy access to bet takers, flexible bets, and credit. Increasingly, the various **state lotteries** are designed to be similar to the illegal game, except that they do not provide credit. In Massachusetts the state's lottery is actually called "The Numbers Game." While credit is not available, it is possible to pay in advance and thereby have an account against which to draw when placing bets. "In New Jersey, a lottery scheme with lower prices and more drawings has reduced the volume of the numbers business by 50 percent. Numbers operators there are said to have been so hard hit that they have reduced their payoff odds to compensate."[29]

However, as yet there is not sufficient data to conclude that state-run legal lotteries significantly reduce participation in the illegal games.[30] The early state lotteries were not competitively designed. Only when daily winners were introduced in New Jersey in 1975, did state-run legal games take on characteristics similar enough to those of illegal operations to compete effectively.

New York State's off-track, pari-mutuel wagering system, introduced in 1970, is another example of the public sector's providing a legal substitute for an illegal activity. By 1974, when a 5 percent surcharge tax was imposed on winnings, thereby reducing legal betting activity, the Offtrack Betting Corporation reported that its activities had cut the bookmakers' share of the horse racing bet in half, and that its competition had forced "a few small bookmaking operations . . . to seek other occupations."[31]

Legal substitutes could also be provided by the private sector. For example, rather than have state-run lotteries or off-track betting, such activities could simply be legalized and left up to private enterprise.[32] The legalized casino gambling in Atlantic City, New Jersey, is an example. Here private industry provides **legal gambling,** which is regulated by the State Casino Gambling Commission.[33] Since the beginning of the 1990s legal casino gambling has been introduced into 34 states in addition to New Jersey and Nevada where it has existed for some time. Additional competition for illegal gambling and for state-run lotteries and casinos is **Internet gambling.** In 1999 there were more than 700 on-line casinos worldwide, 110 sports gambling sites, and 39 lotteries, with most licensed offshore. Their legal status is currently being addressed through the consideration and passage of various state and federal laws.[34]

State lotteries and other forms of legalized gambling are also viewed as important revenue sources for states. Billions of dollars ($14 billion in 2003 from state lotteries alone)[35] are raised annually by this form of "voluntary taxation," with some revenues earmarked for support to education (in sixteen states) and the arts to make legalization more palatable to the electorate. Questions have been raised about legalized gambling's effectiveness as a revenue source, perhaps in part due to the increased competition among legal alternatives and the resulting decrease in monopoly profits of the early state lotteries and casinos.[36] Additionally, the authors of a recent report found that "built into the lottery is the most **regressive tax** we know." Players with incomes under $10,000 spent more of their income on lottery tickets than players from any other income group.[37]

Whether the competition is provided publicly or privately, the question is, "What are the costs and benefits of this kind of public policy?" If the legal activity does compete effectively, the activity is simply shifted from the illegal economy to the legal one. Some of the costs generated by the production and consumption of the good or service (e.g., the negative externalities) will remain, unless these are diminished by the mere fact of legalization. In fact, as we argued in Chapter 7, consumption of the legal products will increase, and therefore some costs to society may increase. Other costs are eliminated by legalization; examples are the lost income taxes on those employed in the production of the product, or the criminal justice costs of attempting to enforce laws against these activities. Legalization also means that legal avenues are available for enforcing discipline in the industry, so that some of the unethical or illegal business practices currently being used may be eliminated.

Whether or not monopoly power and its abuses are eliminated depends on the circumstances. If the public sector provides the legal substitute, then monopoly power is shifted to the public sector, where presumably it is not abused. If the private sector provides the legal substitute—that is, if the activity is simply legalized—then monopoly power may continue, provided that the incentive(s) to be large scale continues. Unless we identify the economic condition(s) which makes large-scale organization necessary and desirable, we cannot predict whether or not monopoly will continue. If it does, then it is quite possible that organized crime will simply become organized noncrime; that is, the same firm or cartel would produce the same products, but everything would now be legal. The advantage, beside those already discussed, is that monopoly abuse could be controlled via antitrust regulations.

Restructuring Urban Environments The last of the preventive approaches is more long term and indirect. The idea is to restructure the urban economic, social, and political environment in order to reduce the demand for organized crime's products or increase its costs of doing business. Several possibilities have been suggested, including eliminating poverty, consolidating the fragmented government units of metropolitan areas, and dispersing strong ethnic neighborhoods.

Eliminating **poverty** is a desirable public policy in any case, but may have some impact on organized crime and/or participation in victimless crimes. Improved legal income opportunities will reduce the supply of criminals in general, and therefore increase labor costs to illegal enterprises. It is also possible that reduced poverty may decrease the demand for certain illegal activities (e.g., gambling or drugs) that may be associated with a poverty culture.

Consolidation of fragmented government units in metropolitan areas is intended to decrease the possibility of corrupting local officials. The importance of corruption to organized crime has already been discussed. Most metropolitan areas today are characterized by a large number of small, independent political jurisdictions, each with its own governing officials. Because of the small size of these jurisdictions, officials are relatively low paid and have small amounts of money available for campaigning. Such conditions make corruption easier. By consolidating, a much smaller number of high-paid, less corruptible professionals would serve in public office. Whether or not this is true is debatable.[38] Either way, there are certainly other strong economic arguments in favor of metropolitan-wide government.

The elimination of strong ethnic neighborhoods is also intended to reduce corruption. Ethnically homogeneous neighborhoods make it easier for organized crime to "deliver the vote" and thus corrupt public officials. Whether or not it is worth it to give up ethnic neighborhoods in order to reduce organized crime is a difficult question to answer. There is also the question of how ethnic neighborhoods could be dispersed both effectively and legally.

Rehabilitation Strategies

The final set of strategies are aimed at rehabilitation. The objective is to treat or rehabilitate the individuals who participate in organized crime so that they no longer have a desire to take part in such activities. This would seem to be the least productive strategy. First, in order to treat or rehabilitate, it is necessary to identify and capture participants. For reasons stated earlier, this is extremely difficult. Second, it is not clear that individuals who participate in organized crime require rehabilitation any more than any other individual who breaks the law, and perhaps less. We have argued that organized crime is best viewed as illegal firms attempting to maximize profits in illegal markets. The profit motive is an accepted and applauded part of American life. Participants in organized crime are simply responding to that motive, albeit in a somewhat discrepant way.

This completes our review of existing or potential strategies for dealing with organized crime. None of the strategies will eliminate organized crime, or at least eliminate the firms which provide the goods and services. At best, some activities can be eliminated while others are legalized. An effectively designed public policy would focus on this trade-off, legalizing those activities in which benefits to society exceed the costs and in which impacts on other markets and the entire underworld economy are given adequate consideration.

REVIEW TERMS AND CONCEPTS

Antitrust regulations
Attrition strategy
Barriers to entry
Bootlegging
Collusion
Conglomerates
Corruption
Efficiency
Equity
Fencing
Financial economies of scale
Gambling
Human trafficking
Immigration
Interstate tax differentials
Law enforcement strategies
Loansharking
Mafia
Market strategy
Monopoly
Monopoly power
Narcotics

National cartel
Negative externalities
Net income
Net profit
Organized crime
Poverty
Preventive strategies
Price discrimination
Profits
Prohibition
Prostitution
Protection costs
Psychic benefits
Psychic costs
Public education approach
Public trust
Racketeering
Regressive tax
Rehabilitation strategies
Technical economies of scale
Underworld economy
Violation strategy

END OF CHAPTER QUESTIONS

1. Which of the following economic concepts best describes organized crime in the U.S.: it is a monopoly or it is a special type of oligopoly known as a cartel?

2. Organized crime is only involved in illegal activities because that's what it does best. True or false and explain.

3. What are some of the negative externalities generated by organized crime?

4. One public policy aimed at combating organized crime is to eliminate business opportunities for the organized firms. What are some examples of the implementation of this policy? Has it been successful?

NOTES

1. Cf. Gordon Hawkins, "God and the Mafia," in John E. Conklin, ed., *The Crime Establishment: Organized Crime and American Society* (Englewood Cliffs, N.J.: Prentice-Hall, 1973), 43–72.

2. President's Commission on Law Enforcement and Administration of Justice, *Task Force Report: Organized Crime* (Washington, D.C.: U.S. Government Printing Office, 1967), 1–2, 6–10.

3. Thomas Schelling, "Economic Analysis and Organized Crime," in Conklin, *op.cit.,* 77.

4. This term is borrowed from economic development theory. See W.W. Rostow, "The Rostow Doctrine," in Gerald M. Meier, ed., *Leading Issues in Development Economics* (New York: Oxford University Press, 1964), Chapter. 1.

5. The following section is based on David A. Caputo, *Organized Crime and American Politics* (Morristown, N.J.: General Learning Press, 1974), 17–20.

6. For a description of the rivalry prior to 1931, see Donald R. Cressey, *Theft of the Nation: The Structure and Operations of Organized Crime in America* (New York: Harper & Row, 1969), Chapter 3.

7. PBS program *Frontline,* February 9, 1993, and Anthony Summers, "Hidden Hoover," *Vanity Fair,* 56, no. 3 (March 1993).

8. The President's Commission on Organized Crime, Report to the President and the Attorney General, *America's Habit: Drug Abuse, Drug Trafficking, and Organized Crime* (Washington, D.C.: U.S. Government Printing Office, March 1986), 5.

9. The low and high estimates for criminal net income for organized crime from narcotics in 1986 were $2.4 billion and $52.7 billion ($4.3 and $93.5 billion in 2005 dollars), with estimates for total net income of $8.1 billion and $80.6 billion ($14.4 and $143.0 billion in 2005 dollars), respectively. The President's Commission on Organized Crime, Report to the President and the Attorney General, *The Impact: Organized Crime Today* (Washington, D.C.: U.S. Government Printing Office, April 1986), Table 8, 463.

10. As reported in U.S. State Department, "Trafficking in Persons Report, June 2004" (www.state.gov/documents/organization/31458.pdf).

11. Francis A. J. Ianni, "Authority, Power and Respect: The Interplay of Control Systems in an Organized Crime 'Family,'" in Simon

Rottenberg, ed., *The Economics of Crime and Punishment* (Washington, D.C.: American Enterprise Institute for Public Policy Research, 1973), 133–153; and Ralph Salerno and John S. Tompkins, *The Criminal Confederation* (Garden City, N.Y.: Doubleday, 1969), 342–344.

12. Selwen Raab, "A Battered and Ailing Mafia Is Losing Its Grip on America," *The New York Times,* October 22, 1990, A1. According to Raab, this is especially true for those areas outside New York City and Chicago.

13. *Ibid.,* B7.

14. The President's Commission on Organized Crime, Report to the President and the Attorney General, *The Impact: Organized Crime Today, op.cit.,* Table 8, 463.

15. Dollar amounts adjusted for increases in the CPI through May 2005. David Boaz, "Drug Legalization, Criminalization and Harm Reduction," Cato Congressional Testimony, June 16, 1999; and "Gambling Boom," CQ Researcher, March 18, 1994, 248.

16. Congressman Charles Rangel, on ABC's *Nightline* of April 8, 1988, indicated the U.S. Congress' concern over the national security issues raised due to the instability in Latin American countries, such as Panama and Colombia, created by the cocaine trade of the Medellin cartel. It was reported on the same show that the cartel offered to pay off the national debt of Colombia, estimated to be $10 billion ($16.3 billion in 2005 dollars), if the government would not enforce the extradition treaty the government signed with the U.S.

17. For an interesting contrast see William J. Chambliss, *On the Take* (Bloomington, Ind.: Indiana University Press, 1978). Chambliss also offers insights into the question of economies of scale in bribery and corruption. See our discussion, which follows.

18. This section is based on Schelling, "Economic Analysis and Organized Crime." Essentially the same paper appears in *The Public Interest,* no. 7 (Spring 1967): 61–78.

19. Paul H. Rubin, "The Economic Theory of the Criminal Firm," in Rottenberg, *op.cit.,* 162.

20. *Ibid.,* 155.

21. *Ibid.,* 158.

22. *Ibid.,* 162.

23. It would be ideal to have an input-output model of the underworld economy which describes the input-output relationships between that economy and organized crime, as well as relationships with the upper-world economy.

24. R. Moran, "Bring Back the Mafia," *Newsweek,* August 7, 1989, 8. Mr. Moran teaches criminology at Mount Holyoke College.

25. This section is based on conversations and communications with Peter Leibowitz, then of the Connecticut Planning Committee on Criminal Administration, which took place when Professor Hellman was a member of that state's Subcommittee on Organized Crime.

26. For a description of how law enforcement information might vary depending on the focus, see Cressey, *op.cit.,* 68.

27. General educational programs for the private sector are recommended by the National Advisory Committee on Criminal Justice Standards and Goals in *Organized Crime—Report of the Task Force on Organized Crime* (Washington, D.C.: U.S. Government Printing Office, 1976).

28. In 2005 state-operated lotteries were conducted in 40 states and the District of Columbia with some form of gambling available in all but two states. Excellent overviews of gambling and state lotteries and issues relating to them can be found in Charles T. Clotfelter and Philip J. Cook, *Selling Hope* (Cambridge, Ma.: Harvard University Press, 1989), and the *National Gambling Impact Study Commission Fund Report.* (govinfo.library.unt.edu/ngisc/reports/fullrpt.html), 1999.

29. Edwin Kriester, Jr., *Crimes with No Victims* (New York: American Jewish Committee, 1972), 32.

30. Commission on the Review of the National Policy Toward Gambling, *Second Interim Report* (Washington, D.C., July 1976); and Cloftfelter and Cook, *op.cit.*

31. Murray Schumach, "OTB Says Bets Reach High of $772 Million in One Year," *The New York Times,* December 29, 1974.

32. For a study of the feasibility and implications of legalizing sports betting and the numbers game in New York, see Fund for the City of New York, *Legal Gambling in New York: A Discussion of Numbers*

and Sports Betting (New York, 1972). For background information on the history of the development of gambling law, see U.S. Department of Justice, Law Enforcement Assistance Administration, National Institute of Law Enforcement and Criminal Justice, *The Development of the Law of Gambling, 1776–1976* (Ithaca, N.Y., 1977).

33. After less than one year of operation, traditionally careful credit sources opened their doors to Atlantic City casino investment interests. Hal Lancaster, "Atlantic City Fever," *The Wall Street Journal,* February 1, 1979, 1.

34. *National Gambling Impact Study Commission Report, 1999 op.cit.,* 2–15, 2–16, and 5-3; and Associated Press, "Internet Gambling Growing"(www.publicagenda.org/issues/news.cfm?issue_type= gambling), February 28, 2000.

35. U.S. Statistical Abstract, *op.cit.,* Table 448, 293. This is total sales net of prizes and operating expenses.

36. Pam Greenberg, "Not Quite the Pot of Gold," *State Legislatures,* 18, no. 12 (December 1992).

37. *National Gambling Impact Study Commission Report, 1999, op. cit.,* 7–10.

38. Contradictory evidence is suggested by the testimony of a county police commissioner, reported in Cressey, *op.cit.,* 76.

10

A Final Note

In the preceding chapters we have tried to present an introduction to the economics of crime with an emphasis on analysis geared to the development and evaluation of public policy. Within the confines of an introductory textbook, it is not possible to cover every subject area in depth or to include some of the more advanced kinds of analysis, particularly when the supportive or advanced material is quantitative in nature. Nevertheless, most of the major issues and subject areas have been covered; research methodologies have been introduced in an elementary way; and advanced treatments or supporting quantitative material have been referenced where appropriate. Thus, it is hoped that this book can serve as a foundation to support additional inquiries into an extremely fascinating subject.

Economic analysis of criminal activity, law enforcement, and criminal justice systems is a relatively new area of applied economics, dating only from the late 1960s. Prior to that time, economic analysis of the law was restricted primarily to the laws concerning regulation of the economy (i.e., anti-trust legislation). Thus, when the President's Crime Commission issued its final report in 1967, the economic community was "either unconcerned or unprepared to contribute to the discussion."[1]

Since that time, considerable progress has been made. At its convention in December 1968, the American Economic Association sponsored a roundtable discussion on "Allocation of Resources in Law Enforcement." Economists began to apply their tools to the analysis of the impact of crime on society, the production of and costs of producing law enforcement and criminal justice, and, from these, the optimum allocation of resources to crime control. Some of this work is summarized and discussed in Chapters 2 and 4 of this book.

Chapter 2 focuses on the economic impact of criminal activity. This type of analysis is an essential forerunner to policy prescription, since it gives us an idea of what it is worth to prevent crime. In that chapter the impact of crime both on society as a whole and on individuals and groups within society is assessed. The ways in which various crimes can affect us are described. This kind of information is necessary in setting budget priorities and developing effective public policy to control crime.

Chapter 4 builds on Chapter 2 and addresses the broader question of optimum allocation of criminal justice resources; that is, it deals with the kinds of decisions which must be made concerning allocating and spending criminal justice resources, and with how economically efficient decisions are implemented. These decisions rely on two primary pieces of information: the benefits to be derived from crime reduction (which depend on the potential impact of crime on society), and the costs of achieving crime reduction in various ways. The chapter is devoted to a discussion of the types of decisions which must be made, how efficient decisions are made, and where the information necessary for decision-making comes from. The issues discussed include the optimum amount of crime prevention, the optimum amount of crime, the optimum "mix" of crime, the optimum allocation of police resources among neighborhoods, and the optimum allocation of resources within courts and corrections, including a discussion of the optimum magnitude or form of punishment for crime. The chapter contains a brief discussion of the production and costs of producing law enforcement. It also includes a discussion of the increasing role played by the private sector in providing correctional services. While Chapter 4 does not address all possible resource allocation questions (e.g., the most efficient method of input combination for producing law enforcement, or the optimum set of criminal justice procedures), it does serve to illustrate the kinds of questions which can be raised and the basic economic approach to answering them.

Economists have also focused on developing an explanation of why an individual or group commits criminal acts. This material was presented in Chapter 3. In that chapter a traditional model of economic choice is presented as one that is capable of explaining the choice to commit a criminal act(s). Application of the model to criminal choice requires the assumption that the potential criminal is rational—that he or she evaluates, however imperfectly or incompletely, the potential gains and losses from engaging in criminal activity. With this model of behavior defined, the types of gains and losses, including expected-punishment costs, are described. A general supply-of-crime function is derived, and the impact of various public policy options on its position and, therefore, on the amount of crime, is analyzed. In the chapter the economist's perspective is expanded to examine the impact of macroeconomic conditions on criminal activity. In addition, a Marxian explanation of criminal behavior and interpretation of the criminal justice system is briefly presented and linked to the more traditional economic approach.

The appendix to Chapter 3 is a necessary methodological complement to the discussion of public policies impacting the supply of crime. It describes the elements of cost-benefit analysis, a technique for evaluating public programs or policy changes from an economic perspective by comparing the benefits of the program or policy with its costs. This type of analysis is the foundation for the more general discussion in Chapter 4. Fundamentals of cost-benefit analysis are presented.

Finally, economists have applied their traditional market analyses to various kinds of illegal activities, including "victimless" crimes, provision of stolen property, and even provision of crimes against persons. Economic analysis of organized crime focuses on market analysis of the various goods and services in which organized crime is involved and/or on the economic theory of the business firm. Market analysis of various crimes and criminal enterprises is the core of chapters 5 through 9.

Chapter 5 is a discussion and analysis of crimes against property. Central to the description and evaluation of public policy alternatives for reducing the number of these crimes is an understanding of the market for stolen property and how it works, including the demand for and supply of stolen goods and the critical role of the fence in its smooth operation. Thus, market analysis is central to the chapter. Chapter 5 also includes a brief introductory discussion of empirical studies of crimes against property and methodological differences among those studies.

Chapter 6 applies the same basic approach to crimes against persons. Again a market framework is central to the chapter. The markets for murder and assault are defined, and links between the two are suggested. A distinction is made between the characteristics of the markets for rational and irrational crimes. Forcible rape is also discussed in a market context.

In Chapter 7 the most common application of market analysis to criminal activity is presented—a discussion of "victimless" crimes in terms of the demand for and supply of illegal goods and services. This general framework is developed and applied, for purposes of illustration, to the market for prostitution. In Chapter 8 the same methodology is applied to the more complicated illegal markets for cocaine and heroin.

Chapter 9 also utilizes a market approach. There an economic analysis of organized crime combines market analysis of the various goods and services in which organized crime is involved with the economic theory of the business firm as applied to illegal enterprises operating in illegal markets. The theme of the chapter is the need to maximize profits in illegal markets. A market analysis of public policy options is therefore required.

This introductory textbook, along with the companion reader, has provided a representative sample of the kinds of work which economists have been doing in the field of the economics of crime over the last twenty years. There is still a great deal of room for additional research, both theoretical and empirical. In this book and in the reader, we uncovered many unsolved issues requiring further investigation.

Beginning in Chapter 2, it was clear that our measurement of the economic impact of crime is inadequate and incomplete. A way to measure the impact of property crime is still required. Can the harm to society be related to the value of the property taken, or must some other method of quantification be devised? In measuring the harm done by crimes against persons, is lost income a valid measure of the worth of an individual? Can additional considerations be included in the measurement? Finally, can we quantify psychic costs or negative externalities? Each of these issues, while ultimately tied to quantification and empirical work, involves a theoretical resolution of the appropriate concept or kind of measurement required.

The discussion of an economic model of criminal behavior in Chapter 3 raises additional questions. Where does the economic model of behavior fit in? Does its appropriateness or validity depend on the characteristics of the crime, the characteristics of the criminal, or other circumstances? Can we generalize about this enough to know when and where to use the economic approach productively? Can it be applied universally? Finally, where we do apply the model, how much of the assessment of the gains and losses to those engaging in criminal activity depends on perceived values of the magnitudes involved as opposed to their actual values? Can the relationship between the two be defined and described so that perceived values can be measured or predictions of impacts on criminal activity can be based on changes in actual values?

Chapter 4 illustrates the need to refine the tools for dealing with questions of optimum allocation of criminal justice resources. Many of the issues raised or suggested are common to other areas of applied economics, such as the appropriateness of the marginal approach to analysis and the need for more theoretical and empirical work on production functions and quantification of production costs. The inability to measure completely and properly the benefits of crime control and criminal justice is related to the problems identified in Chapter 2.

Chapters 5 through 9, which all involved market analysis of criminal activity, share a recognized need—the need to know more about the characteristics of the various markets, including description and measurement of the demand and supply functions in the markets for stolen property, illegal goods and services, and crimes against persons. In the latter case the question of the extent and importance of "irrationality" must be resolved. The infrastructure necessary to support each market must also be defined. This may be particularly important in the analysis of "victimless" crimes and the activities of organized crime. To what extent does organized crime support or facilitate other criminal activities and vice versa? Can a model of the firm be sufficiently adapted to organized criminal enterprises to permit quantification and prediction of the impacts of various actions in the markets for illegal goods and services as well as the entire criminal "underworld"?

These and other questions remain to be answered. From this discussion it is clear that many concepts and dimensions of the criminal problem need to be clarified and quantified before hard public policy decisions can be made. Thus, there is a great deal of work to be done. In addition, there are areas of the study of criminal behavior in which economists have yet to become involved. As an example, urban and regional economists have well-developed theories to explain the locational choice of households and business firms. Yet these theories, or models, have not been applied to the description or prediction of the location of criminal activity—an application which would appear to be particularly useful for public policy, either to reduce crime or to contain it within those geographic areas where it does the least harm.[2]

This and many other applications of economics to the study of criminal behavior and the design of effective public policy for dealing with the crime problem lie in the future. This book is intended to be a link not only to the understanding of additional economic research to come, but to the work being done in other disciplines which study criminal behavior. Economists are relatively new to the field. In almost 35 years of research effort, they have made significant contributions to the study of crime,[3] law enforcement, and criminal justice. But there are others who have made equally important advances by looking at the problems from slightly different perspectives. It is necessary that the work of economists be understood by researchers in other disciplines and that economists learn from the perspectives and experience of others. This brings us back to a statement made in Chapter 1: an adequate understanding of criminal behavior, as well as policy design, probably requires a multidisciplinary approach. Here we focused on the economic perspective in an effort to communicate to a wider audience.

NOTES

1. Martin T. Katzman, "The Economics of Defense Against Crime in the Streets," *Land Economics,* 44, no. 4 (November 1968), 431.

2. For a discussion see Daryl Hellman and Joel Naroff, "Urban Land Use Models: Applications in Criminology," in James Alan Fox, ed., *Models in Quantitative Criminology* (New York: Academic Press, 1981).

3. In 1992, Professor Gary S. Becker of the University of Chicago, won the Nobel Prize in Economics in part for his development of the economic theory of criminal behavior. It forms the basis for the model discussed in Chapter 3.

Bibliography

AARONSON, DAVID E., C. THOMAS DIENES, and MICHAEL C. MUSHENO. "Changing the Public Drunkenness Laws: The Impact of Decriminalization." *Law and Society Review,* 12, no. 3 (Spring 1978), 405–436.

ALLISON, JOHN P. "Economic Factors and the Rate of Crime." *Land Economics,* 48, no. 2 (May 1972), 193–196.

American University Law School, Institute for Advanced Studies in Justice, Employment and Crime Project. *Crime and Employment Issues.* Washington, D.C., 1978.

ANDERSON, DAVID. "The Aggregate Burden of Crime." *Journal of Law and Economics,* October 1999.

ANDERSON, R.W. "Towards a Cost-Benefit Analysis of Police Activity." *Public Finance,* 22, no. 1 (1974), 1–18.

ARCHER, DANE and ROSEMARY GARTNER. *Violence and Crime in Cross-National Perspective.* New Haven, Ct.: Yale University Press, 1984.

ASSOCIATED PRESS, "Internet Gambling Growing." February 28, 2000, www.publicagenda.org/issues/news.cfm?issue_type=gambling.

Attorney General's Commission on Pornography. *Final Report.* Washington, D.C., July 1986.

AVIO, KENNETH. "An Economic Analysis of Criminal Corrections: The Canadian Case." *Canadian Journal of Economics,* 6, no. 2 (May 1973), 164–178.

_____. "Recidivism in the Economic Model of Crime." *Economic Inquiry,* 13, no. 3 (September 1975), 450–456.

BARNETT, ARNOLD, DANIEL J. KLEITMAN, and RICHARD C. LARSON. "On Urban Homicide: A Statistical Analysis." *Journal of Criminal Justice,* 3 (1975), 85–110.

BARNETT, HAROLD C. "Wealth, Crime and Capital Accumulation." *Contemporary Crises,* 3 (1979), 171–186.

_____. "The Distribution of Crime and Punishment." Paper presented at the Western Economics Association Meeting, San Francisco, June 24, 1976.

BARTEL, A.P. "Women and Crime: An Economic Analysis." *Economic Inquiry,* 17, no. 1 (January 1979), 29–51.

BECK, ALLEN, and CHRISTOPHER MUMOLA, "Prisoners in 1998." Washington, D.C.: U.S. Department of Justice, Bureau of Justice Statistics, August 1999.

BECKER, GARY S. "Crime and Punishment: An Economic Approach." *Journal of Political Economy,* 76, no. 2 (March–April 1968), 169–217.

BECKER, GARY S., and WILLIAM M. LANDES, eds. *Essays in the Economics of Crime and Punishment.* New York: National Bureau of Economic Research, 1974.

BENSON, BRUCE L. "Do We Want the Production of Prison Services to be More 'Efficient'?" Florida State University, Department of Economics Working Paper Series, no. 91–06–6, 1991.

BLACK, CHARLES L., JR. *Capital Punishment: The Inevitability of Caprice and Mistake.* New York: W.W. Norton, 1974.

BLUMSTEIN, ALFRED, and RICHARD LARSON. "Models of a Total Criminal Justice System." *Operations Research,* 17, no. 2 (March–April 1969), 199–231.

BLUMSTEIN, ALFRED, JACQUELINE COHEN, and DANIEL NAGIN, eds. *Deterrence and Incapacitation: Estimating the Effects of Criminal Sanctions on Crime Rates.* Washington, D.C.: National Academy of Sciences, 1978.

BOAZ, DAVID. "Drug Legalization, Criminalization and Harm Reduction." www.cato.org/testimony/ct-dbz061699.htm, June 16, 1999.

BOWERS, WILLIAM J., and GLENN L. PIERCE. "Deterrence, Brutalization, or Nonsense: A Critique of Isaac Ehrlich's Research on Capital Punishment." *Yale Law Journal,* 85, no. 1 (1975–76), 187–208.

_____. "Arbitrariness and Discrimination under Post-Furman Capital Statutes." *Crime and Delinquency,* 26, no. 4 (October 1980), 563–635.

_____. "Deterrence or Brutalization: What Is the Effect of Executions?" *Crime and Delinquency,* 26, no. 4 (October 1980), 453–484.

BRANTINGHAM, PATRICIA L., and PAUL J. BRANTINGHAM. "Residential Burglary and Urban Form." *Urban Studies,* 12, no 3 (October 1975) 273–284.

BRZEZINSKI, MATTHEW. "Re-engineering the Drug Business," *The New York Times,* June 23, 2002.

Business Software Association, "Worldwide Business Software Piracy Losses Estimated at Nearly $11 Billion in 1998." www.bsa.org/pressbox/enforcement/927637266.html.

CAPUTO, DAVID A. *Organized Crime and American Politics.* Morristown, N.J.: General Learning Press, 1974.

CARPENTER, TED. "Collateral Damage: The Wide-Ranging Consequences of America's Drug War." www.cato.org/realaudio/drugwar/papers/carpenter.htm.

CATALANO, SHANNAN. "Criminal Victimization, 2003," (Washington, D.C., Bureau of Justice Statistics, September 2004).

CAULKINS, JONATHAN, PETER REUTER, MARTIN IGUCHI and JAMES CHIESA. "How Goes the 'War on Drugs'?" Santa Monica, CA: Rand Corporation, 2005.

CHAMBLISS, WILLIAM J. *On the Take.* Bloomington: Indiana University Press, 1978.

CHAPMAN, JEFFREY I., and CARL W. NELSON. *A Handbook of Cost-Benefit Techniques and Applications.* Washington D.C.: American Bar Association, Correctional Economics Center, July 1975.

CHILTON, ROLAND J., and ADELE SPEILBERGER. "Increases in Crime: The Utility of Alternative Measures." *Journal of Criminal Law, Criminology, and Police Science,* 63, no. 1 (March 1972), 68–74.

CLARK, LORENNE M.G., and DEBRA J. LEWIS. *Rape: The Price of Coercive Sexuality.* Toronto: Women's Press, 1977.

CLOTFELTER, CHARLES T. "Public Services, Private Substitutes, and the Demand for Protection Against Crime." *American Economic Review,* 67, no. 5 (December 1977), 867–877.

CLOFTFELTER, C., P. COOK, et al., "State Lotteries at the Turn of the Century: Report to the National Gambling Impact Study Commission." Washington, D.C.: National Gambling Impact Study Commission, April 1999.

COCHRAN, JOHN K. and MITCHELL B. CHAMLIN. "The Influence of a Cost-Benefit Function on the Supply of Economic Crimes: A Specific Test of the Profit Maximizing Thesis." *Journal of Crime and Justice,* xv, no. 2 (1992), 53–68.

COHEN, MARK A. "The Cost of Crime to Victims." Vanderbilt University, Owen Graduate School of Management, Working Paper No. 86-29 (October 1986).

_____. "A Note on the Cost of Crime to Victims." *Urban Studies*, 27, no. 1 (1990), 139–146.

COHEN, MARK A., ROLAND T. RUST, SARA STEEN, and SIMON T. TIDD. "Willingness-to-Pay for Crime Control Programs," *Criminology*, Vol 42, Number 1, February, 2004.

COLEMAN, JAMES W. *The Criminal Elite.* New York: St. Martin's Press, 1985. Commission on the Review of the National Policy Toward Gambling. *Second Interim Report.* Washington, D.C., July 1976.

CONKLIN, JOHN E., ed. *The Crime Establishment: Organized Crime and American Society.* Englewood Cliffs, N.J.: Prentice-Hall, 1973.

CONNER, ROGER L. and PATRICK C. BURNS, "The Winnable War: How Communities are Eradicating Local Drug Markets." *The Brookings Review* (Summer 1992), 26–29.

COOK, PHILIP. "The Demand and Supply of Criminal Opportunities," in M. Tonry and N. Morris, eds., *Crime and Justice: An Annual Review.* Chicago: The University of Chicago Press, 1986, 1–28.

COOK, PHILIP, and GARY ZARKIN. "Crime and the Business Cycle." *The Journal of Legal Studies,* xiv(1) (January 1985), 115–128.

CRESSEY, DONALD R. *Theft of the Nation: The Structure and Operations of Organized Crime in America.* New York: Harper & Row, 1969.

CUNNINGHAM, WILLIAM C., JOHN J. STRAUCHS, and CLIFFORD W. VAN METER. *Private Security Trends 1970 to 2000.* Boston: Butterworth-Heinemann, 1990.

_____. *Private Security: Patterns and Trends.* Washington, D.C.: U.S. Department of Justice, National Institute of Justice (Research in Brief), August 1991.

DANZINGER, S., and D. WHEELER. "The Economics of Crime: Punishment or Income Redistribution." *Review of Social Economy,* 33, no. 2 (October 1975), 113–131.

Death Penalty Information Center, "Millions Misspent: What Politicians Don't Say About the High Costs of the Death Penalty." www.essential.org/dpic/dpic.r08.html.

DEITH, LILIAN, and DAVID WEINSTEIN. *The Impact of Legalized Gambling.* New York: Praeger, 1974.

De IULIO, JOHN J., JR. "A Limited War on Crime That We Can Win." *The Brookings Review* (Fall 1992), 6–11.

DENNIS, RICHARD J. "The Economics of Legalizing Drugs." *The Atlantic Monthly,* November 1990, 126–132.

DEZHBAKHSH, HASHEM, PAUL RUBIN and JOANNA SHEPPHERD. "Does Capital Punishment Have a Deterrent Effect? New Evidence from Postmoratorium Panel Data," *American Law and Economics Review,* (Fall 2003), 344-376.

DIAMOND, MILTON and AYAKO UCHIYAMA. "Pornography, Rape and Sex Crimes in Japan," *International Journal of Law and Psychiatry,* 22(1) (1999), 1–22.

DONOHUE III, JOHN and STEVEN LEVITT. "Legalized Abortion and Crime," *Quarterly Journal of Economics,* 116:2, May 2001, 379–420.

DONOHUE III, JOHN and STEVEN LEVITT. "Further Evidence that Legalized Abortion Lowered Crime," *Journal of Human Resources,* Vol. 39, no. 1, Winter 2004, 29–49.

DOUGLASS, JOSEPH D., JR. "Assessing Progress in the 'War on Drugs.'" *The Journal of Social, Political and Economic Studies,* 17, no. 1 (Spring 1992), 29–42.

Drug Control: Status Report on DOD Support to Counternarcotics Activities. Washington, D.C.: U.S.G.A.O. Report to the Chairman, Subcommittee on Legislation and National Security, Committee on Government Operations, House of Representatives, June 1991.

EHRLICH, ISAAC. "Participation in Illegitimate Activities: A Theoretical and Empirical Investigation." *Journal of Political Economy,* 81, no. 3 (May–June 1973), 521–564.

_____. "The Deterrent Effect of Capital Punishment: A Question of Life and Death." *American Economic Review,* 65, no. 3 (June 1975), 397–417.

_____. "Capital Punishment and Deterrence: Some Further Thoughts and Additional Evidence." *Journal of Political Economy,* 85, no. 4 (August 1977), 741–788.

EHRLICH, ISAAC, and GARY S. BECKER. "Market Insurance, Self-Insurance and Self-Protection." *Journal of Political Economy,* 80, no. 4 (July–August 1972), 623–648.

ERBE, NANCY. "Prostitutes: Victims of Men's Exploitation and Abuse." *Law and Inequality,* 2:609 (1984), 609–628.

ERICKSON, PATRICIA G., et al. *The Steel Drug: Cocaine in Perspective.* Lexington, Mass.: Lexington Books, 1987.

FERRY, JOHN, and MARJORIE KRAVITZ. *Issues in Sentencing.* Washington, D.C.: U.S. Department of Justice, Law Enforcement Assistance Administration, National Institute of Law Enforcement and Criminal Justice, March 1978.

FLYNN, STEPHEN. "Worldwide Drug Scourge: The Expanding Trade in Illicit Drugs," *The Brookings Review* (Winter 1993), 6–11.

FOX, JAMES ALAN, ed. *Models in Quantitative Criminology.* New York: Academic Press, 1981.

FOX, JAMES ALAN, and MARIANNE W. ZAWITZ. "Homicide Trends in the United States: 1998 Update," *Crime Data Brief,* Washington, D.C.: U.S. Department of Justice, Bureau of Justice Statistics, March 2000.

FOWLER, THOMAS B. "Winning the War on Drugs: Can We Get There From Here." *The Journal of Social, Political and Economic Studies,* 15, 4 (Winter 1990), 403–421.

FREEH, LOUIS J. "Statement for the Record of Louis J. Freeh, Director Federal Bureau of Investigation, on Cybercrime." www.fbi.gov/pressrm/congress/congress00/cyber021660.htm.

FREIMUND, JUSTUS, and MARJORIE KRAVITZ. *Police Productivity.* Washington, D.C.: U.S. Department of Justice, Law Enforcement Assistance Administration, National Institute of Law Enforcement and Criminal Justice, May 1978.

FRIEDMAN, MILTON. "The War We Are Losing," in M. Krauss and E. Lazear, eds., *Searching for Alternatives: Drug-Control Policy in the United States.* Stanford, Ca.: Hoover Institution Press, 1991, 53–67.

FUGII, EDWIN T. "Heroin Addiction and Public Policy." *Journal of Urban Economics,* 2, no. 2 (April 1975), 181–198.

Fund for the City of New York. *Legal Gambling in New York: A Discussion of Numbers and Sports Betting.* New York, 1972.

GEIS, GILBERT, and ROBERT F. MEIER. *White Collar Crime.* New York: The Free Press, 1977.

GIBBS, JACK P. "Death Penalty, Retribution and Penal Policy." *Journal of Criminal Law and Criminology,* 69, no. 3 (Fall 1978), 291–299.

GILLIARD, DARRELL, *Prison and Jail Inmates at Midyear 1998,* Washington, D.C.: Bureau of Justice Statistics, March 1999.

GOLDBERG, ITZHAK. "Public and Private Protection: Substitutability or Complementarity." Stanford, Ca.: Stanford University, Hoover Institution, Center for Econometric Studies of the Criminal Justice System, Domestic Studies Program, Occasional Paper Series, April 1977.

GOLDFARB, RONALD. *Jails.* New York: Twentieth Century Fund, 1975.

GORDON, DAVID M. "Class and the Economics of Crime." *Review of Radical Political Economics,* 3, no. 3 (1971), 50–75.

GREENWOOD, MICHAEL J., and WALTER J. WADYCKI. "Crime Rates and Public Expenditures for Police Protection: Their Interaction." *Review of Social Economy,* 31, no. 2 (October 1973), 138–151.

GRIFFIN, SUSAN. "Rape: The All-American Crime." *Ramparts,* 10, no. 3 (September 1971).

HANN, ROBERT G. "Crime and the Cost of Crime: An Economic Approach." *Journal of Research in Crime and Delinquency,* 9, no. 1 (January 1972), 12–30.

HARRIS, JOHN R. "On the Economics of Law and Order." *Journal of Political Economy,* 78, no. 1 (January–February 1970), 165–174.

HARWOOD, H., D. FOUNTAIN, and G. LIVERMORE. *The Economic Costs of Alcohol and Drug Abuse in the United States— 1992, Executive Summary.* Rockville, MD: U.S. Department of Health and Human Services, National Institute on Drug Abuse, September 1998.

HAY, JOEL W. "The Harm They Do to Others: A Primer on the External Costs of Drug Abuse," in M. Krauss and E. Lazear, eds., *Searching for Alternatives: Drug Control Policy in the United States.* Stanford, Ca.: Hoover Institution Press, 1991, 200–225.

HEINECKE, J. M. "An Econometric Investigation of Production Cost Functions for Law Enforcement Agencies." Stanford, Ca.: Stanford University, Hoover Institution, Center for Econometric Studies of the Criminal Justice System, Domestic Studies Program, Occasional Paper Series, August, 1977.

HELLER, NELSON B., and ROBERT E. MARKLAND. "A Climatological Model for Forecasting the Demand for Police Service." *Journal of Research in Crime and Delinquency,* 7, no. 2 (July 1970), 167–176.

HELLMAN, DARYL A. "Social Welfare Implications of Sentencing Policy: An Economic Perspective." *Legal Studies Forum,* XXII, no. 1 (1988).

HELLMAN, DARYL, and JOEL NAROFF. "The Impact of Crime on Urban Residential Property Values." *Urban Studies,* 16, no. 1 (February 1979), 105–112.

HELLMAN, DARYL, JOEL NAROFF, SUSAN BEATON, and BAR-BARA IANZITI. *Incentives and Disincentives to Crime Prevention*

Behavior. Washington, D.C.: National Institute of Law Enforcement and Criminal Justice, 1978.

HENDRICKSON, ROBERT. *Ripoffs—A Complete Survival Guide.* New York: Viking Press, 1976.

HOBBLER, THOMAS, and DOROTHY HOBBLER. *Drugs & Crime.* New York: Chelsea House Publishers, 1988.

HOLMES, STEVEN. "Look Who's Questioning the Death Penalty." *The New York Times, News of the Week in Review,* April 16, 2000.

ICHNIOWSKI, CASEY. "The Persistence of Organized Crime in New York City Construction: An Economic Perspective." *Industrial and Labor Relations Review,* 42, no. 4 (July 1989), 549–565.

INTERNATIONAL CRIMINAL POLICE ORGANIZATION (INTERPOL). *International Crime Statistics for 1987–88.* St. Cloud, France: INTERPOL, 1991.

JOHNSON, BRUCE, ANSLEY HAMID, and HARRY SANABRIA. "Emerging Models of Crack Distribution," in T. Mieczkowski, ed., *Drugs, Crime, and Social Policy.* Boston: Allyn and Bacon, 1992.

JOHNSON, BRUCE D., et al. *Taking Care of Business: The Economics of Crime by Heroin Abusers.* Lexington, Mass.: Lexington Books, 1985.

Judicial Conference of the United States, *Federal Death Penalty Cases: Recommendations Concerning the Cost and Quality of Defense Representations.* Washington, D.C.: Administrative Offices of the U.S. Courts, May 1998.

KAPLAN, JOHN. "Taking Drugs Seriously." *The Public Interest,* no. 92 (Summer 1988), 32–50.

KATZ, LAWRENCE, STEVEN LEVITT and ELLEN SHUSTOROVICH. "Prison Conditions, Capital Punishment and Deterrence," *American Law and Economics Review,* Fall 2003, 318–343.

KATZMAN, MARTIN T. "The Economics of Defense Against Crime in the Streets." *Land Economics,* 44, no. 4 (November 1968), 431–440.

KERACHER, JOHN. *Crime—Its Causes and Consequences.* Chicago: Charles H. Kerr, 1937.

KERRY, JOHN. *Drugs in Massachusetts: The Domestic Impact of a Foreign Invasion.* Washington, D.C.: U.S. Senate, Committee on Foreign Relations, January 1990.

KIM, ILJOONG, BRUCE BENSON, DAVID RASMUSSEN, and THOMAS ZUEHLKE. "An Economic Analysis of Recidivism

Among Drug Offenders." Florida State University, Department of Economics Working Paper Series. no. 91–02–10 (May 1991).

KLEIMAN, MARK A. R. *Against Excess: Drug Policy for Results.* New York: Basic Books, 1992.

_____, and JONATHAN P. CAULKINS. "Heroin Policy for the Next Decade." *The Annals of the American Academy of Political and Social Science,* 521 (May 1992), 163–174.

KRAUSS, MELVYN B. and EDWARD P. LAZEAR, eds. *Searching for Alternatives: Drug-Control Policy in the United States.* Stanford, Ca.: Hoover Institution Press, 1991.

KRIESTER, EDWIN, JR. *Crimes with No Victims.* New York: American Jewish Committee, 1972.

LANDES, WILLIAM. "Copyright Protection and Appriopriation Art," culturalpolicy.uchicago.edu/conf1999/landes.html.

_____. "An Economic Analysis of the Courts." *The Journal of Law and Economics,* 14, no. 1 (April 1971), 61–107.

LEONHARDT, DAVID. "As Prison Labor Grows, So Does the Debate." *The New York Times,* March 19, 2000.

LESSAN, GLORIA T. "Macro-economic Determinants of Penal Policy: Estimating the Unemployment and Inflation Influences on Imprisonment Rate Changes in the United States, 1948–1985." *Crime, Law and Social Choice,* 16, no. 2 (September 1991), 177–198.

LEVINE, MICHAEL. "Fight Back: A Solution Between Prohibition and Legalization," Washington, D.C.: Cato Institute, www.cato.org/realaudio/drugwar/papers/levine.htm.

LEVITT, STEVEN. "Understanding Why Crime Fell in the 1990s: Four Factors that Explain the Decline and Six that Do Not," *Journal of Economic Perspectives,* Vol. 18, no. 1, Winter 2004.

LEVITT, STEVEN and SUDHIR VENKATESH. "An Economic Analysis of a Drug-Selling Gang's Finances," *The Quarterly Journal of Economics,* August 2000.

MacCOUN, ROBERT. "Are the Wages of Sin $30 an Hour? Economic Aspect of Street-Level Drug Dealing." *Crime and Delinquency,* 38, no. 4 (October 1992).

McMANUS, WALTER S. "Estimates of the Deterrent Effect of Capital Punishment: The Importance of the Researcher's Prior Beliefs." *Journal of Political Economy,* 93, no. 2 (April 1985), 417–425.

McPHETERS, LEE R., and WILLIAM B. STRONGE. "Law Enforcement Expenditures and Urban Crime." *National Tax Journal,* 27, no. 4 (December 1974), 633–643.

_____, eds. *The Economics of Crime and Law Enforcement.* Springfield, Ill.: Charles C. Thomas, 1976.

McPHETERS, LEE R., R. MANN, and D. SCHLAGENHAUF. "Economic Response to a Crime Deterrence Program: Mandatory Sentencing for Robbery with a Firearm." *Economic Inquiry,* 22, no. 4 (1984), 550–570.

MATHIAS ROBERT A. *The Road Not Taken: Cost-Effective Alternatives to Prison for Non-Violent Felony Offenders in New York State.* New York: Correctional Association of New York, September 1986.

MAUER, MARC. "Americans Behind Bars: U.S. and International Use of Incarceration, 1995." Washington, D.C.: The Sentencing Project, 1997.

MEAD, A.C., and H.C. BARNETT. "Regional Crime Patterns: A Question of Stability?" *Growth and Change,* 15, no. 3 (July 1984), 10–14.

MIECZKOWSKI, THOMAS, ed. *Drugs, Crime, and Social Policy.* Boston: Allyn and Bacon, 1992.

_____. "Some Observations on the Scope of Crack Use and Distribution." *Ibid.*

MILLER, ROD, GEORGE SEXTON, and VICTOR JACOBSEN. "Making Jails Productive," Washington, D.C.: U.S. Department of Justice, National Institute of Justice Research in Brief, October 1991.

MILLER, TED, MARK COHEN, and BRIAN WIERSEMA. *Victim Costs and Consequences: A New Look.* Washington, D.C.: National Institute of Justice, January 1996.

MOCAN, H. NACI and TURAN BALI. "Asymmetric Crime Cycles," www.aeaweb.org/annual_mtg_papers/2005/0108_1430_1303.pdf, December 2004.

MOORE, MARK H. *The Economics of Heroin Distribution.* Croton-on-Hudson, N.Y.: Hudson Institute, 1970.

_____. "Supply Reduction and Drug Law Enforcement." Mimeo, March 1, 1989.

MUSTO, DAVID F. "Opium, Cocaine and Marijuana in American History." *Scientific American,* July 1991, 40–47.

NADELMANN, ETHAN. "An End to Marijuana Prohibition—The Drive to Legalize Picks Up," National Review, July 12, 2004, 1–7.

_____. "The Case for Legalization." The Public Interest, no. 92 (Summer 1988), 3–31.

_____. "Drug Prohibition in the U.S.: Costs, Consequences, and Alternatives," Thomas Mieczkowski, ed., op.cit.

National Advisory Committee on Criminal Justice Standards and Goals. Report of the Task Force on Organized Crime. Washington, D.C., 1976.

National Commission on the Causes and Prevention of Violence, Firearms and Violence in American Life, by G. D. Newton, Jr., and F.E. Zimring. Washington, D.C., 1969.

National Commission on Marijuana and Drug Abuse. Drug Use in America: Problem in Perspective. Washington, D.C., 1973.

National Drug Intelligence Center. "National Drug Threat Assessment 2005," February 2005.

National Gambling Impact Study Commission Report, 1999. Washington, D.C.: National Gambling Impact Study Commission, June 1999.

National Narcotics Intelligence Consumers Committee. The NNICC Report 1997: The Supply of Illicit Drugs to the United States. Washington, D.C.: U.S. Department of Justice, Drug Enforcement Administration, November 1998.

National Narcotics Intelligence Consumers Committee. The NNICC Report 1985–1986: The Supply of Illicit Drugs to the United States from Foreign and Domestic Sources in 1985 and 1986. Washington, D.C., June 1987.

_____. The NNICC Report 1991: The Supply of Illicit Drugs to the United States. Washington, D.C.: U.S. Department of Justice, Drug Enforcement Administration, July 1992.

NOAM, ELI, M. "A Cost-Benefit Model of Criminal Courts." Research in Law and Economics, 3 (1981), 173–183.

Office of National Drug Control Policy. "Drug Use Consequences," www.whitehousedrugpolicy.gov/publications/policy/03ncds/.

_____. "Fact Sheets" (various), www.whitehousedrugpolicy.gov/publications/facts/.

_____. "Measuring the Deterrent Effect of Enforcement Operations on Drug Smuggling, 1991–1999," August 2001.

_____. "The Economic Costs of Drug Abuse in the United States, 1992-2002," Washington, D.C., December 2004.

_____. "Measuring the Deterrent Effect of Enforcement Operations on Drug Smuggling, 1991–1999," Washington, D.C., August 2001.

_____. *The National Drug Control Strategy, (various issues),* Washington, D.C.: Executive Office of the President.

_____. *Pulse Check: National Trends in Drug Abuse,* Washington, D.C.: Executive Office of the President, Spring 1996.

_____. *What America's Users Spend on Illegal Drugs, 1988–1993,* Washington, D.C.: Executive Office of the President, Spring 1995.

_____. *Drug Use Trends.* Washington, D.C.: Executive Office of the President, June 1999.

_____. *Drug Data Summary.* Washington, D.C.: Executive Office of the President, April 1999.

_____. "The Price and Purity of Illicit Drugs: 1981 through the Second Quarter of 2003," November 2004.

_____. "The Price of Illicit Drugs: 1981 through the Second Quarter of 2001," October 2001.

Office of Technology Assessment. *The Border War on Drugs.* Washington, D.C., March 1987.

ORSAGH, THOMAS J. "The Determinants of Major Crime in California in 1960." *Western Economic Journal,* 8, no. 3 (September 1970), 326. Abstract only.

_____. *Judicial Responses to Crime and the Criminal: Utilitarian Perspective.* Washington, D.C.: Bureau of Justice Statistics, May 1982.

OSTROWSKI, JAMES. "Thinking About Drug Legalization," *Policy Analysis,* May 25, 1989.

PASSALL, PETER, and JOHN B. TAYLOR. "The Deterrent Effect of Capital Punishment: Another View." *American Economic Review,* 67, no. 3 (June 1977), 445–451.

PEELE, STANTON. Addiction Web Site, www.peele.net/Faq/addicts .html.

Pennsylvania Program for Women and Girl Offenders. *The Decriminalization of Prostitution—The Movement Towards Decriminalization.* Philadelphia, 1975.

PERRY, CATHERINE D. "Right of Privacy Challenges to Prostitution Statutes." *Washington University Law Quarterly,* 58:439, Number 2, 439–480.

PHILLIPS, LLAD, and HAROLD L. VOTEY, JR. "Black Women, Economic Disadvantage and Incentives to Crime." *American Economic Review,* 74, no. 2 (May 1984), 293–297.

_____. "The Choice Between Legitimate and Illegitimate Work: Micro Study of Individual Behavior." *Contemporary Policy Issues,* v, no. 4 (October 1987), 59–72.

PHILLIPS, LLAD, HAROLD L. VOTEY, JR., and DAROLD MAXWELL. "Crime, Youth and the Labor Market." *Journal of Political Economy,* 80, no. 3 (May–June 1972), 491–503.

PIERCE, GLENN L., and WILLIAM J. BOWERS. "The Bartley Fox Gun Law's Short-Term Impass on Crime in Boston." *The Annals of the American Academy,* 455 (May 1981), 120–137.

PILLER, CHARLES. "Cyber-Crime Loss at Firms Doubles to $10 Billion." *The Los Angeles Times,* March 22, 2000, Part C.

PLATTNER, MARC F. "The Rehabilitation of Punishment." *The Public Interest,* no. 44 (Summer 1976), 104–114.

POWER, RICHARD. "2000 CSI/FBI Computer Crime and Security Survey." *Computer Security Issues & Trends,* Vol. VI, No. 1, Spring 2000.

President's Commission on Law Enforcement and the Administration of Justice. *The Challenge of Crime in a Free Society.* Washington, D.C., 1967.

_____. *Task Force Report: Crime and Its Impact: An Assessment,* by J. Vorenberg and H.S. Ruth. Washington, D.C., 1967.

_____. *Task Force Report: Organized Crime.* Washington, D.C., 1967.

_____. *Task Force Report: Science and Technology.* Washington, D.C., 1967.

President's Commission on Obscenity and Pornography. *Technical Report of the Commission on Obscenity and Pornography.* Washington, D.C., 1971.

President's Commission on Organized Crime, Report to the President and the Attorney General. *America's Habit: Drug Abuse, Drug Trafficking, and Organized Crime.* Washington, D.C., March 1986.

_____. *The Impact: Organized Crime Today.* Washington, D.C., April 1986.

President's Working Group on Unlawful Conduct on the Internet. *The Electronic Frontier: The Challenge of Unlawful Conduct Involving the Use of the Internet.* Washington, D.C., March 2000.

PRESSMEN, ISRAEL, and ARTHUR CAROL. "Crime as a Diseconomy of Scale." *Review of Social Economy,* 29, no. 2 (September 1971), 227–236.

Prostitutes Education Network. "Prostitution in the United States—The Statistics." www.bayswan.org/stats.html.

PYLE, DAVID J. *The Economics of Crime and Law Enforcement.* New York: St. Martin's Press, 1983.

QUINNEY, RICHARD. *Class State and Crime.* New York: David McKay, 1977.

RAPHAEL, STEVEN and RUDOLF WINTER-EMBER. "Identifying the Effect of Unemployment on Crime," *Journal of Law and Economics,* v. 44, issue 1, April 2001, 259–283.

RENNISON, CALLIE MARIE. "Criminal Victimization 1998." Washington, D.C.: Bureau of Justice Statistics, July 1999.

REUTER, PETER. "Can the Border be Sealed?" *The Public Interest,* no. 92 (Summer 1988), 51–65.

_____. "The Limits and Consequences of U.S. Foreign Drug Control Efforts." *The Annals of the American Academy of Political and Social Science,* 521 (May 1992), 151–162.

REUTER, PETER, and MARK KLEIMAN. "Risks and Prices: An Economic Analysis of Drug Enforcement." In M. Tonry and N. Morris, eds., *Crime and Justice: An Annual Review of Research.* Chicago: University of Chicago Press, 1986, 289–340.

REUTER, PETER, ROBERT MacCOUN, and PATRICK MURPHY. *Money from Crime: A Study of the Economics of Drug Dealing in Washington, D.C.* Santa Monica, Ca.: The RAND Corporation, June 1990.

REYNOLDS, HELEN. *The Economics of Prostitution.* Springfield, Ill.: Charles C. Thomas, 1986.

RIAA (Recording Industry Association of America). "Issues: Anti-Piracy," www.ria.com.

ROGERS, A.J. *The Economics of Crime.* Hinsdale, Ill.: Dryden Press, 1973.

ROHTER, LARRY. "Colombia Adjusts Economic Figures to Include Its Drug Crops." *The New York Times,* June 27, 1999, A3.

ROTTENBERG, SIMON. "The Clandestine Distribution of Heroin, Its Discovery and Suppression." *Journal of Political Economy,* 76, no. 1 (January–February 1968), 78–90.

_____. ed. *The Economics of Crime and Punishment.* Washington, D.C.: American Enterprise Institute for Public Policy Research, 1973.

SALERNO, RALPH, and JOHN S. TOMPKINS. *The Criminal Confederation.* Garden City, N.Y.: Doubleday, 1969.

San Francisco Task Force on Prostitution. "Final Report 1996," www.bayswan.org/5cost.html.

SCHELLING, THOMAS. "Economics and Criminal Enterprise." *The Public Interest,* no. 7 (Spring 1967), 61–78.

SCHMIDT, PETER, and ANN D. WITTE. *An Economic Analysis of Crime and Justice.* Orlando, Fla.: Academic Press, 1984.

SCHUR, EDWIN M. *Crimes Without Victims: Deviant Behavior and Public Policy: Abortion, Homosexuality, Drug Addiction.* Englewood Cliffs, N.J.: Prentice-Hall, 1974.

SCHUR, EDWIN M., and HUGO BEDAU. *Victimless Crimes: Two Sides of a Controversy.* Englewood Cliffs, N.J.: Prentice-Hall, 1974.

Security Industry Association. "Economic Crime Cost Reaches $200 Billion in 2000." Security Industry Association Research Update, Report for 1st Quarter 2000.

_____. "The Security Industry: An Invisible Giant." SIA Press Room. www.siaonline.org/wp_giant.html.

SESNOWITZ, MICHAEL. "The Returns to Burglary." *Western Economic Journal,* 10, no. 4 (December 1972), 477–481.

SHEPHERD, JOANNA. "Murders of Passion, Execution Delays, and the Deterrence of Capital Punishment," *Journal of Legal Studies* (June 2004), 283–321.

SHOUP, CARL S. "Standards for Distributing a Free Governmental Service: Crime Prevention." *Public Finances/Publiques,* 19, no. 4 (1964), 383–394.

SIMON, CARL P., and ANN D. WITTE. *Beating the System: The Underground Economy.* Boston: Auburn House Publishing Company, 1982.

SIMON, DAVID R. and FRANK E. HAGAN. *White-Collar Deviance.* Boston, MA: Allyn & Bacon, 1999.

SINGER, MAX. *Policy Concerning Drug Abuse in New York State: The Basic Study,* vol. 1. Croton-on-Hudson, N.Y.: Hudson Institute, 1970.

SJOQUIST, DAVID L. "Property Crime and Economic Behavior: Some Empirical Results." *American Economic Review,* 63, no. 3 (June 1973), 439–446.

Small Business Administration. *Crimes Against Small Business.* Washington, D.C., 1969.

SNELL, TRACY. "Capital Punishment 1998." *Bulletin,* U.S. Department of Justice, Bureau of Justice Statistics, December 1999.

STEPHENS, RICHARD C. "Psychoactive Drug Use in the U.S. Today: A Critical Overview." in Thomas Mieczkowski, ed., *Drugs, Crime, and Social Policy.* Boston: Allyn and Bacon, 1992.

STIGLER, GEORGE. "The Optimum Enforcement of Laws." *Journal of Political Economy,* 77, no. 3 (May–June 1970), 526–536.

Substance Abuse and Mental Health Services Administration. (2004). "Results from the 2003 National Survey on Drug Use and Health: National Findings," (Office of Applied Studies, NSDUH Series H–25, DHHS Publication No. SMA 04–3964). Rockville, MD.

_____. "The ADSS Cost Study: Costs of Substance Abuse Treatment in the Specialty Sector," Rockville, MD.

SUTHERLAND, EDWIN H. *On Analyzing Crime.* Chicago: University of Chicago Press, 1973.

TABASZ, THOMAS F. *Towards an Economics of Prisons.* Lexington, Mass.: Lexington Books, 1975.

THORNTON, MARK. "Do Economists Reach a Conclusion?," Economic Journal Watch, (www.econjournalwatch.org/pdf/ThorntonDoEconomistsApril2004.pdf), April 2004, 82–105.

THUROW, LESTER C. "Equity Versus Efficiency in Law Enforcement." *Public Policy,* 18, no. 4 (Summer 1970), 451–459.

TULLIS, LA MOND. *Handbook of Research on the Illicit Drug Traffic.* New York: Greenwood Press, 1991.

TULLOCK, GORDON. "Does Punishment Deter Crime?" *The Public Interest,* 36 (Summer 1974), 103–111.

_____. "An Economic Approach to Crime." *Social Science Quarterly,* 50, no. 1 (June–September 1969), 59–71.

TURNER, DAVID. "Pragmatic Incoherence: The Changing Face of British Drug Policy," in M. Krauss and E. Lazear, eds., *op.cit.,* 175–190.

United Nations, Office on Drugs and Crime. *World Drug Report 2005,* www.unodc.org/unodc/en/world_drug_report.html.

United States Courts. *Report to Congress on the Optimal Utilization of Judicial Resources.* Washington, D.C.: United States Courts, Administrative Office, February 2000.

U.S. Department of Health and Human Services. *1998 National Household Survey on Drug Abuse.* Washington, D.C.: Department of Health and Human Services, August 1999.

U.S. Department of Health and Human Services, National Institute of Drug Abuse. *Relapse and Recovery in Drug Abuse.* Washington, D.C., 1986.

_____. Self-Report Methods of Estimating Drug Abuse: Meeting Challenges *to Validity.* Washington, D.C., 1985.

U.S. Department of Justice, Bureau of Justice Statistics, "Census of State and Federal Correctional Facilities, 2000" Washington, D.C., August 2003.

_____. "Prison and Jail Inmates at Midyear 2004," Washington, D.C., April 2005.

_____. *Sourcebook of Criminal Justice Statistics* (various years). Washington, D.C..

_____. "The Electronic Frontier: The Challenge of Unlawful Conduct Involving the Use of the Internet." Washington, D.C.: U.S. Department of Justice, March 2000.

_____. "Justice Expenditure and Employment in the United States, 1995." November 1999.

_____. *Expenditure and Employment Extracts Program* (various years). Washington, D.C.: Bureau of Justice Statistics.

_____. *Dictionary of Criminal Justice Data Terminology.* Washington, D.C., 1981.

_____. *BJS Data Report,* 1988. Washington, D.C., April 1989.

_____. *Criminal Victimization,* (various years). Washington, D.C..

U.S. Department of Justice, Drug Enforcement Administration. "Drug Trafficking in the United States," www.usdoj.gov/dea/concern/durg_traffickingp.html.

U.S. Department of Justice, Federal Bureau of Investigation. *Crime in the United States: Uniform Crime Reports* (various years). Washington, D.C..

_____. "Structure and Implementation Plan for the Enhanced UCR Program," mimeo, nd.

U.S. Department of Justice, Law Enforcement Assistance Administration, National Institute of Law Enforcement and Criminal Justice. *The Development of the Law of Gambling, 1776–1976.* Ithaca, N.Y., 1977.

_____. National Evaluation Program: *Operation Identification Projects: Assessment of Effectiveness.* Washington, D.C., August 1975.

_____. *Citizen Patrol Projects.* Washington, D.C., January 1977.

_____. *Citizen Crime Reporting Projects.* Washington, D.C., April 1977.

U.S. Department of Justice, National Drug Intelligence Center. "National Drug Threat Assessment 2005," Johnstown, PA, February 2005.

U.S. Department of Justice, National Institute of Justice. *Criminal Justice 2000,* (Washington, D.C., July 2000).

_____. *Research in Brief: Drug Use Forecasting.* Washington, D.C., February 1992.

U.S. Department of State. *International Narcotics Control Strategy Report, 1998.* Washington, D.C.: U.S. Department of State, Bureau for International Narcotics and Law Enforcement Affairs, February 1999.

U.S. Government Accounting Office (G.A.O.), *Drug Control: Status Report on DOD Support to Counternarcotics Activities, Report to the Chairman, Subcommittee on Legislation and National Security, Committee on Government Operations, House of Representatives.* Washington, D.C., June 1991.

U.S. Internal Revenue Service, Criminal Investigations Division. *FY 1998 Annual Report.* www.treas.gov/irs/ai/annual_report/progbk 98.htm.

VORENBERG, ELIZABETH, and JAMES VORENBERG. "The Biggest Pimp of All: Prostitution and Some Facts of Life." *Atlantic Monthly,* 239, no. 1 (January 1977), 27–38.

WALSH, MARILYN E. *The Fence: A New Look at the World of Property Theft.* Westport, Conn.: Greenwood Press, 1977.

WANDLING, THERESE M. "Decriminalization of Prostitution: The Limits of the Criminal Law." *Oregon Law Review,* 55, no. 4, 553–566.

WEICHER, JOHN C. "The Allocation of Police Protection by Income Class." *Urban Studies,* 8, no. 3 (October 1971), 207–220.

WILSON, JAMES Q. *Thinking About Crime.* New York: Basic Books, 1975.

_____. "Who Is in Prison?" *Commentary,* 62, no. 5 (November 1976), 55–58.

WILSON, JAMES Q. and BARBARA BOLAND. "The Effect of the Police on Crime." *Law and Society Review,* 12, no. 3 (Spring 1978), 367–390.

WILSON, JAMES Q., MARK H. MOORE, and DAVID WHEAT, JR. "The Problem of Heroin." *The Public Interest,* no. 29 (Fall 1972), 3–28.

WILSON, M., and P.B. HIGGINS. *Television's Action Arsenal—Weapon Use in Prime Time.* Washington, D.C.: U.S. Conference of Mayors, 1977.

WITTE, ANN D. "Estimating the Economic Model of Crime with Individual Data." *Quarterly Journal of Economics* (February 1980), 57–84.

WOLFGANG, MARVIN, et al. *The National Survey of Crime Severity.* Washington, D.C.: U.S. Department of Justice, June 1985.

ZIMMERMAN, PAUL. "State Executions, Deterrence, and the Incidence of Murder," *Journal of Applied Economics,* May 2004, 163–193.

ZIMRING, FRANK E. "Federal Arms and Federal Law: The Gun Control Act of 1968." *Journal of Legal Studies,* 4, no. 1 (January 1975), 133–199.

_____. "Determinants of the Death Rate from Robbery: A Detroit Time Study." *Journal of Legal Studies,* 1, no. 2 (June 1977), 317–332.

Index

replacement cost
net realiz. value